Edelman, Hope.
Mother of my mother [large
print] : the intricate bor
between generations

Mother of My Mother

G·K
Hall
&Cº

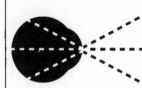

This Large Print Book carries the
Seal of Approval of N.A.V.H.

Mother of My Mother

The Intricate Bond
Between Generations

Hope Edelman

G.K. Hall & Co. • Thorndike, Maine

Published in 2000 by arrangement with Dial Press, an imprint of the Bantam Dell Publishing Group, a division of Random House, Inc.

G.K. Hall Large Print Nonfiction Series.

Acknowlegdments may be found on pages 357–358

The text of this Large Print edition is unabridged.
Other aspects of the book may vary from the original edition.

Set in 16 pt. Plantin by Minnie B. Raven.

Printed in the United States on permanent paper.

Library of Congress Cataloging-in-Publication Data

Edelman, Hope.
    Mother of my mother : the intricate bond between generations / Hope Edelman.
      p. cm.
    Originally published: New York : Dial Press, 1999.
    Includes bibliographical references.
    ISBN 0-7838-9029-X (lg. print : hc : alk. paper)
    1. Edelman, Hope — Family. 2. Grandmothers — United States — Biography. 3. Granddaughters — United States — Biography. 4. Grandparent and child — United States. 5. Mothers and daughters — United States. 6. Intergenerational relations — United States. I. Title.
HQ759.9.E34 2000
306.874′3—dc21   00-022629

For my grandmother, Faye,
my mother, Marcia,
and my daughter, Maya

Sons branch out, but one woman leads to another. Finally, I know you through your daughters, my mother, her sisters, and through myself.

— Margaret Atwood,
Five Poems for Grandmothers

Contents

Introduction

My grandmother lived in a town called Mount Vernon, and for most of my early childhood I thought that meant George Washington had once been her neighbor. There was a legitimate old-world feel to her street: gabled roofs, imposing oak trees, trellises, gazebos. Her house was a Cape Cod–style with a century-old maple tree anchored near the curb. Inside, the walls were painted slate blue and the blinds always drawn, and the living room smelled of electric heat and boiled chicken and week-old fruit slowly going soft in a large wooden bowl. My mother bounced her right foot anxiously whenever she sat in the room and my father had to step outside periodically for fresh air, but even when my grandfather sat in his salmon upholstered lounge chair and trapped me between his crossed ankles, refusing to release me until I said the magic words, *Open sesame,* I never felt the desperate need to escape. I drew great comfort from a room where the walnuts on the end table were the same walnuts I'd seen there last year, a room where the type of holiday cards displayed on the mantel were the only evidence of the passage of time.

It did not take me long to understand that

rooms were predictable but the people in them were not. My parents, relatively even-tempered in our home, were capable of anything in my grandparents' presence — irritation, laughter, indifference, anger. My grandparents, it seemed, could transform from doting elders to meddling intruders in the span of one carefully timed comment. Then my grandfather died unexpectedly the summer I was twelve, a passage I learned about weeks later when I returned from summer camp. In my memory he's a large, gentle man with a shoebrush moustache who stands at the perimeter of every room. Funny, really, since he always sat in a lounge chair in the center or in a seat at the table's head, a commanding presence in his own right, but in my mind my grandmother's personality pushes him aside. Where he was Laurel, she was Hardy. Where he was yin, she was yang.

I never had the kind of grandmother who wore aprons and spectacles and pulled warm cookies from the oven, the kind who exists more often in children's books than in real life. I didn't have the kind of grandmother I saw on television, either. She was neither as sage as Grandma Walton nor as goofy as Granny on *The Beverly Hillbillies*. You couldn't reduce her to a single dominant trait the way you could say Aunt Bee was cheerfully domestic or Maude acid-tongued. The grandmother I knew was colorful, opinionated, ubiquitous, stubborn, loving, patient, devoted, intelligent, intrusive, funny, tragic, uncontrollably obsessive, wildly superstitious, and capable of both astonishing acts of compassion and unpredictable fits of rage. She had little in common with the "New American Grandparent," of the 90s, the one who mall-walks and e-mails and moves down to Florida to remarry at seventy-five. My grandmother wore suits, but they weren't the kind you jogged in. She lived in the same house from 1952 until she died.

Because Mount Vernon was an easy thirty-minute drive from my parents' home in Spring Valley, New York, my grandmother was a staple of my childhood. I questioned her presence no more than I questioned the existence of my swing set, or of lunch. She was just, simply, there. Several days a week she crossed the Tappan Zee Bridge and showed up at our door, usually without warning, always carrying gifts. Plastic snowshakers, Lucite coin banks, those little upright metal calendars where you turned a tiny knob to change the date. She drove over during the day, while my father was at work. It was not unusual for me to come home from school and find her sitting in the kitchen with my mother, drinking coffee in her coat, or for my mother and me to return from an ice-skating lesson or shopping trip to find her parked in front of the house, listening to AM radio in her car. Only now do I realize that means all those years she never had a key.

I imagine that was because my mother knew the risks involved in giving her mother unrestricted access to our house. Whenever my grandmother baby-sat while my parents were away on vacation she immediately combed through the refrigerator and medicine cabinets, discarding all the foods she thought to be bad for us and stocking up on supplies she believed ensured good health. After my parents returned, my mother did a search of her own, pushing the containers of witch hazel to the back of our linen closet and pouring bottle after bottle of castor oil down the kitchen sink. My father watched from the background with his hands on his hips, swearing, "Goddammit, I'm *never* leaving that *woman* alone in *this* house *again*." Nobody took this seriously. We all knew that the next time my parents prepared to leave town, my grandmother would come driving up with her suitcase and a vaporizer. Despite her idiosyncrasies, my parents knew there was no one they could trust with their children more.

But none of this describes her relationship with me. After she died in 1996, one of my cousins was surprised by the depth of my sadness, having known my grandmother to be difficult, stubborn, and driven by crisis. I knew her in those capacities too. But when I push past the images of her standing in the middle of our living room in her coat and hat, stamping her foot and shouting *"Listen* to me! Would you just *listen* to me?" or standing on our front step, banging on the door and demanding to be let back in, I find other memories, softer ones, of times we spent together, just us two. Of her in 1981 sitting patiently outside a department store dressing room for hours, wearing her wool coat and clutching her pocketbook in her lap, while I tried on pants and sweaters for the new school year the first autumn after my mother died. Or an even earlier memory, one of my first, of her teaching me to read when I was two, afternoon after patient afternoon of alphabet flashcards on the living room sofa, sounding out the letters until I recognized each one. *Ah, Beh, Cuh, Duh.* Back then, she carried a black patent leather handbag stuffed beyond hope of closure with empty lipstick containers, dried-up pens, six-month-old receipts, telephone numbers scribbled on paper scraps, stray coins, unopened junk mail, lengthy notes to herself, and loose ten-dollar bills. "Grandma, your pocketbook is pregnant!" I told her when I was six, and she laughed and agreed yes, it was. As if in testimony, the next time she visited she reached into her shopping bag and pulled out a black patent leather purse for me, a miniature version of her own. She was trying to teach me about reproduction, I think, but I learned more about love.

Our relationship was easy then, an aging woman guiding a child who had not yet learned how to discriminate or to judge. Arthur Kornhaber, M.D., a child psychiatrist and the author of several books on the relationships between grandparents and their grandchildren, says that part of the magic between the genera-

13

tions exists because children haven't yet con-
formed to societal ideals of youth and beauty,
because they ignore signs of aging or disabilities
and respond instead to a grandparent's inherent
goodness. And it is true, there was a time when I
loved my grandmother with a pure and simple
love, before I could distinguish between acceptable behavior and objectionable behavior, before
I one day understood what my parents had been
complaining about for all those years. Until
then, I was still my grandmother's ally, sitting
knee-to-knee with her on our brick front steps
after she'd once again been banished from our
home. "Why do they do this to me?" she
moaned. "Why?" I grasped my ankles and
shrugged. Like her, I didn't know. "Maybe you
shouldn't yell so loud," I suggested. Then, one
day when I was eleven or twelve, she asked the
same question — *Why do they do this to me?* —
and I knew. It was the day I joined my parents on
the other side of the door.

I knew, for as long as I can remember, that if I
wanted to complain about my grandmother, my
mother was the wrong parent to approach. In
private, she might roll her eyes at her mother's
obsessions or laugh at her superstitions, but she
never extended an invitation for me to join in. I
might have seen commiserating about my
grandmother as an opportunity for my mother
and me to bond, a chance for the two of us to
drink coffee together at the kitchen table in-

stead of the two of them, but my mother wouldn't tolerate my acting with such lack of respect. It was a position, I suspect, similar to the one I now take with her. I give myself license to say whatever I choose about her, but if someone else remembers her critically, or even in a slightly unfavorable light, I immediately leap to her defense.

The bonds between mother and daughter are primal, immutable, revered. Between grandmother and granddaughter they're never as direct. My grandmother, no matter how large a role she played in my childhood, was always the mother of my mother, one generation removed from me. The powerful attachment they shared was the central drama of my family, the story around which all the others revolved, often leaving me swinging my legs impatiently at the kitchen table while they reprised roles first staged long before my birth. No matter how essential a part of their lives I imagined myself to be, the intimacy between them didn't include me. I found some relief in this, knowing I was outside of that exitless loop, but I also felt excluded, aware that I was more observer than participant — and oftentimes even incidental — to events that unfolded before me. As Carole Ione writes about her mother and maternal grandmother in her memoir *Pride of Family: Four Generations of American Women of Color*, "They were caught up in their own story, and I felt like an intruder in their lives."

As contradictory as this may sound, my ability to feel close to my grandmother grew out of this distance between us. Because grandmothers and granddaughters leapfrog over the emotionally charged mother–daughter bond, it was easier for me than for my mother to overlook my grandmother's behaviors, to regard her with compassion or even indifference. Mothers and daughters own each other, with one's behaviors always feeling like a comment, a judgment, a rejection on the other. My grandmother, on the other hand, always felt like a separate entity to me. Whereas my mother was often disrupted, angered, or shaken by her mother's attempts to intrude or control, I could observe my grandmother from a distance and with a greater degree of objectivity. What I found funniest about my grandmother my mother often found troubling; what I found endearing often annoyed my mother the most.

Joy Horowitz, the author of *Tessie and Pearlie: A Granddaughter's Story*, a memoir about her two nonagenarian grandmothers, remembers how her parents considered her maternal grandmother, Pearlie, manipulative and controlling at times. "But I always thought it was a total kick, how Pearlie managed to get whatever she wanted," Horowitz recalls. "I think that when you're the child of those behaviors you can feel suffocated, but as a grandchild I thought the way she could maneuver herself through situations was a riot."

In her collection of prize-winning columns *Living Out Loud*, Anna Quindlen called this "the familiar dance of the generations, the minuet in which the closer we are the more difficult relations become. We are able to accept, even love, things in our grandparents that we find impossible to accept in their children, our parents. The reverse is true, too: in us they can take the joys without the responsibilities. In the family sandwich, the older people and the younger ones can recognize one another as the bread. Those in the middle are, for a time, the meat."

From the start, the expectations a granddaughter places on a grandmother are different and, in most respects, lower than those placed on a mother. We invest mothers with awesome powers, with the ability to soothe all hurts, right all wrongs, to nurture without any concept of self. Not so the grandmother. Her, we permit to make mistakes and to fail. We feel safe in the belief that her actions, no matter how outrageous, don't make statements about our intelligence, our sanity, or our worth. When we step up to the mirror it's usually our mothers, not our grandmothers, whom we're afraid to see.

Yet this permissiveness also gives us a false sense of immunity, encouraging us to believe that the connection between granddaughter and grandmother barely matters at all. For some women, particularly those who never knew their maternal grandmothers, this may feel true. But in the lives of many others a grandmother occupies an essential role, as a primary nurturer, a confidante, a family nemesis, or the hub around which the whole wheel revolves, playing a direct and significant role in her granddaughter's emotional development.

Even though affluence and mobility have transformed the extended family system, where multiple generations live under the same roof, into extended family networks, where the generations live close by, many grandmothers have remained highly involved in the lives of their kin, offering emotional, financial, and day-to-day support. Women raised in close contact with these grandmothers often point to them as the source of their female identity, the wellspring from which many of their values, behaviors, idiosyncrasies, mannerisms, desires, and fears flow.

Particularly when a grandmother functions as co-parent with the mother, the three-generational relationship can act as the backbone of the family, providing nurturing and support for all its members. This type of three-generation female family system has rapidly grown over the past twenty years, largely as a result of single motherhood and divorce. According to the U.S. Bureau of the Census, between 1970 and 1993 the number of children under the age of eighteen living in their grandparents' homes with their mothers, but not their fathers, present rose 98 percent.

Today, at least 1.6 million children are being raised by their grandmothers and mothers in the grandmother's home. That's about one out of every fifty children, including 6 percent of all African-American children, 3 percent of Hispanic children, and 2 percent of Caucasian children. And those figures are deceptively low, since they don't include situations where the grandmother has moved into her daughter's home, or informal arrangements where a child lives with a grandmother for part of the year. An additional one million children in the United States — one out of 100 — are being raised by grandmothers with neither biological parent present, a ratio that has remained relatively stable for the past twenty-five years. For these granddaughters, a grandmother is hardly a secondary character of childhood. In many cases, she's the only mother figure they have.

When I first started writing this book, I intended to examine the relationship between grandmothers and granddaughters, to explore the types of connections that skip a generation and to discuss the impact I felt my grandmother had on me. I read books about grandparenting and aging, spoke with psychologists and sociologists, interviewed 70 women in six cities, and surveyed 186 more by mail. My findings were closely aligned with what other researchers had revealed: that women are more likely to have close relationships with maternal grandmothers than with paternal grandmothers;[*] that these relationships evolve in a distinct and predictable manner as both women age; that the granddaughter–grandmother relationship can absorb more ambivalence than the mother–daughter relationship; and that many women feel they have more in common with their maternal grandmothers than they do with their mothers. Nearly all of the women I interviewed had lived closer to a mother's mother than to a father's mother while growing up, saw her more often, and felt she'd had the greater influence on their lives. The connection they'd developed with their maternal grandmothers was the strongest grandchild–grandparent bond most of these women had known.

The strongest, perhaps, but not necessarily the easiest. Most of these women, like myself, did not have grandmothers who stayed home and commandeered the oven but instead recalled women who were vibrant, nurturing, meddlesome, wise, matriarchal, highly critical, and fiercely protective of their clan. These Grandmas, Grannies, Nanas, NooNoos, Mimis, Omas,

[*]This is uniformly true in contemporary culture, with only a few notable exceptions: women from Asian families and other cultures where aging parents have traditionally been cared for by their sons' families, and rural children raised on farms, where fathers and sons often live nearby and work the land together (King and Elder, 1995).

Nonnas, Savtas, Obasans, Mamacitas, Mormors, and Mamons were role models and rulers, confidantes and instigators, just as likely to be sources of conflict as pillars of support. Many of them, like my grandmother, were both.

I started writing about these types of grandmother–granddaughter relationships, but I was interrupted by a visitor I hadn't expected to see. It was my mother, who kept showing up in the stories about my grandmother. Trying to write about one without writing about the other became as futile as trying to separate the rain from the cloud. My mother's appearances quietly but forcefully reminded me that every grandmother–granddaughter relationship is connected by two mother–daughter bonds. She, I realized, was a critical part of any interaction I had with my grandmother, both of them defining the terms *mother, daughter,* and *woman* for me. The three of us, in my memory, are separate yet linked, like sequential pearls on a strand. It quickly became clear that a book about relationships between granddaughters and grandmothers, especially one about my relationship with my grandmother, had to include mothers, too.

And then into the middle of this threesome arrived my daughter, who'd been little more than a vision when this book was first conceived. Back then, I was single and childless and my grandmother was still alive. I'd begun the book to help myself sort through the affection and exasperation and sadness and guilt I'd always felt toward

21

my grandmother, racing against the clock for answers as her mental and physical health chased each other down a steep decline. But in that respect, I ran out of time. I was only a few months into the book when my father called me at home. *I have bad news,* he said. *It's your grandmother.* I slowly sank into an armchair. *Ohhhh,* I said, like air escaping from a balloon. I hung up the phone and sat for a long time in my living room, staring at the floor. There was something solemn about the moment, respectful and hushed, as the steam-heat pipes hissed in the background and the cat silently padded across the hardwood floor. I thought I should be crying, even recognized the preparatory tight spot at the base of my throat, but the tears were out of reach. Instead, I felt scooped out, hollowed, emptier than I could ever remember feeling before.

How do I describe the experience, two days later, of standing alongside her grave in the light rain? Family members surrounded me, but in my memory I stand there alone. I was acutely aware that without my mother or my grandmother I was the only woman left in my direct maternal line, a matriarch without a queendom at thirty-two. But then, only a month later, came the unexpected bright pink line on the home pregnancy test my boyfriend and I bought at the local drugstore for $12.99.

The baby was, of course, a girl.

I say "of course" because I believe in the regenerative properties of nature, in the process by which old growth is replaced by new. I live in the midst of a California fire zone, where hills that are charred and black one season return the next as verdant. Who's to say it's any different in a family, with one generation's demise creating an opportunity for the arrival of the next?

Perhaps my grandmother sensed this the last time I saw her, on an autumn visit I made to her home. By that time she was living alone, predeceased by her husband and both sisters who'd later moved in, and cared for by a full-time aide. It was the last in a series of difficult, draining visits I was never quite sure were made out of obligation or out of love. Or empathy or respect or fear. As so often happened when I spent time with my grandmother, one emotion quickly tangled up in another. Compassion invited irritation, which immediately intertwined with guilt. As an adult, I'd never felt stable or consistent around her, never felt my course of action couldn't be swayed. I constantly abandoned good sense in favor of preserving peace. It wasn't until the very end of her life when I held her hand and told her stories from her past, by then our roles completely reversed, that I felt secure in my position and my response. That afternoon was the first time I could say I trusted, even liked, the person I was in her presence. But by then, it was too late. I'd spent too many years ignoring her phone calls and requests, too much time in retreat. During the last six months of her life, each time I visited she asked for my mother but claimed not to remember me.

"*Hope,* Grandma," I'd explain as I sat alongside her on the slate-blue couch. "I'm your granddaughter, Hope. You had three daughters. The oldest one was Marcia. Marcia's oldest daughter is named Hope." Each visit would dissolve into this perverse exchange, with me shouting "Hope!" into the hearing aid of a frail, sickly woman, like some kind of relentless command, and her insisting "Hope? I don't know any Hope."

So this last time, she surprised me when she said, seemingly apropos of nothing, "I want you to get married," with the emphasis on the *you.* It took me a moment to understand she was responding to a reference to my cousin's wedding I'd made a half hour before. Though my grandmother was always awake and alert when I visited, she had a tenuous grasp of the immediate. She might suddenly answer a question you'd asked six questions back, as if the synapses had finally, after a prolonged and great effort, connected for a brief moment and then separated again. Or, perhaps, as if she'd caught the question the first time but had to wade through a sea of competing distractions to reach the answer on the other side.

"I want *you* to get married," she said.

"Why, Grandma?" I asked, carefully, trying to hold her in the moment. "Why do you want me to get married?"

She answered in a tone that sounded annoyed

to be stating the obvious. "So you can have a *ba*by," she said.

My daughter was born one year later, almost to the day. She will grow up knowing my grandmother only through the stories she hears, which is just another way of saying she'll know her mostly through the stories I tell. Choose to tell. Already, I feel the impulse to censor myself in her presence, to share with her only the narratives that portray the women in my family as heroines, as anchors, as champions of the fold. But I do my daughter no favor by telling her an incomplete story. As much as this book is for me, to help me unravel the threads that tie me to my grandmother and my mother and examine each one, and for other women who are trying to do the same, it is also for my daughter, who will one day have to go through a similar process with me. And with the women who came before her, the ones she's never met.

I don't expect to tell my daughter, or even claim to know, exactly who my grandmother was. I just want to convey who my grandmother was to me. Perhaps it will help her understand what I come from, what shaped me, and what will therefore, inevitably, shape her. She belongs not just to me but to all the women who preceded her. Another daughter born into this chain of mothers. Sometimes I look at her upturned face, her smile so quick and so earnest, her eyes locked so intently on mine, and I think, Here is where it begins. One generation at a time.

PART I

Grandma and Me

1

Through a Child's Eyes

My grandmother had red hair. I don't know when she started coloring it. She was fifty-eight when I was born, and I never saw any gray. This was back when women went to the beauty parlor once a week for a wash and set and slept on their backs with their curls tucked into protective nets. My grandmother always wore a hat during the day. When I was a child, I used to think she wore it indoors because she'd forgotten to take it off. As a teenager I thought it was because she was an observant Jew. Only later did I realize a hat is the perfect antidote to a bad-hair day. Probably all three were true.

She wore her hair up in a bun or a twist, always on the crest of her head. One afternoon, when I was about three, my mother and I walked into a salon in the suburban New York town where my grandmother lived. A woman with hair the same shade as my grandmother's was leaning back in the beautician's chair, her waterfall of dark orange hair spilling halfway to the floor.

I tugged on my mother's hand. "Where's Grandma?" I asked. We were supposed to be meeting her for lunch.

My mother jutted her chin toward the chair. "Over there," she said.

I tugged again. "That's not Grandma," I insisted. Even at three I knew such vibrant hair belonged to younger women. When the beautician spun the chair toward us and I saw my grandmother's crinkled, welcoming face surrounded by that extraordinary halo, I screamed. Screamed and screamed. She held out her arms, laughing. "It's only Grandma," she said, but I wouldn't let go of my mother's legs. I had to be carried outside until my grandmother's hair was piled back on top of her head.

My mother thought this was a funny story, and we added it to the list of anecdotes I liked to hear about my toddler years. *Tell me about the time I didn't recognize Grandma. Grandma, remember the time I didn't know you were you?* My mother later told me she thought I was scared because I'd never seen my grandmother out of her usual context before, which might well be true. But there was also something a little wild, something a little unrestrained about the way my grandmother's hair flowed so freely down her back in the beautician's chair, and it frightened me. I recognized something decidedly uninhibited about my grandmother that day, and I think perhaps that is why I was not entirely surprised when, in later years, a lack of control began to characterize her relationships with both my mother and me.

What is there to say about a grandmother who

loved with a force so powerful it could lose all sense of proportion? That she used to hug me so hard I had to struggle to breathe, that she visited every Friday loaded down with shopping bags full of challah bread and fruitcakes that no one ever ate, that after she got back into her Oldsmobile and slowly drove home alone my parents inevitably closed their bedroom door and the shouting began?

They argued about the strength of my mother's bond with her mother, about her difficulty asserting her autonomy with any real success. If my grandmother saw her eldest daughter as separate from herself, it was likely to be more by accident than as a result of my mother's ardent attempts to wrench free from her mother's grasp. Though these efforts never succeeded in loosening the emotional bond, I do know my mother tried. She rejected much of my grandmother's parenting advice, most of which was based on Eastern European traditions that did not easily transfer to contemporary suburban New York. I remember how my parents used to sit in the front seat of the car on the way back from a visit with my grandparents, laughing about my grandmother's fears of ice cream (which she was certain caused the common cold and maybe worse); the color black (which she forbade us to wear in her presence); and the number thirteen (which she avoided to such a degree that she refused to take Exit 13 off the New York Thruway to reach our house, even though Exit 12 took her five miles out of the way). The first time I heard the word *cockamamy* used was when my father attached it to my grandmother's ideas. Many times, my mother stomped out of a room in frustration, leaving my grandmother behind to clench her fists and squeeze her eyes shut, lamenting, "Oh, Oh, Oh . . . if *only* your mother would listen to me."

But listen to what? My grandmother was ruled by superstition and what we called "her theories," and it did not seem to occur to her that her beliefs might be wrong. She would close her eyes, pinch her lips, and shake her head rhythmically from side to side whenever anyone introduced information that contradicted her ideas. It was impossible to argue, let alone reason, with a woman who held so firmly to her viewpoint that she left no room for an alternative. Disagreeing with her only set off a barrage of late-night phone calls and unexpected visits that could go on for weeks. Her tactic was never to convince anyone else that they were wrong, only to prove that she was right. In an interesting twist to what otherwise might have been a straightforward matriarchy, however, she had limited success winning others to her side and even more trouble keeping them there.

Yet for all her obstinance, my grandmother was not a mean-spirited woman in any way. Quite the contrary, in fact, her obsessions and concerns always focused on someone else's health or happiness, and nothing could upset her more than the suspicion that one of her loved ones might be suffering. When my mother struggled with infertility in the early '60s, my grandmother spent weeks interviewing doctors, reading about endometriosis in medical libraries, calling university clinics, and writing away to Italy for supposed miracle drugs. If others accused her of meddling, then so be it. She knew what they thought of her, but her desire to be of help eclipsed her self-restraint. It's impossible to stay angry at someone motivated by pure benevolence, or at someone with a love so huge, especially when you're one of its principal beneficiaries.

Forever concerned about preserving peace between her mother and her husband, my mother understood it was often easier to fake compliance than to openly rebel. This was not, however, in her mind, the equivalent of giving in. Throughout my childhood I was witness to the small deliberate acts of subversion she committed to prove her solidarity with my father without triggering her mother's alarms. I remember how she used to dash around the kitchen, hiding all the unkosher food and processed meats while my sister and I shouted progress reports from the living room window — "She's getting out of the car . . ." "She's halfway to the door . . ." Once I heard her tell my grandmother, who was terrified of air travel, that we were taking the train to Florida for our vacation, and then immediately hang up and call Delta to confirm our airline reservations. She later complained about the secrets I kept from her, without realizing she was the one who taught me how to sneak around.

My father, an outsider from the start, wanted nothing to do with these shenanigans. After a perfunctory greeting, he usually retreated to his bedroom. If he heard agitation brewing, he emerged and insisted that my grandmother leave. *"Fa-aye,"* he said, just that one word, stretching it into two syllables as a warning. But there were certain obligations and so forth, including my father's position in the family business and my grandparents' periodic financial support. The strings were taut, but in no danger of snapping, and even during the worst of times my grandmother and my mother spoke nearly every day. I remember, mostly, the midmorning phone calls my mother took in her nightgown or housedress, sitting at the built-in desk at the kitchen, twisting the cord from the wall phone around and around her left hand. Sometimes she doodled on a pad as they spoke. Afterward, I saw how the penciled curlicues got darker and tighter as they migrated down the page.

Yes, Mother. We're having turkey breast and carrots. Uh-huh. She's got a slight fever. A hundred point two. No, I'm taking her to the doctor at three. It's not that cold out, and I bundle her up. A hat and mittens. I bundle her up. Mo-ther. No. No. I don't need anything. I don't need anything, Mother.

The conversations began tamely enough, but

they could turn a corner quickly. I could tell when by the way my mother's voice started closing in on itself, the way she would say "Mo-*ther*," with a sharp edge on that last syllable. This usually meant my grandmother had started obsessing about our health, or insisting we all take a tablespoon of castor oil in the morning, or follow some piece of unconfirmed medical advice she'd just read about in *Prevention* magazine. She had a constant fear of impending calamity and some unusual ideas about cause and effect. I learned at an early age not to mention allergies, stomachaches, or sore throats in her presence. At a booth in a Hebrew National delicatessen when I was six, I discovered, the hard way, that hot dogs were also a smart topic to avoid.

I learned to be careful in my mother's house, as well. The word *crazy* was not to be used in the same sentence as *Grandma*, ever. I wasn't even supposed to think it. "Difficult," my mother called her, and left it at that. If anyone complained about my grandmother's behaviors, my mother would raise her open palms in a gesture indicating "What can you do?" But underneath her attempt to dissociate was something else — a concern? a fear? Once my father casually said to her in the course of an otherwise innocuous conversation, "What are you talking about? Are you crazy?" and she spun around from the kitchen sink with a wild look in her eyes. "I am *not* crazy!" she shouted, slamming her yellow rubber dishwashing gloves onto the counter so hard, they bounced. "Don't you *ever* call me crazy again! Do you hear?"

I heard. Sprawled across the backseat of the car, tangled up in my sister's legs and feigning sleep as we drove back from my grandparents' house at night, I listened to my parents' low murmurs in the front. "Marcia, you've got to listen to me," my father pleaded. "That kind of behavior is *not normal.*"

My mother shrugged. She looked out the passenger window. "You know how she is," she said.

I quietly repositioned myself to direct an ear toward their voices. I wanted to know how, exactly, my grandmother was, but my father let the conversation die. He was looking for affirmation, not excuses. And it was clear no one wanted to keep his suspicions alive.

If this grandmother had been the only grandmother I knew, I might have believed, in the way every child believes her own family defines "normal," that all grandmothers were similar to mine. But I had a basis for comparison, my father's mother, who'd died when I was nine. We'd called her Nana, and she'd lived in a low pink house by the beach with a tidy rectangle of grass in the backyard and garbage pails built into the ground at the front curb. These are the things a child remembers. The hard licorice candies she kept in a glass bowl on her coffee table. The scents of perfume and shoe leather in her walk-in closet; the soft chimes of multiple strands of beads.

Nana was charmed by her grandchildren, but by the time I, her fifth one, was born we were not the focal point of her days. She was newly remarried and cultivating that next phase of her life, which is to say that each time I saw her we ran toward each other with our arms flung open wide, but she was neither the primary grandmother of my childhood nor a continual presence in my early years. At most, we saw her four or five times a year. Even so, I absorbed the message she was stable and predictable, the parent my parents always called first when in need of serious advice. Even if I didn't fully understand what my father meant by *not normal,* I had a sense of what, at least in his estimation, something closer to "normal" might be.

But how much of this really mattered to me then? Children form general impressions about a person; they don't analyze. What I knew, or needed to know, about my mother's mother distilled to very few details. She was patient with me. She called our house every day. She brought me gifts. She could yell very loud. To me, these were facts, not criteria for judgment.

She cooked food I didn't like. She wore scratchy wool suits. She was short. *Tiny,* actually. When she drove, she had to pull the front seat of the car close in to the steering wheel, and from a distance all you could see above the top of her dashboard were her eyes and her wool beret. I once asked her, as I settled into her passenger seat, if she wanted to borrow one of our phone books to sit on, and she laughed with a little "heh-heh-heh," a low, measured three-step that might have been mistaken for a modest clearing of the throat if not for the way her eyes crinkled at the outer corners when she smiled.

In photographs I see she wasn't always as small as I remember, probably about five feet three at my parents' wedding when she was fifty-three. But in later years age reduced her, skimming a few inches off the top. As I began my early ascent, she was already in the midst of her decline. From third grade to fourth to fifth, we catalogued my growth by comparing my height to hers. I would stand and face her, my nose inches away from her wool lapels, her painted lips, her brown beret. At eight my head fit under her chin; at eleven, I looked her in the eye.

"Heh-heh-heh," she chuckled, pleased with my progress. "Are you growing or is Grandma shrinking?"

During those years, little my grandmother did seemed unquestionably objectionable to me. Her daily phone calls, filled with mundane questions — What did you do this morning? What are you cooking for dinner? — were often a source of irritation to my mother, who interpreted them as insinuation that she couldn't care for a family or a home without constant supervision. Before long I would understand how a mother's barrage of questions could feel like an intrusion, but at the time my grandmother's inquiries seemed only an expression of genuine interest. If I happened to answer the phone, I was pleased to answer her questions. Who else cared that much about the minutiae of my days? *I watched Scooby Doo and then I got dressed and then Michele and I played Monopoly and I got to be the banker because she doesn't know how to subtract yet.* My mother sometimes had to pry the receiver away from my ear.

My grandmother and I shared an appreciation for detail, and perhaps for an audience as well. She would tell me stories of her childhood in Newark as the fourth child of five in an immigrant Russian family, her father a pious man who made his living as a junk dealer and fruit peddler — "What kind of fruit?" I asked her. "Bananas, I think," she said. Me, again: "Did he have a cart with a horse?" — and her mother a seamstress (and bathtub bootlegger, as I later learned) and a resourceful cook. She finished high school early and found work as a legal secretary to help support her family, a job she held for the next twelve years. She could have become a lawyer, she maintained, if only she'd had the money to take the exam. I believed her then, and I still do.

The childhood poverty my grandmother alluded to but never dwelled on was a concept at once romantic and elusive to me. One afternoon, in an attempt to experience some of the deprivation she might have known, I cooked myself a potato for lunch and sliced it into six discs, spearing each one with my fork and eating it plain. It was my idea of a poor immigrant's lunch, born from reading too many books about the Irish potato famine and watching *Little House on the Prairie*. Of course, the fact that I took the potato from a refrigerator filled with other food and cooked it in a toaster oven diluted the experience significantly. But while slowly eating my lonely potato at the kitchen table, I could close my eyes and conjure up brief flickers of simplicity and longing, which helped me, even if only for a moment, imagine myself as a child in Newark in 1915, the year my grandmother turned nine.

Several times, usually as gift-giving occasions approached, she told me how as a child she had once cut the hair off her only doll, believing it would grow back, and had to wait nearly a year before her parents could afford a replacement. Of all the stories my grandmother told me, this one left the most lasting impression. By then, I understood remorse, and I recognized the tiny shocks that accompanied each little bit of innocence lost. But even more so, I loved the naiveté and imagination behind her act. Sometimes when I looked at my grandmother I tried to imagine her as that little girl, clutching her single, hairless doll close to her at night. The knowledge that she ever had to do without an object as basic and comforting as a pristine doll was one of the few thoughts during childhood that could move me to tears.

More than anyone else in a family, young children respond to a grandparent based on the way that grandparent makes them feel. It's a simple equation, really: Granddaughters who feel comfortable and loved when they're with the grandmother usually want to be in her presence, and those who feel bothersome or overlooked don't. Most granddaughters I've met describe a feeling of calm and peace in their grandmother's presence, a sense that the daily pressures of home and school no longer exist. They draw comfort from the folds of her body and lilt in her voice.

In Dorothy Allison's novel *Bastard Out of Carolina*, the child narrator, Bone, spends long, peaceful summer afternoons on her aunt's porch with her cousins, supervised by a grandmother who offers a welcome respite from a childhood marked by poverty and violence. Describing one of those late afternoons, Bone recalls,

I edged forward until I could put my hand on Granny's chair, fingers sliding over the smooth, worn trellis of woven slats to feel the heat of her body through her cotton dress. The laughter echoed around me, the music, truck brakes ground up on the highway, and somebody started shouting far off as the dark descended and the fireflies began to flicker past the boys' heads. Granny put her arm

41

down and squeezed my wrist. She leaned over and spat a stream of brown snuff off the side of the porch. I heard the dull plopping sound it made as it landed in the dusty yard. I slipped under her shoulder, leaned across the side of the rocker, and put my face close to her breast . . . Granny was ugly herself, she said so often enough, though she didn't seem to care. Her wide face was seamed and spotted with freckles and long deep lines. Her hair was thin and gray and tied back with one of the little black strings that came off a snuff pouch. She smelled strong — bitter and salt, sour and sweet, all at the same time. My sweat disappeared into her skirt, my arms wrapped around her waist, and I breathed her in like the steam off soup.

Like many of the women interviewed for this book, forty-two-year-old Phyllis says she can't quite explain the powerful connection she felt to her maternal grandmother. When she tries to transform emotion into words, even she, a writer by profession, feels she shortchanges the essence of the bond. Dr. Arthur Kornhaber nods when I relate this story. As a child psychiatrist who's researched and written extensively about the grandparent–grandchild bond, he's heard this before. "It's not an identification with their grandmothers that these women are talking about, because that's a psychological phenomenon," he explains. "And it's not a form of awareness, because that's an intellectual recognition. This is a spiritual, emotional attachment we're talking about here, almost an ego fusion. So they feel it exists, but they don't have a word for it. There really *are* no words for it, but it's extremely powerful."

Phyllis knows only that her attachment to her grandmother was strong and intuitive and made her want to be in her grandmother's presence as often as possible. "For as long as I can remember, my grandmother was always my favorite person," she recalls. "I just loved being around her. It seemed like she was the person who understood me best. When I was three years old, I started . . . it wasn't exactly running away from home, because there was nothing wrong at home. It was just that I wanted to be with my grandmother. Even as young as three years old I got my snowsuit on and tried to take a city bus to the town 120 miles away where she lived. When I was about five, I found a suitcase under the bed that my older sister had packed. She said she was going to visit our grandmother, and I said, 'I won't tell as long as you take me with you.' It took months of planning, but we collected dimes and all kinds of money and we took off. We got a taxi and made it to the bus terminal. My sister insisted that we call our parents so they wouldn't be worried, and of course the second we did they came down and got us. I was very, very angry at my sister, but it turned out that she had never intended to really go. It was just a fantasy she had that I had forced by my enthusiasm and insistence."

When Dr. Kornhaber conducted a videotaped study of toddlers interacting with various family members, he found that the children received the most peaceful affirmations and validating responses from their grandmothers. "It was the most smooth, non-performance-oriented, joy-in-the-action-together interaction we saw," he says. "It was an example of what I call the 'ethos of being.' Just being together and enjoying one another's essence without doing an activity. The grandmother affirms the existence of the granddaughter, even more so than the grandsons. And you could see the granddaughters mimicking their grandmother's actions, and absorbing their ideals. When you think about that, you realize that grandmothers have traditionally raised granddaughters to ensure the integrity of the tribe. We're so preprogrammed and hard-wired for this."

Early bonding between young granddaughters and their grandmothers often occurs in what Dr. Kornhaber calls "feeling places," special sites usually somewhere in or around the home — a kitchen, a yard, a sitting room, a front porch — without parents or siblings to disturb them. In this shared space, communication is often silent. The grandmother doesn't need to focus her attention exclusively on her granddaughter. Instead, she goes about her ordinary business and allows the child to enter her world, introducing

44

her to a different way to "be" without being judged or evaluated for her efforts or results. Children relax around a grandmother, and the grandmother, finished with the full-time responsibilities of child rearing, can take her hands off the wheel in this relationship and coast.

Evelyn Bassoff, Ph.D., a psychotherapist in Boulder, Colorado, and the author of several books on mother–daughter relationships, recalls a childhood with a beloved maternal grandmother who lived in her home. "One of the things I loved most about my grandmother was that she shared my sense of time, a child's sense of time," Dr. Bassoff explains. "The adults around me all worked. They were rushed and didn't have patience for the little things that interested me, but my grandmother did. She had slowed down to the point where she had time for that. We did so much observing and exploring of the world together."

Children are limited (or blessed, depending on your point of view) by a cognition that matures slowly, piece by piece, and their responses to a grandmother correspond with whatever level of development they've achieved at their particular age. Very young children, still in an egocentric phase of development and thus able to perceive other people only in relation to themselves, prefer indulgent grandmothers who bring them treats and toys. By age eight, most granddaughters have the capacity to understand and enjoy mutuality, and prefer the company of grandmothers who join them in fun activities, such as doing puzzles or playing cards. A few years later, when a granddaughter has mastered more abstract thought, she'll start to identify qualities in her grandmother that exist independent of their relationship, such as "She's a good person" or "I think she's very smart." By age twelve and the onset of adolescence, however, preferences for an indulgent grandmother often reemerge and interest in shared activities starts to decline.

Psychologists who study grandparents and grandchildren like to categorize; they'll create five or six labels and ask granddaughters to select the one that describes their grandmothers best. Was she a formal grandmother, with a focus on instruction and discipline? Fun-seeking, with an emphasis on shared activities? A reservoir of family wisdom? Intimate? Or distant? I'm thankful such a questionnaire was never administered to me. Where was the category for all and none of the above? As I started to develop a more sophisticated awareness of the adults around me, I became increasingly conscious that my grandmother was not a woman who could be reduced to a single term. Even by simplest definition, she was two grandmothers to me: the patient, doting, storytelling Good Grandmother with the sweet smile and the tight hug I knew from our private time, and the meddling, shrieking Bad Grandmother whose outbursts and accusations caused my parents to quickly send me to my room or start heading for the car. Though the Good Grandmother was the one I always expected to answer the door at her house or drive up to ours, I never knew when the Bad one might appear. Without a static image of my grandmother to fasten on, my feelings toward her began to fluctuate in sync with her mood. When she was indulgent or playing games with me, I adored her; when she was causing conflict with my parents, I felt that familiar tightening inside my rib cage and silently prayed for her to leave. The first and only song I ever composed at the piano, when I was about ten, was entitled "The Grandma Song," and the lyrics went something like "Please come and stay/Why don't you go away?" When my mother walked in from the kitchen and heard what I was doing, she bit her lips and stood still, watching me with a pinched expression on her face. She must have realized at that moment how successfully her own mixed feelings toward her mother had filtered down to me.

The inconsistency with which I began to respond to my grandmother — comfortable in her presence one day, edgy and irritable the next — was strikingly similar to the way I perceived my mother felt toward her too. Some days I'd come home from school and find the two of them sitting together at the kitchen table and gossiping like schoolgirls, drinking coffee from the electric percolator my mother lugged upstairs only for dinner parties and her mother's visits. Other days she'd take the telephone receiver from my hand with an expression that could be described as nothing other than sheer dread.

Whether or not my mother truly did feel such ambivalence toward her mother actually matters less than my observation that she did, since an older child's feelings of closeness toward her maternal grandmother typically depend on how close she *perceives* her mother and grandmother to be.[*] In other words, granddaughters who think their mothers and grandmothers have a good relationship are much more likely to feel emotionally close to those grandmothers than granddaughters do who believe their mothers and grandmothers don't get along. It follows, then, that three-quarters of the women interviewed for this book who described their mothers and maternal grandmothers as emotionally close say they felt close to those grandmothers, too.

Phyllis, the granddaughter who tried to run away to her grandmother's house when she was five, cites her mother's intimate bond with her grandmother as the basis for her constant desire to be in her grandmother's presence. "We went to see my grandmother frequently, on weekends

[*]A child's feelings toward her paternal grandmother seem to depend more on how she thinks both her father *and* her mother get along with that grandmother. In the case of maternal grandmothers, however, only the mother's relationship with her seems to matter.

and for every holiday, because my mother was very, very close to her mother," Phyllis explains. "When my mother talked about going to see my grandmother she always talked about going 'home.' And there was a time during our teenage years when my sisters and I got furious that she thought of *that* as her home, instead of where *we* lived. I think my mother was part of my, in a sense, deflection toward my grandmother, because she created this other place, where my grandmother lived, as her home. So there was a way in which my feelings of devotion toward my grandmother were probably fed by my mother's attitude toward her mother, who was a god to her, too."

A mother's negative opinion of her own mother can work in the opposite direction, damaging a daughter's relationship with a grandmother before it has a chance to develop on its own. Bitterness or anger toward the maternal grandmother — sometimes the result of legitimate abuse or neglect but often the result of a mother's immature vision of her mother, which prevents her from accepting her mother as imperfect and with human limitations — can be unconsciously passed down to a granddaughter who adopts these emotional responses as her own. This is especially the case when a granddaughter's physical contact with her grandmother is sparse. A 1987 study of 126 triads of young-adult granddaughters, their mothers, and their maternal grandmothers found that granddaughters who had less than monthly contact with their grandmothers tended to adopt their mothers' feelings toward that grandmother instead of developing opinions of their own.

But granddaughters having extensive contact with their grandmothers are far more likely to form independent relationships with them and separate themselves from a mother's negative opinion. Thirty-one-year-old Rachel, for example, remembers how her mother and grandmother fought throughout most of her childhood, highly critical of one another's life choices. Rachel remembers her maternal grandmother, however, as the adult who consistently offered her structure and advice, especially after her father died and her mother began experimenting with alternative lifestyles. When Rachel left home at twelve for boarding school, her grandmother remained a family anchor, calling her once a week, writing letters, and mailing her sweaters in the winter.

"My mother still talks very harshly about her mother, who's now been dead for almost ten years, and we get sort of testy about it with each other," Rachel says. "I tell her, 'You can pick on her all you want, but she was my grandmother and I find it offensive. She wasn't all those bad things to *me*.' "

Rachel developed a bond with her grandmother by spending consistent one-on-one time with her as a child during weekly visits without her mother present. The importance of physical contact between granddaughters and grand-mothers cannot be underestimated. Seventy-eight percent of the women surveyed for this book who saw their maternal grandmothers once a month or more during their childhoods said they'd felt emotionally close to them, compared to only 45 percent who'd seen them less.

Despite their angry outbursts and their tensions, my mother and grandmother shared a deep, abiding, and immutable love. Because they spent so much time together, and because I knew my mother trusted her mother enough to often leave the two of us alone, my grandmother and I had the opportunity to develop an intimate relationship of our own. On the other hand, if my mother had refused to see her mother during those years, or if we'd lived farther away and seen her only infrequently, I would have been cut off from my grandmother until I became old enough to establish and maintain contact myself. By that time, probably early- to mid-adolescence, it might have been too late.

A grandchild's first seven years are the most critical period for developing close bonds with grandparents, Dr. Kornhaber explains. "After then, kids start to run experience through their intellect," he says. "They get into 'Should do this' and 'Right' versus 'Wrong.' When they're younger, their way of operating with a grand-parent is through example and non-verbal ado-ration that's not complicated by the psycho-logical baggage that parents and kids have." The opportunity for a pure spiritual connection with a grandmother diminishes greatly once judgment and opinion arrive on the scene. Children who form a close bond with a grandmother from the start inevitably have a firmer foundation with her than those who, for example, try to start cultivating it at age ten.

"A grandchild's connection with grandparents also plays a role in behavior modification, in the sense that shame and guilt come into play with a grandparent," Kornhaber continues. "Most children will not hurt a grandparent, where they will hurt a parent. In other words, the parents are the bad guys and the grandparents and the grandchildren are the victims of the parents' oppression."

I never would have showed my grandmother the piano song I wrote. I hid it in the walnut piano bench between some Judy Garland sheet music and two concertos by Chopin, careful to prevent her from coming across it by accident. Despite my growing ambivalence, I couldn't bear the thought of hurting her. Though I was capable of screaming at my mother until my throat burned raw, I never once raised my voice to my grandmother. "Grandma, *please!*" was as close as I could get. Even as a child, especially as a child, I could sense that underneath her fierce and often combative armor lay a soft and gentle core I needed to protect.

2

Mount Vernon: 1971

It's the first night of Passover, and we arrive at my grandparents' house before sundown. I'm six and a half years old. Watch me tumble out of my parents' red Oldsmobile and across my grandparents' lawn, my black patent leather Mary Janes making satisfying little smacks against the flagstones as I hurtle toward the front door. I'm wearing a navy blue, shiny vinyl miniskirt with a matching vest, and my pigtails are tied with mustard-colored bows. "Don't run!" my mother calls from the car. I slow down to let my sister catch up, and we bound up the front step together. Before I can reach the round, gray slatey button that rings the bell, my grandmother pulls open the wooden door, welcoming us with a "How'd ya do, how'd ya do?" as she leans out to push open the screen.

The house's warmth envelopes me as I gallop into the dim foyer. It's like heading into a womb, only noisier. There's a sudden burst of pandemonium as my sister and I pass through: the shouts of "Hi, Grandma!" the loud screech of the screen door swinging shut, the crush of too many active bodies in too small a space; and my grandmother calling over our heads in her high, sweet voice, "Ta-ahm! Look who's he-ere!"

She's never not happy to see us. *Never.*

My mother walks in holding a Pyrex bowl with a cellophane lid in both hands. It's filled with *haroseth,* a mixture of apples and walnuts and wine that she made this morning for the Seder. She lifts the bowl above her head to keep it safe, her greeting of "*Hel*-lo, *Hel*-lo" mingling with both of my grandparents' "hul-*lo,* hul-*lo*s" in a discordant echo. "Mother," she says as she leans over to kiss my grandmother on the cheek. She calls her mother "Mother" and her father by the informal "Daddy," which has never made sense to me. When I once asked her why, she looked momentarily confused. "That's a good question," she said. "I don't know." I asked if it was because she liked her father better, and she said, "Of *course* not," but I vowed to be especially nice to my grandmother the next time I saw her anyway.

We're the first family members to arrive, so my sister and I head straight for the dining room buffet where my grandmother keeps the books and toys. Some of them she bought for us, some we've accidentally left here and now don't bother bringing home, and some are left over from her three daughters, now all grown. Even this young, I'm aware that my grandmother saves everything. *Ev-er-y-thing.* The elegant mahogany furniture is piled high with books and cards and photographs and papers, clutter skimming the surface of the rooms like a thick layer of uneven frosting. The buffet is crammed with dozens of coloring books and board games, all haphazardly jammed in. I'd never get away with this kind of organization at home. My mother keeps the books on my shelf neatly lined up, spines facing out, and the games in my closet form tidy piles, with the largest ones on the bottom and the smallest on the top.

At Grandma's house the rules are considerably more relaxed. It's the only place I ever go where I don't have to worry about being impeccably behaved. Here, anything I do is golden. If my crayon shoots off the paper and marks up the table, it's treated like artwork. If I forget to flush the toilet or leave toys on the floor, she never complains.

And the toys she has! Princey, a black-and-white metal horse attached to its frame by tightly coiled springs; a little cardboard dollhouse with a tiny pink family dressed in cloth clothes; an Autoharp I strum with a quarter when I can't find the guitar pick. My grandfather runs a manufacturing business, but in his free time he's an inventor who's elevated tinkering to a semifunctional art. The house is filled with items he's crafted, several of them involving cigar boxes and doorbells. The house is a child's paradise. Only later will I realize that no one else I know lives in the midst of such an excessive volume of detritus and junk.

While my mother helps my grandmother prepare for the Seder in the kitchen, and my father talks business with my grandfather on the back porch, my sister and I settle with our coloring books into the kitchen's blue vinyl wraparound booth. At one corner of the table, my grandmother is arranging items on the silver Seder plate. A hard-boiled egg, some sprigs of parsley, a shankbone, and a small mound of the *haroseth* my mother made. *It's supposed to remind us of the mortar the Jews put between bricks a long time ago,* my grandmother explains as she spoons it onto the plate. Behind her, pots of chicken soup and brisket simmer on the stove.

The doorbell rings, and rings again. All my grandmother's brothers and sisters and their spouses are here, as well as my aunts and uncle, and a friend. The rooms hum above my head. We're seventeen in all. Every surviving member of my grandmother's family moves into her dining room, taking their seats along the sides of the mahogany table. My grandfather lowers himself into a chair at the table's head and my grandmother shares a piano bench with her sister Nell at the other end, with easy access to the kitchen's swinging door. Between them lies the same spread that connects them on Passover every year: the matzo plate in front of my grandfather covered with a cloth napkin; the browned, braided challah bread lying on a scratched silver platter; the symmetrical silver candelabra in the center, its two white candles steadily burning down into thick rivulets of wax; the parallel rows of china dinner plates rimmed with burgundy and gold; and, placed at strategic intervals down the table's length, the rectangular bottles of Manischewitz Concord Grape wine.

There are some things you can count on, that you believe will never change.

My grandmother is peaceful tonight, surrounded by the people she loves most. They're all healthy and everyone looks happy; for once, there's no reason for concern. There will be no disruptions tonight, no unexpected emotional displays. We will look and act every bit the close-knit family she so badly wants us to be. I take my seat between my parents. My grandmother at one end of the table and my grandfather at the other bracket all of us like bookends, containing a whole family in between. Tonight, my grandmother's house is a safe, warm place. My grandfather opens his Haggadah. My grandmother looks up at him and smiles. We begin.

3

The Eternal Grandmother

"Perhaps nothing is more valuable for a child than living with an adult who is firm and loving," Margaret Mead wrote in her autobiography, *Blackberry Winter*. "My mother was trustworthy in all matters that involved our care. Grandma was trustworthy in quite a different way. She meant exactly what she said, always."

Dependable, predictable adults are the foundation of a child's world. In the child's mind, grandparents serve as backup parents, the net that will break the family's fall. They know that if their greatest fear — something happening to their parents — comes true, as long as they have grandparents who love and trust them they'll never be left unprotected and alone.

Thirty-six-year-old Marion was eight when her parents died, and her maternal grandparents stepped in to raise her and her fifteen-year-old brother. "My grandparents always lived right next door and were around our house all the time," she recalls. "They were very good, warm people, and though it was awful to lose my parents, they were the best substitutes we could have found. Soon after my brother went into the army, my grandfather died of a stroke and then it was just me and my grandmother at home. She was a heavyset woman, very soft-spoken. I used to get up in the mornings and go in to lay my head on her to start my day. She was already in her sixties when we went to live with her, and it wasn't easy for her to raise a child and a teenager but she did it. She was always there for me, every day, waving to me from the window when I walked home from school. I'm just so grateful to her. I mean, where else could my brother and I have gone? What would have happened to us if she hadn't been there?"

Children need one stable adult they can depend on, and their emotional development depends more on having such a person than it does on that person being the mother. Marion's grandmother became the "secure base" she could return to at moments of insecurity or distress, giving her the foundation she needed for forming secure attachments with others as well as developing empathy, self-reliance, and self-esteem.

"Sometimes I'm simply appalled by some of the case histories that I take from adult women in the course of my treatment plan," says Marilyn Boynton, R.N., M.Ed., a psychotherapist in Toronto and a co-author of *Goodbye Mother, Hello Woman: Reweaving the Mother–Daughter Relationship.* "When I hear some of the losses and some of the abuse that a woman has gone through, I think, How could these women have functioned considering all this? And more for my own sake, I try to think about what or who has sustained them. Inevitably, when I ask, 'Has there been or is there a grandmother somewhere in the picture?' the answer is yes, and the grandmother emerges as a figure who has been warm and supportive. Some women dismiss her as not being very important because she's only a grandmother. They're focusing instead on the people who weren't there and who should have been. So I get to turn it around and point out that they've identified the one person in all of the family who may have given them what they needed in order to grow. It's like having a fairy godmother."

Especially when a mother is unable to fill her parenting role adequately, a warm and loving grandmother can help soften a granddaughter's feelings of abandonment or rejection. The message the child receives is *I'm still a worthy person, even if my mother doesn't treat me so.* When an adult woman reviews her childhood and concludes, "My grandmother saved my life," what she often means is the grandmother salvaged or repaired her fragile and emerging self-esteem.

To these girls, the awesome power of the mother isn't eliminated, just reduced. A daughter will still look to her mother for acceptance, and will still feel rejected and angry in its absence. A father's harsh treatment may also erode her emerging sense of self-worth. But the security she derives from knowing she has at least one source of consistent, unconditional love in the home helps compensate for some of what she's lost.

"I just thank God that my grandmother had a place in my life," says thirty-eight-year-old Jan, who describes a childhood with parents who physically and emotionally abused her. "I do believe I'd be institutionalized if I didn't have her in my upbringing. All the values and beliefs that are important to me now came from her. I don't know how my grandmother, who was such a loving person, produced my mother, who was so angry and violent. I feel kind of ungenerous toward my mother, because I really don't know what she went through when she was growing up. I feel I should be more understanding of what caused her to turn out the way she did. But my grandmother was, and still is, really, the only source of unconditional love I've ever known. She very often tried to put herself physically between my mother and me when my mother was beating me up. My mother would never touch me affectionately, but I loved being physically close to my grandmother. She was my safe haven, as much as there could be one in that household. I still struggle with a lot of self-loathing and depression today, which I know is the identity my mother gave me, but I also know that my grandmother thought I was a good girl. Whatever strength and fortitude I have today definitely came from her. I think of myself as very self-sufficient and I'm good at speaking up for myself and for other people, too. That came from my grandmother, because that's what she did for me."

In any family system, children are highly attuned to what each adult is capable of offering them and amazingly adept at getting their needs met, quickly learning whom they can approach for what. "Resourceful children are like scavengers," Evelyn Bassoff explains. "What they can't get from one person they look for in another."

As a child, it didn't take me long to figure out that if my mother answered a request with a no, an appeal to Grandma usually elicited a yes. And if I had a concern I felt wasn't receiving the regard it deserved, I knew where to turn. I was a naturally dramatic child and always hungry for attention, liable to inflate a situation way out of proportion just to direct the focus toward me. My mother didn't appreciate this tendency toward melodrama; she called me a little Sarah Bernhardt. But my grandmother understood the importance of an occasional well-timed emotional display. If I felt a performance coming on, I knew I could find a receptive audience in her. Even if I just needed acknowledgment or praise, I knew whom to call.

"In an isolated single parent family or in coupled families that are distanced from the extended family, no one is there to make up for the limitations of the parents and the child is shortchanged," Dr. Bassoff says. "The emotional problems of a parent are much more magnified when no one else is there to balance them out.

My mother was extremely anxious when I was a child, in large part because of her experiences during the Holocaust. My grandmother was unbelievably not anxious. If my mother had been my whole environment, I think I would have grown up to be very fearful, but my grandmother kept off-setting that because she was brave and unafraid, and at moments of stress I looked to her for that."

When twenty-two-year-old Kristen was a child and her mother, a single parent, could no longer handle the demands of two small children, her maternal grandmother stepped in to offer Kristen the structure and nurturing she needed. From ages five through twelve, Kristen lived with the woman she called "Mor-mor," Swedish for "mother's mother," visiting with her biological mother after school and one or two nights a week. The two women divided Kristen's care between them, but Kristen's warmest memories of childhood all involve times spent with Mormor.

"Every Saturday night I used to take a bath and she would curl my hair in rags. I'd eat my ice cream and we'd watch *The Love Boat* together. Every Saturday night," she recalls. "If I was really good, I got to stay up for *Fantasy Island*, which wasn't too often. Then on Sundays after church we'd go to the bakery and buy fresh bread. I'd get a jelly donut and then I'd go home and watch *The Three Stooges* and *The Little Rascals* and part of an Abbott and Costello movie before she sent me out while she cleaned the house. She did everything for me. She made me eat all my vegetables, drove me to summer camp, took me to Girl Scout events. When I lived with her, I was happy. I never even questioned why I was there, because I didn't want the situation to change. Mormor was the stability in my life. The way most children bond with their mothers, I bonded with her."

The day Kristen got her first period, she and her grandmother went out for dinner and a movie to celebrate. "I vividly remember the drive home," Kristen says. "My grandmother was complaining that her arm hurt and that she had angina. Being twelve, you don't realize that those are signs of heart trouble. I was supposed to go to my mother's that night and I remember Mormor asking me, 'Why don't you just come home? Don't go there,' and I was like, 'No, I have to go to my mom's. I have to go there.' Something told me not to stay at Mormor's. She died that night in her sleep. From what I understand, she sat in her chair and was watching TV, and fell asleep there and died."

Like most granddaughters raised by grandmothers, Kristen experienced Mormor's death as a crushing blow. The subsequent emotional devastation she goes on to describe is similar to the type suffered by girls who lose their mothers. Mormor, as Kristen's primary nurturer, *was* like a mother to her.

After Mormor's death, Kristen moved into her mother's house, where she walked around in a stupor for several months, unable to adjust to the news. "I freaked out really bad," she says. "My parents were giving me sedatives to calm me down so I could sleep, because otherwise I'd stay up all night and at the crack of dawn I'd leave, saying I was going to walk to school. They used to catch me walking past my grandmother's house instead. I wouldn't go to school, I'd just walk around all day. I don't even remember where I'd go. And I was fighting terribly with my mother. I hadn't lived with her for seven years, which is a big chunk of your life when you're twelve. One day I was leaving her house, and she asked, 'Where are you going?' I said, 'I'm going to Mormor's,' and my mother just said, 'She's dead.' It was months after the fact, and that's when it just hit me. I couldn't handle her dying at all.

"A few months later, I moved in with my father," Kristen continues. "He worked a lot, and I had to learn how to cook and take care of myself. Mormor had done everything for me — wash my clothes, make my bed, clean everything. When I lived with her, I basically did nothing but live my happy little life. After she died, I had to grow up really fast. Within a year, I'd changed dramatically. With her, I was still like a little girl, very innocent. After she died I became very bad and rebellious. It's not like she was doing anything wrong by doing too much for me; she was doing everything right. She knew how to love me. She was just there for me. My parents were there, too, but they didn't give me the kind of love I'd received from my grandmother and that I still needed. So I became very independent and not really close with them. Since my grandmother died, I've basically been on my own." Even though both her parents were still alive, when Mormor died Kristen's secure base vanished, and with it her belief that she would be protected and provided for as a child.

By contrast, in families where a child's parents are her primary nurturers and a grandmother plays an important but secondary role, a young granddaughter is often affected as much by her mother's response to the grandmother's death as she is by the actual loss. Fifty-two-year-old Gloria's most vivid memory of her grandmother's death when she was eight is of her mother's breakdown and month-long recuperation in another state. "I was terrified for her, terrified that I might lose her, too," Gloria recalls. "I'd been very attached to my grandmother, but her death completely took a backseat to my fear that something awful had happened to my mother and that she'd never return. I don't know if I ever even mourned for my grandmother, but I know I mourned the month-long loss of my mother."

Acutely sensitive to any shifts in her mother's composure, a young child may need first to feel assured that the mother is through the worst of her mourning before she allows herself to start grieving for a lost grandmother. She may not start acting out her grief for as much as six months to a year after the death, long enough for the adults around her to miss the connection between her current behavior and the loss of her grandmother many months before.

For most children, the loss of a grandparent marks a first experience with death. Their response to the loss depends on several factors: the nature of the relationship with the deceased grandparent; the family's collective response to the death; and their age at time of loss. That last factor is perhaps the most significant, since it indicates how much intellectual awareness a grandchild has of death and how capable she may be of handling strong feelings of grief.

Very young children, up to about age seven, lack a basic understanding of what death means. They often interpret euphemisms such as "Grandma went to heaven" or "Nana is in a very deep sleep" literally, expecting Grandma to return or Nana to wake up. My father's mother died just after I'd turned nine, and that afternoon my father sat me down in my bedroom to break the news. "We lost Nana," he told me, and my immediate thought was Why can't we go and find her? I remember feeling sad when he explained I wouldn't see her again — no more trips to her house? no more presents brought back from her vacations? — but I lacked the capacity to understand the deeper implications of *forever.* The phrase *Nana is dead* was virtually meaningless to me at the time. Though I'd loved her absolutely, I'd seen her only a few times a year, and the impact the loss had on my father, leaving him despondent and irritable for months afterward, affected me much more than her sudden absence. The alarming shock of hearing him cry, a foreign, jagged sound far worse than any I could have imagined, stayed with me for years, long after the point that I fully understood my beloved nana was lost to me for good.

Three years later, when my maternal grandfather died, I had a much firmer grasp of what *We lost Grandpa* meant. When I cried, I did so not out of confusion or fear this time but because I knew I would miss him, and I felt sad. Those three years between nine and twelve spanned an intellectual awakening, since *forever* was no longer an inaccessible concept to me. At age nine it was still too abstract for me to grasp, but by age twelve I understood it meant longer than I could possibly imagine, and then some more.

Most children don't have what's called a full adult understanding of death — meaning it's inevitable, it's irreversible, and it happens to everyone — until they've reached the "operational thinking" stage, characterized by the ability first to think logically and then to think abstractly, which begins around age seven and takes about five years to develop fully. This adultlike concept of death hasn't been observed in children younger than seven, and typically doesn't appear until ages ten to twelve. Those are roughly the same years that a child's intellectual maturity reaches a point where she can also accept and adjust to a loved one's death, but she doesn't yet have the emotional skills to handle the sadness or fear this awareness usually provokes. Children of this age who lack a stable adult who can help them mourn are the ones most likely to stuff their emotions and delay their mourning, sometimes for years, until they feel more capable of handling the emotional distress on their own.

Parents, often and understandably absorbed by their own grief after losing a parent, frequently underestimate the strength of a child's attachment to a grandparent. Although many bereavement centers in this country provide support programs for children who've lost a grandparent, directors of these centers say grandchildren rarely walk through their doors. When you consider that a child needs her parent to acknowledge she needs such bereavement support and then seek it out for her, this absence makes sense. First the parent has to recognize the magnitude of the child's loss, and that's where many families get stuck.

"I really don't think my mother had any idea how devastating the loss of my grandmother was to me," says thirty-three-year-old Julie, who was thirteen when she lost the grandmother who helped raise her throughout childhood. "Because she considered herself my primary parent, she didn't understand how completely lost I felt for months afterward. She was caught up in her own guilt and grief because she hadn't realized how sick my grandmother was until it was too late, and so I felt like I pretty much had to get over the loss on my own. My mother is just starting to figure out how orphaned I felt back then, and I think it's been a little shocking for her. She sends me cards on St. Patrick's Day in my grandmother's memory now, because it was my grandmother's favorite holiday."

In any family, the death of a beloved grandmother has the potential to rock a child's world. Grandmothers, being older than parents, are often perceived by their grandchildren as all-powerful figures who live close to God and will always exist to nurture and protect. Discovering otherwise is a profound shock to a granddaughter's belief in a safe and predictable universe. "To me, my grandmother was eternal," Julie explains. "I honestly didn't expect her to die. Ever."

4

Conflict and the Emerging Self

When we sit down to fashion personal narrative out of life events, the moments that stand out in boldest relief are always those that contain the most conflict and drama. So it's not surprising that when I interviewed women who identified their grandmothers as significant influences in their lives, for every anecdote I heard about how warm and loving a grandmother was, I heard two about how difficult or negative she'd been.

Not all grandmothers are family sweethearts: I need to make that clear. Lois Banner, Ph.D., a professor of history at the University of Southern California and the author of *In Full Flower: Aging Women, Power, and Sexuality*, especially warns against romanticizing the grand-daughter–grandmother relationship. Raised by her grandmother in an extended-family household after her mother died when she was a teen, Banner's memories of her grandmother are not uniformly pleasant. "My grandmother was a very powerful and extremely unhappy woman," Banner explains. "After my mother died she took over raising the children who were left in the home, but after losing her daughter she was extremely depressed, so it wasn't a positive experience for me."

While women whose grandmothers were harshly critical or abusive certainly can emerge from those relationships with a damaged sense of self-worth, most of the women I met spoke instead of feeling a low-level tension toward difficult grandmothers, often the result of obscuring conflict between their grandmothers and their parents. They frequently reverted to a child's terminology to describe how they'd felt. "Sometimes I was afraid of her," they said, or "I didn't like her all the time."

Learning to cope with resentment toward or fear of a grandmother occasionally led these young granddaughters to occasions of early epiphany, in which an important awareness or a moment of personal growth occurred. "I was about nine when I realized my grandmother wasn't really as nice a person as my parents wanted me to believe," twenty-eight-year-old Gretchen recalls. "And I realized then that I could have my own opinion about her, or about anything really, even if it meant I was the only one who held it. That gave me an enormous feeling of power as a child, knowing I had access to independent thought."

But ongoing conflict with a grandmother can also influence a child's emerging personality in a negative manner, forcing her to adopt artificial coping strategies. Twenty-four-year-old Leila, for example, remembers a childhood with a maternal grandmother who was often generous and protective but was also prone to unpredictable fits of hysteria and rage. "You had to be careful what you said around her," Leila explains. "Anything could do it, depending on her mood. Sometimes she'd be fine for months and then one day she'd just go off. It was completely irrational, like nothing you'd ever seen before. One time my sister and I had a friend over after school and my grandmother was in my mother's room, cleaning up. My friend and I were in there talking to her, and my friend lay down on the bed. My grandmother had just made the bed, and that set her off. She had been cleaning the room for my mother who worked so hard, and my friend was in someone else's home, and how could she be so inconsiderate? She didn't say it that calmly, either. My friend was just terrified. She started to cry. And that wasn't the only friend of ours she did that to. We had to warn everyone we knew and everyone who might come to our house to be careful around her, because it was scary when she went off like that.

"I knew this kind of behavior wasn't normal, because my mother had explained to me that Grandma had some problems," Leila continues. "I didn't see my mother acting like that, and when I went to other people's houses I didn't see their families react that way either. We just tried to work around it in our house, in our own ways. I was extra sweet with her so she would never have an excuse to act that way around me. My sister went in the opposite direction, especially when she was young. She would try to argue or reason with my grandmother, and that just made the situation worse."

The childhood coping mechanisms Leila relied on — *be sweet; be calm; don't challenge Grandma's authority* — earned her peace with a grandmother who adored her soft-spoken, even-tempered granddaughter. But tiptoeing around her grandmother had a hidden long-term cost. Leila says she now doesn't know how to handle anger, at all. She's afraid to inspire it in others and unable to feel it herself. "I'm afraid of being or looking like my grandmother if I get angry," she admits, "so I don't get angry. I really just don't ever feel anger. I feel either happy or sad. I used to break down and cry a lot when I was about twelve. I told my mother I thought it was because I couldn't get angry and that maybe I should see a counselor. We went to one and he gave me some books to read, but I know I have to do the work myself. I'm very aware of that, but right now it's still too hard."

Children who are raised by such unpredictable grandmothers suffer many of the same psychological injuries as children raised by inconsistent or abusive parents, including damaged self-esteem; feelings of diminished self-worth; the excessive desire to please others, even at the expense of their own well-being; self-blame; and difficulty forming secure attachments to others. Psychiatrist Francine Cournos, in her memoir of early orphanhood, *City of One*, describes spending the two years after her mother's death with a maternal grandmother who was slipping into senility and who fluctuated between episodes of intense devotion and unpredictable anger.

For months after her mother's death, an eleven-year-old Cournos, her younger sister, and her grandmother cried together every night about their loss, an evening ritual involving bear hugs and loud wails. "Then, when Grandma was mad at us one night," Cournos writes, "she ended our routine with a nasty twist. 'If your mother hadn't been so busy taking care of you,' she said, 'she could have gone to the doctor in time and she wouldn't have died.' I was horrified to discover that Grandma blamed us for Mom's death. For an instant, I stopped experiencing Grandma as a helpless companion and saw her as a witch. When we were adults, my cousin Marlene described our grandmother: 'She was the incarnation of selfishness and evil, the source of all her children's impairments.' But I was depending on Grandma; I had to see her in the best possible light." Tightly focused on her own survival, Cournos blocked out any evidence of her grandmother's instability, and this became a defense mechanism against further pain.

A child's sense of self is highly dependent on her interactions with the adults around her, particularly those who raise her. When a grandmother is an important but secondary figure in

75

the family, however, conflicted feelings toward her are less likely to evolve into disastrous internal results. "As a child, you orient yourself in relation to the generations," explains Naomi Lowinsky, Ph.D., a psychotherapist in Berkeley, California, and the author of *The Motherline: Every Woman's Journey to Find Her Female Roots*. "Even if the grandmother is a negative force, you have a sense of who you are in relation to her." Grandmothers who are harsh, judgmental, critical, or otherwise difficult to get along with can even contribute positively to a granddaughter's development, adds Valerie Kack-Brice, CSW, a psychotherapist in Grass Valley, California, and the editor of the anthology *For She Is the Tree of Life: Grandmothers Through the Eyes of Woman Writers*. "A granddaughter will often push against that and become her own person as a result of that pushing away," she explains. "It's almost like she can't lose. That negative relationship still has some benefit."

I'm reminded of a woman I'll call Erin, who's now forty-two years old. Unlike the other granddaughters I interviewed for this book, Erin's maternal grandmother had been institutionalized and absent for most of her childhood, and her father's mother became the dominant grandmother of her childhood.

A self-described good little Catholic girl, a people-pleaser until the age of twelve, when "a bomb went off — because who can be that perfect forever?" Erin remembers her grandmother as an authoritative Irish matriarch who lorded it over her only son and, indirectly, over Erin's entire nuclear family. Erin resented her grandmother's power, especially when it monopolized her father's attention or minimized her mother's role. "I once said to my grandmother, 'He's *my* father, not yours,' because I felt that when she was around, my father's devotion was to her, not to us," she recalls. Because Erin's mother, whom she describes as "coming from a place of total love," never stood up to her mother-in-law, Erin adopted the role of family provocateur, refusing to bend to her grandmother's will.

"In church, all the little girls had white gloves and a little purse," she recalls. "You weren't supposed to put your hands to your mouth in church, and you never went to the altar with gloves on. Never. Whenever my grandmother came to church with us, I would go to the altar with gloves on and come back with my hands at my mouth. I could see her shaking with anger. At home, I would walk into the room, she would look at me, I would look at her defiantly, and *then* I would sit down. I don't know why I felt I had the right or the power to act that way with her, because I didn't feel it with anybody else. It was the only time I felt full of myself as a child. I felt secure in my dislike for her and in my position in the family.

"I think maybe that's how I survived what came next," she continues. "Maybe that's what allows me to be able to sit here and talk with you today. Because I really put myself through the wringer the rest of my life. Car accidents. Abortions. Split-ups. Drugs. My mother used to say, 'Why do you insist on living this kind of life?' I made it as difficult for myself as I possibly could. I'm not sure why — I think I felt I had to punish myself for something. I think there was a lot of self-hate. But I also think now that what pulled me through those years was that strong sense of self I developed as a child, because there was always something in me that kept me going."

Erin's parents never knew how strongly defiant she felt toward her grandmother. They might well be surprised by the clarity and conviction with which she tells her story today. In much the same way, my family is often startled by the vivid memories I have of my grandmother's outbursts during my childhood, the images I still have of her standing in our living room in her wool coat, her hair poking out from under her hat in disarray, punching the air with her upraised fist for emphasis, or of the sound of steady banging on our front door with the accompanying, even shouts of "LET ME IN! LET ME IN!" I don't remember what the arguments were about; my parents tried to shuffle me off behind a closed door as quickly as they could. I don't even remember if the arguments were frequent; they could have happened three or three dozen times. The most dramatic events from childhood grow in significance over the years; their emotional content swells. The noise and the heightened emotion are what I remember most, the way that for those few minutes, time seemed to stand still. That, and the absolute terror of seeing my otherwise calm and patient grandmother explode. My stomach would clench tight as I waited on my bed, hugging my Raggedy Ann, praying for the screaming to stop. Afraid that it never would. Not yet understanding how apology and reconciliation always arrived with the morning and how, with mechanical powers of recovery, we would all go on as usual, as if the night before had never occurred.

5

We All Go to Florida: 1976

Picture a paved road leading through a gated entry, past a guard issuing a two-finger wave, past turnoffs lined with low beige-stucco town houses and coconut-laden palm trees, past a clubhouse on the shore of a man-made lagoon. Picture men in plaid pants zipping across the road in golf carts. Make a right onto the inexplicably named Luxembourg Court; past the tennis courts and the swing sets and the painted metal horses that bounce on springs; past the heated pool where your sister is learning to jump in alone. Stop in front of the building marked 4465. Walk past the row of silver mailboxes set into the wall, past the communal laundry room and the elevator you ride for fun when it rains. Wonder why all the apartments open to the outside, like rooms in a motel. Walk through the door marked 105 and down the short hall carpeted in white shag, past the tiny, bright kitchen on the left, past the spare bedroom with the identical twin beds arranged in what your mother describes as "catty-corner" and the corner nightstand with a built-in radio that picks up only AM. Feel the humidity. Enter the big room, where an elderly red-haired woman in a bathrobe (your grand-mother) sits around a beige dining room table with a middle-aged woman (your mother), who squints at her row of tiles, and a dark-haired eight-year-old girl (your sister), who balances first on one foot and then the other, whining, "When do *I* go?" See that the game has just started. Realize it is your turn. Sit down.

We're playing Scrabble in my grandparents' condominium in Lake Worth, Florida. "We" being my grandmother, mother, sister, and me. My four-year-old brother is asleep on one of the twin beds and my grandfather is watching *The Rookies* in the master bedroom in the back. My father is still in New York, finishing the work week before he flies down to meet us Friday night.

We took the train down a few days earlier, twenty-six hours of screeching brakes and back-to-back Nancy Drew mysteries. "We" this time meaning my mother, brother, sister, grand-mother, and me. My grandfather flew ahead of us, for several days of solitude and golf. The train costs less than the airplane, but not by much. We took it mostly because my mother didn't want to travel alone with three children, and my grand-mother won't fly. Something about witnessing a barnstormer's crash back in the 1920s. Don't try to convince her that flying is safer than driving. It doesn't work.

All the sleeping compartments were booked

by the time my mother figured out my grand-mother really *wasn't* going to get on an airplane, which meant we had to sleep sitting up. Except for my brother, who's still small enough to lie with his head on my mother's lap. Which makes my sister unbearably jealous. She threw a tantrum in Penn Station when my father dropped us off because my mother was paying too much attention to Glenn. All those suitcases and over-head announcements and she was stamping her feet and screaming underneath the arrivals and departures board. "Come with me, Michele, we'll go over there and buy you a toy," my grandmother suggested, and I saw my mother mouth a silent "thank you" as they walked away.

Remarkably, for the next twenty-six hours we all get along. For most of the trip my mother and grandmother sit side by side while my brother runs the length of the car or plays with his G.I. Joe dolls on the floor. My mother does most of the talking. My grandmother rests in the aisle seat with her hands folded gently in her lap and her eyes closed, wearing her coat and hat. From time to time she nods or shakes her head. She's the only one of us who sleeps all night, right through the shuffling and grunting that goes on in the front seat of our car at 5:00 A.M., when the muscular man who got on in North Carolina goes to sit with the blond woman who got on in Baltimore.

The next morning my mother asks me if I heard the couple having sex in the front seat. I don't really understand what she means but she says it like I'm supposed to, so I say yes. "I thought so," she says. "I think it's better if you don't mention it to Grandma."

I add this to the list of things I'm not supposed to tell my grandmother, most of which she already knows. For example: that I'm planning to go swimming and wear shorts all week. For example: that we have airline reservations to get back home. But the surprise is all mine, because once we arrive in Florida my grandmother as I've always known her disappears. She's replaced by a woman who wears golf skirts and attractive chain-link belts and no hat. You'd be hard-pressed to find a bottle of castor oil anywhere in her condo.

The condo: That's the biggest surprise of all. Last April, not long after my grandparents bought the place as a winter golf getaway, my parents brought us to Florida for vacation while my grandparents were back up in New York. We drove our rented K-car through the gated entry and down the immaculately landscaped main boulevard, pulling up in front of the three-floor apartment building indicated on our directions sheet. My parents were silent the whole way in. You could almost hear my mother thinking, My parents have a place *here?* As we walked up to the apartment door and my father turned the key, she said a little singsong "Here we go-o," half expecting, as we all were, to walk into a smaller version of my grandparents' dark, cluttered house in New York.

Instead, we walked from room to room in a state of mute amazement. Bright yellow and white furniture, a few carefully selected ceramic knickknacks on the wall units, new mustard-and-white Melmac dishes in the kitchen cupboards. And central air-conditioning that worked. The air in the apartment was heavy with a month's worth of moisture and the faint smell of mildew. My father flicked the air-conditioning control switch to On and the familiar hum of imminent comfort vibrated around us. In the living room, a watercolor of an orange and yellow sailboat hung above the orange-and-yellow-flowered couch. "Did they hire a decorator?" my mother asked no one in particular.

It was difficult for any of us to imagine my grandmother cooking brisket and gravy or lighting her Shabbos candles in such a place, but traces of her littered the apartment like deliberate clues. A *Reader's Digest* on the rectangular glass coffee table. A squeezed tube of Fixodent in the bathroom. Even a pair of used women's scuffed white golf shoes on the floor of the master bedroom closet. I'd never known she played.

When she comes down here, my grandmother is lighter. New York weighs on her, with its winter coats and china cabinets and siblings with faltering health. But Florida is all paper napkins and short sleeves. Our first morning after the train ride she cooks scrambled eggs for breakfast

and helps me use a styrofoam cup to catch a sala-
mander that's trapped in her screened-in back
porch. My brother swings a golf club on the back
lawn, wearing only his underpants, and there is
no talk of catching cold.

But: She won't let us turn on the air-
conditioning. During the day it's unbearably hot
both inside and out. We go to the pool between
breakfast and lunch, and then we've done that.
My grandfather doesn't want anyone else driving the car, so all afternoon we sit in the living
room idly flipping through books and maga-
zines. My mother brushes my brother's damp
hair across his forehead. The yellow vinyl swivel
chairs stick to our legs. My grandfather returns
from his golf game, red and blue tees still poking
from the band in his hat. He suggests a fifteen-
minute drive to Cushman's fruit stand to mail
boxes of oranges and grapefruit to our family
and friends back home. My mother perks up; it's
something to do.

Cushman's is a long, low building with an
awning that reaches almost to the side of the
road. Rows of cardboard crates tilt toward us,
their orange and yellow citrus gifts packed in
with shredded fake grass. Behind the fruit there's
a gift shop. We can tell from the closed glass door
that inside it must be cool. Immediately, my
mother, brother, sister, and I head for the door.

The air thins considerably as soon as we cross
the threshold. Inside, the shelves are a monu-
ment to mid-seventies tropical kitsch. Troll dolls

in bikinis, Pet Rocks, and a row of aluminum cans with colorful labels that read "Florida Sunshine!" I pick one up and shake it. Its content feels like nothing, which is exactly, my mother informs me, what it is. Still. I imagine peeling off the lid in the middle of a New York winter, the scent of oranges and chlorine and Bain de Soleil emanating into my bedroom in a blinding ray of light. I sniff around the edge of the can. "Probably it smells like car exhaust in there," my mother says.

My sister is playing with a small green plastic tube with a pointy corkscrew on one end that, we conclude, is a straw for oranges. You screw one end right through the rind and suck out the juice from the other end. "How about that?" marvels my grandmother, who's just joined us in the air-conditioned room, leaving the tinkle of door chimes behind her. She's cradling a sack of oranges in one arm as if it were an infant. I can see my grandfather through the glass door, standing at the cash register and riffling through a wad of bills with his thumb.

"It's for oranges," I tell her.

She rips through the plastic netting of her bag and hands one orange to me, one to my sister. "Why don't you give it a try?" she asks.

If I hesitate, it's because I know you're not supposed to put an item in your mouth before you buy it. There's something a little thrilling about the idea of doing this backward, use now, pay later, but I know my mother won't want to pay for something as frivolous as this little sucking pipe — that's what fathers are for in our house — and that trying it in the store is akin to letting my grandmother buy it for me. This may or may not bother my mother. Usually she objects to my grandmother's indulging us when my father is around, but when he's not there she lets my grandparents pay for everything without a fight. I'm not supposed to notice that, though, because it undermines her theory that her younger sisters get and have always gotten more from their parents than she does, a claim that loses most of its credibility anyway the moment you start acknowledging my grandparents' nearly obsessive generosity to all their children and grandchildren — which on this vacation includes all of our train tickets, all of our meals, and all of the numerous trinkets and toys we accumulate during the week. My grandfather buys us whatever we want with a shrug. He's not worried about my parents' response. My grandmother, on the other hand, will buy us small toys with the caveat "Don't tell your mother," which means we have to hide the offending item until a certain danger zone has passed. Around my mother and grandmother I spend a lot of time trying to keep straight what I can and can't notice and what I'm not supposed to say to whom.

But the idea of sucking juice straight out of an orange is too tantalizing to resist. I take the orange from my grandmother and try to screw the pipe into its side, but it gets stuck in the rind.

"Let me see it," she says, and pushes the tube through in two sharp twists. She's stronger than I think. It's not such a great toy after all, though, because you have to suck *really* hard to get any liquid and I suspect all sorts of internal problems like seeds and veins are getting in the way. I'm dragging on the pipe with such force that my eyes are bulging and my cheeks are completely concave, when my mother walks over and gives me a funny look.

"What's wrong with you," she says.

I show her the orange with the little pipe sticking out. "It doesn't work."

"Give it here," she says, showing me her open palm. She unscrews the pipe, extracts a piece of rind with her fingernails, and screws it back in. Then she sucks on it a few times and gives a little laugh. "Good idea," she says, handing it back to me. "Tell Grandma you want two."

Back at the apartment, my sister and I poke holes in another four or five oranges before the novelty wears off. Then we take turns sneaking over to the refrigerator where we've stored the box of coconut patties we bought at Cushman's. If we leave them on the counter, the dark chocolate coatings will start to melt. At six o'clock, even with the sun down, even with the front and back screen doors open to encourage a cross breeze, the effect is still something like being wrapped in a wet blanket. My mother can't handle it. She keeps walking out to the parking lot with my brother, pacing between the rows of cars. My grandparents are calm, reclining in their chairs and watching the news, reports of robberies and record temperatures punctuated by commercials for personal-injury attorneys, all of which add to my mother's anxiety. I'm starting to feel tense, too. I don't want to look like I'm choosing sides by sitting here, but I don't want to stand outside and listen to my mother ask what's the point of having an air conditioner if you never use it in this kind of heat.

Finally, after an hour of this, she asks my grandparents to take us for a ride. At least with the windows down we'll get a breeze. So we go cruising slowly on Okeechobee Boulevard in my grandfather's big Cutlass Supreme, past the used-car dealers and the new strip malls and all-you-can-eat seafood restaurants. My mother sits in the passenger seat with my brother on her lap and my sister, grandmother, and I share the back. The windows are rolled halfway down, and the first breeze of the day swipes past my cheek. I can relax back here, knowing my mother is comfortable now, feeling my grandmother peaceful beside me, all of us protected and content in our mobile pocket of family and fresh air.

And then. We stop for a red light and my brother reaches out and starts turning the FM dial like he always does in our car at home, looking for a song he recognizes. *I love you-u-u, Show me the way* . . . static static . . . *favored in the upcoming Pennsylvania Democratic primary . . . lay down and boo-gie and play that funky music till you die.* He stops when he finds "Rhinestone Cowboy" and starts bouncing on my mother's lap, singing loudly: *Doo-doo! Ridin' out on a horse in a star-spangled ro-de-o, doo-doo!* The light turns green; the car to our left revs its engine and peels off. *Doo-doo! Getting cards and letters from people* — And then suddenly there's no background music, just the sound of my brother shouting *"I don't even know!"* a cappella into a quiet car before any of us realize my grandfather has reached over and switched off the radio without warning.

My brother starts to wail when he figures out what's happened. It's so completely out of character for my grandfather to do this that no one really knows how to respond. "Tom, he was having fun," my grandmother protests, but it's too late. My mother is stroking my brother's hair to calm him down, already filing the incident away as ammunition for the phone call she'll make to my father when we get back to the apartment, the one pleading with him to cut the work week short and go stay with her in a hotel. "The kids can stay here," she says, "but I've *had* it. You know what my father did tonight in the car?" When my father refuses on the grounds that his boss, who happens to be my grandfather, is also out of the office this week, my mother will hang up the phone with an expression of grim resignation and start putting my brother to bed in the guest room, with the AM radio turned down low.

She finds the Scrabble game on a shelf in the

guest room closet while she's putting away my brother's clothes. It's a recent edition, probably left behind by one of my aunts, and it's only eight-thirty, so why not? We arrange ourselves at one end of the dining room table, with my grandmother at the head, me at her left and my mother and sister to her right, and pass the bag of tiles around.

They let me keep score because I'm the only one who doesn't need to use my fingers to add seven and nine. Also I just won the sixth-grade spelling bee in my school, which matters less than you'd think in Scrabble if you pick crappy letters, which I do. None of us manage to fashion words longer than four letters, but we're creative within those limits. My mother comes up with words like QUIP and ABET. My sister gives up after WAG and CUP and dumps her tiles back into the bag, joining my mother's team. "It's your turn, Mother," my mother gently reminds my grandmother at the beginning of every round. "Oh!" she says, startled every time. "Me, already?"

On the way back from the bathroom, my grandmother notices the tiles on my rack forming a parade of vowels. While we're waiting for my mother to take her turn, I feel a little tap-tap on my right thigh. I reach down to investigate and feel my grandmother pressing two tiles into my hand. When I'm sure no one's looking, I look at them: an *R* and an *M*. I give her a look that signals "What are you *doing?*" and she gives me a

91

little wink with her left eye. So I slide my rack close to the edge of the table and sneak her an *E* and a *U* in return.

It's peaceful here in the living room, the only sounds muted ones — the low buzz of the refrigerator, my mother and sister whispering as they consult about a word, the murmur of the *Marcus Welby* theme song coming from behind a closed door. It's getting late and we're tired; there's no energy left to argue or complain. Even my sister smiles at me when I tally up the score and announce that I've won. "All right, girls," my mother says as she packs up the box, code words for "It's time for bed." When we beg her to please, *pleeze* let us stay up a little longer, she doesn't resist. My grandmother brings out a tray of challah bread, kosher dill pickles, and margarine, and we make thick sandwiches we wash down with club soda and orange juice. When my sister punches a hole in the middle of a slice of challah and sticks it on her nose, we all laugh — my mother a quick giggle, my grandmother a deep heh-heh-heh.

I wish I could take my Scrabble pencil and draw a circle around us now, corralling everything that exists inside this space. All of it — the pickles, the margarine, the nightgowns, my mother's good mood, my grandmother's smile. This is my family, these women. I want to find a way for us to wake in the morning without letting this hour drain away into our pillows during the night. But I'm only eleven and a half, and I don't yet know how to make a moment last.

My father will arrive three nights later, on a direct flight from New York. We'll all go to meet him at the West Palm Beach airport, relieved he is here, ecstatic he is here, craning our necks for the first glimpse of his aviator glasses and long sideburns as soon as the passengers start gliding through the gate. We crowd around him as we walk through the airport, touching his hands, tugging on his sleeves. He is our savior, arrived to rescue us from ourselves. But even as we hurry together toward the Hertz rental car desk with the promise of air-conditioned hotels and beaches and FM radio urging us on, I can't quite shake the feeling that we're leaving something important behind.

PART II

The Three of Us: Grandmothers, Mothers, and Granddaughters

6

Adolescence

"When I was beginning adolescence, I started to clash with my grandmother," recalls fifty-year-old Marjorie, who grew up a half hour's drive from her maternal grandparents and visited with them every Sunday throughout her childhood. "I would cry. I wouldn't listen to her. She would say to me, 'You used to be such a nice girl. What happened?' "

Ten- to twelve-year-olds still value grandparents as companions and confidants, but early adolescence, from about ages thirteen to fifteen, is often a time when distance emerges between the generations. Grandmothers who felt adept at meeting a child's needs for companionship or play don't always feel competent handling a capricious teen, and granddaughters of this age tend to become more critical of all adults around them, including their grandparents, occasionally treating them with a loving form of condescension. As young teenagers make the shift from family-oriented activities to an immersion in the world of their peers, grandparents are often the first family members to get left behind.

"When I was a child, my grandmother was the

center of my world," explains twenty-eight-year-old Allison. "She would do my hair and treat me like a little dolly. I always wanted to be with Grandma. But when you enter your teenage years, your grandparents, as much as you love them, aren't the center of your universe anymore. In fact, they're pretty peripheral. We still had family dinners together every Sunday, but I didn't want to spend the whole weekend sitting around the pool with Grandma. And I think that hurt her deeply. She always made me feel guilty for not spending enough time with her. Which, of course, would make me want to see her less."

My grandmother continued to show up unannounced at our house before dinner and on the weekends a few times a month throughout my early adolescence, but my one-on-one time with her slowly dwindled down to visits during school vacations and summer break. Because I couldn't yet drive, this involved her transporting me, usually out for lunch at Howard Johnson's with her two sisters, or for a shopping trip to White Plains.

"Grandma, you can drive faster," I urged her, when I couldn't stand the slow road pace anymore. She rarely drove the speed limit. Off the highway she felt safest doing thirty-five.

"Slow and steady wins the race," she insisted, gripping the steering wheel tightly at ten and two o'clock. My parents used to complain she drove with her left foot on the brake. I didn't understand how it was possible to brake and accelerate at the same time, but when I checked below her dashboard I saw the square toe of her beige leather shoe resting gently against the brake pedal, ready to second-guess any potential calamity on the road. Within a few years she gave in to my impatience and just handed me her keys.

Already past the developmental stage in which they idealize most adults, teenagers no longer see their elders as flawless. Whereas children may think of a grandmother as older and wiser, teens observe her fall from grace. *Older* starts meaning *old*, *wiser* a synonym for knowledge that may or may not have any relevance to an adolescent's worldview. Thirty-four-year-old Deborah remembers how her relationship with her grandmother started changing during her adolescence, how the nana who'd been a roommate and confidante to a child was transformed into a grandmother who was irritating and embarrassing to a teen.

"I had to share a bedroom with my grandmother from the time I was two until I was about sixteen," Deborah recalls. "So I had a very intense relationship with her, in the same small room. During my early years, it was sort of fun, because she was my nana. She played with me and protected me. When I was sent to my room without dinner, she used to sneak up food in the pockets of her apron so I wouldn't go hungry. And she was the one who would come upstairs and hold me if I was crying, or when my mother would yell at me, or when I got spanked. She was my friend. She taught me how to be light and funny, and to enjoy the little things in life. I have a vivid memory of being five or six and sitting on her lap on a rainy day with the JC Penney catalog and she made me laugh about everything she pointed out in the catalog. There was one picture of a kid's training potty, and because she had a Greek accent she'd say 'potty' but it would sound like 'party.' She'd say, 'That's the party,' and I'd say, 'Nana, that's not a party! That's the potty where you go —' We were laughing and laughing about this potty-party thing.

"But then when I turned about twelve, I wanted my privacy. And I resented her very much for being in the same room with me. I was a teenager with my *grandmother* in my bedroom. We started to lose the friendship part of our relationship. When you're a teenager, you don't want to be friends with your grandmother, you want to be friends with your friends. I was embarrassed by Nana, just like I was embarrassed by having my mother around. As I started dating and my boyfriends would bring me home, Nana would be sitting in the middle of everything. My parents would go upstairs to leave my date and me alone downstairs to talk and I'd be like, 'Nana, could you go?' I was incredibly resentful. I did not have *any* privacy. And I had to work through the guilt I felt for that afterward. I remember sitting in church at her funeral when I was twenty-two, just weeping my eyes out. Bad enough that we'd lost her, but the *guilt* I felt. I felt so awful for the way I'd treated her during those years."

Deborah's adolescence coincided with her grandmother's slow descent into Alzheimer's disease, which gradually turned a sweet-natured matron into a confused and angry older woman. The diagnosis, however, was handed down only after Deborah had finished her teens. Until then, her family mistakenly believed her grandmother was naturally growing more difficult as she aged, and was frustrated, often treating her with anger for her lack of self-control.

If her grandmother had not begun this mental decline during Deborah's late teen years, Deborah probably would have started developing a more mature, balanced view of their relationship at about age sixteen. Two important events occurred simultaneously in her life at that time. First, her brother left for college and she moved into her own bedroom. Second, she reached the developmental stage when alienation between the first and third generations begins to disappear. Granddaughters ages sixteen to eighteen typically start seeing grandmothers in a more abstract and differentiated manner, and treat them with more consideration and indulgence. Not yet prepared to have a woman-to-woman relationship with their mothers — that won't occur for about another ten years — granddaughters in their mid- to late-teens often reconnect with a grandmother first, and begin to identify the traits and characteristics they most admire in her.

Of course, some granddaughters never experience this emotional separation from a grandmother, considering her a close friend and advisor throughout their teen years. A 1976 survey of 920 girls ages twelve to eighteen revealed that next to parents, a grandmother was the family member they confided in most. Other studies conducted with young adults looking back on adolescence have revealed that a majority of grandchildren feel their relationships with grandparents are important to them, and that their interactions with grandparents were satisfying during their high school years.

Sometimes granddaughters will even permit a grandmother to tread on territory where a mother is not allowed. Nineteen-year-old Elisa, for example, is in the midst of a difficult adolescent separation from her single mother, who raised her from birth with the help of Elisa's grandmother. Last year Elisa started college sixty miles from home and moved into her own apartment, but she remains in close touch with both women. When she describes her mother's daily phone calls and requests for information about the smallest details of her day, her frustration and anger are evident. "My mother calls me about eight times a day, literally," Elisa says. "She starts at six-thirty in the morning and doesn't leave me alone until three. She calls all the time for no reason. She'll say, 'Oh, what are you doing?' I'll say, 'I'm doing my homework. That's why I live here.' 'Oh, okay, are you going out tonight? Call me when you get in.' I say, 'No! I haven't lived with you in years. Please leave me alone!' I'm even in therapy now to figure out how to deal with this."

By contrast, her grandmother's daily phone calls aren't a source of anxiety to Elisa at all. She and her grandmother have remained emotionally intimate throughout her adolescence. In fact, during the past few years they've even drawn closer together, spending more time together than Elisa now spends with her mother.

"My grandmother is really hip for a grandmother," Elisa explains. "I took an urban history class and she came up and went on all the walking tours with me. When I was in high school we took a class together at the local community college called Horror from Mary Shelley to Stephen King. We go everywhere together. She took me to Hawaii for three weeks when I was in eighth grade, the first time she ever flew. We used to go to Gettysburg and Lancaster, Pennsylvania, once a year for years. It's weird, my grandmother and I are much closer than my mother and I. She's an inspiration to me because she's really independent and she doesn't care what other people think."

A girl's adolescence is a time of inner chaos, as she tries to resolve the conflict between wanting to become an independent adult yet wanting to remain a protected child. Mother–daughter tension typically increases during these years, with a daughter trying to break away while her mother struggles to hold on. A grandmother can act as a much-needed emotional sanctuary at this time, providing a granddaughter with a refuge from her home life, a fresh perspective on the mother's behaviors, or just a sympathetic ear.

"A mother and daughter can get so polarized," explains Naomi Lowinsky. "But the grandmother has a larger view that doesn't take it all so seriously. She can see that the granddaughter is a teenager and she's driving her mother crazy, and that the mother is afraid her daughter is going to be taken away from her in some way. The grandmother can support both the mother's and the daughter's points of view. If a granddaughter doesn't have access to that overview, the tension feels much more immediate and more desperate. It feels like she has no refuge."

Though grandmothers may offer suggestions or opinions, they often act less as oracles than as sounding boards, and granddaughters go to them as much for silent support as for advice. Gayle, thirty-six, recalls her maternal grandmother as someone with whom she, as a teenager, could openly communicate about peer pressure, doubts about the future, and problems at school. "We talked things out," Gayle explains. "If I hadn't had someone like that to bounce ideas off, I probably would have gotten more involved in the drug scene, been a little more crazy and less responsible. I probably wouldn't have gotten my bachelor's degree or gone on to college at all. That was important to my grandmother, that I have a goal and follow through with it. I'd always been a responsible kid, but in high school I didn't want to be responsible anymore. Everybody goes through that, I guess, but I had my grandmother to discuss things with. That was about the time my parents' marriage started falling apart, and I must have sensed stuff was going on with them. That's probably why I would go to my grandmother's house a lot. I'd go for long walks at night and end up there. My mother hated when I wanted to leave the house at night, so I'd say, 'I'll call you when I get to Gram's.' I remember how my gram used to tuck me into bed in her pull-out couch and kiss me good night."

At this point in our conversation, Gayle's voice cracks and she pauses briefly as she tries to stop her tears. "There's emotion there, thinking about that," she continues, dabbing at her eyes, "because I miss that sense of safety and comfort most. It was so long ago. Oh, boy."

At a time when Gayle's nuclear family was breaking apart, her grandmother represented stability and constancy. Of course Gayle's long walks led her to Grandmother's house: at a time of turmoil, both within herself and in her family, she needed a person with whom she could regress to an earlier state of dependency and feel cared for and reassured, and a place where she could escape the intense emotions of her nuclear

105

family. A grandmother who would play cards with her and tuck her into bed, who offered the simple comforts of companionship and compassion that help a sixteen-year-old feel protected and safe, gave Gayle the security she needed to navigate her way through those difficult years.

According to Valerie Kack-Brice, even harsh or unemotional grandmothers can offer adolescent girls relief by providing a change of atmosphere when the one at home feels too suffocating or intense. "It's like having another home to go to," Kack-Brice explains. "It's also important, as children, to have other adults in our lives who can provide a sense of reflection, reminding us that we're not just daughters or children — that, in fact, we're human beings."

Thirty-four-year-old Lucy remembers an incident that took place during a trip she and her mother took to visit her maternal grandmother in London, when she was sixteen. She and her mother had had a volatile relationship throughout her adolescence, and in Lucy's account of this story, her grandmother emerges as the savior who rescues her from a disastrous mother–daughter exchange.

"My mother and I had gone out to lunch together, and on the way back we had an argument in the middle of Trafalgar Square," Lucy recalls. "She basically said 'Fuck you,' and walked away, leaving me standing there alone in the middle of London with maybe fifty dollars in my pocket. Bear in mind, I'm sixteen years old in the middle of a country where I don't know where I am or what I'm doing and my mother says 'Fuck you,' and walks away. That kind of sums up my relationship with my mother at that point. I was just devastated. I remember standing there thinking, *Thank God my grandmother is here. What would I do if she weren't and I didn't have a place to go and my mother just left me here in the middle of this pigeon-infested hellhole?* I found my way back to my grandmother's house and told her what had happened. From that point on, the trip was really good. My grandmother and I went everywhere together and had a great time. But she never forgave my mother for doing that. The week before my grandmother died, the last time I saw her, she actually brought it up. She said, 'Never forget your mother walking away from you in Trafalgar Square and remember never to do that to anyone else, ever.' "

I wish my story had more in common with these granddaughters for whom grandmothers became emotional refuges or confidantes. Instead, as I passed through adolescence and picked up more sophisticated methods for assessing the adults around me, starting to analyze family relationships rather than blindly accepting them, I slowly began to realize that my grandmother was not the type of person with whom I could share heart-to-heart communication. Candor as I knew it from late-night conversations with girlfriends and tearful exchanges with my mother would elicit only a thoughtful or distracted "Un-huh" from my grandmother or provide her with new material for concern. After my grandfather died in 1976 she seemed to recede farther into an interior world, still highly interested in reading, learning, and visiting her family but increasingly more preoccupied with churning new information around and around through the established schemata in her mind. From time to time she'd come up with declarations or accusations that had no apparent relationship to the facts at hand, making me wonder, "What was *that* all about?" But I was accustomed to unusual behavior from my grandmother. To me, also absorbed in my own thoughts at the time, this new development meant only that I needed to be more careful about self-revelation, to scrupulously edit my conversations with her and strip them of surprises, sticking only to the barest, blandest facts.

Instead of developing into a relationship of reciprocity and disclosure, ours remained relatively lopsided and service-oriented throughout my adolescence. Mostly, it relied on what my grandmother was willing to do for me. And I was willing to accept those conditions, because to reject them would have meant to reduce our relationship to those superficial exchanges, the snippets of information about my classes and friends conveyed in the brief moment between the time I answered the phone and my mother picked up an extension in another room.

When conversation failed us, we compensated

with motion. We drove. We lunched. We shopped. Throughout her life my grandmother was generous almost to a fault, giving away money to a point where she barely saved any for herself. It was not unusual for her during these years to take me shopping and spend several hundred dollars on Junior department clothes. This was back in 1978 or 1979, and that was no small sum. She was not an extravagant woman, but she appreciated good taste. She was the person who taught me it's better to have a single suit of good quality than three inferior ones. At the same time, she could never quite get past the guilt she felt for having more — of anything — than someone else. She once called me on the phone an hour after she'd dropped me off at home, asking me to return a pair of Gloria Vanderbilt corduroy jeans and matching sweatshirt we'd just bought. "I'm worried you're going to make the other girls at school jealous," she explained. Only my repeated insistence that the other girls already had similar outfits (not exactly true) could alleviate her concern. At the time, I thought she was being unnecessarily dramatic. Now I understand what she meant and that she had a point.

Despite all this, my grandmother never represented a sanctuary to me during my adolescence; for that, I would have needed to feel comfort in her presence, which I no longer did. Her house, once a place of wonder and warmth to me, by then felt darker and even more cluttered, with an elderly sister now installed in each bedroom and a high-strung standard poodle that barked and jumped on every visitor who walked through the door. Shortly after my grandfather died, we'd stopped spending holidays there and started gathering in public places instead. I couldn't use my grandmother as a sounding board, either. I was acutely aware that complaining to her about either of my parents would elicit only worry, not advice.

But my grandmother did offer me something no one else in the family could at that time: the chance to feel like an adult. By then, she was already starting to treat me like one, engaging me in the sort of conversation I heard her having with my mother in the kitchen or over the phone. *I'm very worried about your father* (or *your mother* or *your brother* or *Aunt Rea*), she'd begin as her car pulled away from the curb. I would sit quietly as she talked, fiddling with the window-control button, directing the glass a few inches down and back up. I wasn't entirely comfortable hearing intimate details about other family members, but I got a small, secret thrill from being confided in as if I were no longer a child. I understood my grandmother defaulted into these conversations only when my mother refused to listen anymore, but that was acceptable to me. I welcomed any opportunity to offer what sounded like an adult opinion, even if I didn't feel entirely confident in my maturity yet.

Having watched my mother and grandmother

have this type of exchange countless times before, I understood it was my responsibility, as
the listener, to calm my grandmother down. I
tested responses I imagined my mother would
offer, the words virgin and unfamiliar in my
voice, not yet sullied by innuendo or overuse. *If
this is the most we have to worry about, we're lucky.
I'm positive they make the children wait an hour
after eating before they can go swimming. He's a
very good doctor who I think we can trust.* It was a
form of play-acting, since I never stopped to
consider whether I even agreed with what I said.
This marked the beginning of a lifelong habit of
assessing what other people want to hear and
then delivering exactly that, so focused on
averting conflict that I ignore the potential re-
percussions of my words.

It was not difficult during my teen years for me
to feel superior to my grandmother. How do I
say this without sounding like the arrogant child
I fear I was? Even at fourteen I felt more self-
possessed than she was, at times even more mature. She often acted with little regard for my
definition of social conduct, leaving me with the
distinct feeling that no one was in charge. So
each time she ignored the social norms I'd been
raised to obey, the ones that told me not to complain too much, challenge authority too loudly,
or initiate intimate conversations with strangers,
I planted my feet more firmly within their
boundaries, espousing an increasingly conserva-
tive line.

In retrospect, little my grandmother did was truly offensive, her actions probably provoking more amusement in others than outright scorn. But as a teenager I was highly self-conscious and hypersensitive to any behaviors that might direct unwanted attention to me. Even standing in front of a cash register while my grandmother slowly removed each item from her overstuffed pocketbook, looking for her checkbook and gently murmuring to herself, "Grandma's purse is a mess," as the sales clerk impatiently tapped her pen against the counter felt like more than I could handle. So from a fairly early age I took on the self-appointed role of social conscience when my grandmother and I were together, gently placing my hands on her shoulders and steering her out of situations that might disconcert or irritate someone she'd just met.

I didn't particularly like the persona I began to adopt around my grandmother, the patronizing, almost condescending attitude that emerged. At times I could feel as annoyed with myself as I did with her. Perhaps I would have been better off exploding at a restaurant table or on a Bloomingdale's escalator — *I can't take this anymore!* — as I'd seen my mother do. At least she managed to release all that ire quickly, and after a few clipped exchanges with my grandmother the two of them could walk on and enjoy the next few hours as if nothing extraordinary had just occurred. But I didn't have that kind of relationship with my grandmother, even if she would have accepted such an outburst from me. I couldn't imagine myself speaking harshly to her, or, even worse, accepting myself as the type of person who would treat her with such impatience and anger. Not that my quiet condescension was any better, but at least it freed me from the guilt I'd otherwise feel from acting with such overt disrespect.

My grandmother endured my attitude silently, perhaps feeling she hadn't a right to complain. Or maybe believing it was my mother's responsibility, and not hers, to reprimand or criticize me. I don't know what sort of recriminations or resentments might have been churning around in her mind. Surely she noticed my behaviors. Certainly she knew how inappropriate they were. Yet somehow I never managed to convey how embarrassed I was by her actions. Once, when I was about sixteen, I stayed behind to use a restaurant bathroom and emerged to find my grandmother already in the parking lot, absorbed in conversation with a man dressed in khakis and a polo shirt who looked to be about twenty-five. He'd been entering the restaurant as she was coming out, she explained on our way home, a nice young man who was hoping to go back to school to study law. "I tried to get him to take your phone number, but he said you were too young for him," she said. In response to my admonition *"Grandma!"* she added, with a tone of bemusement, "I thought all the men were interested in younger girls these days."

As always, her intentions were benevolent: what she'd had in mind for me was dinner and a movie, innocent enough. And if it happened to lead to an actual romance — with a law student! — well, then, even better. But didn't she recognize the danger inherent in giving my phone number to a complete stranger? A year and a half after my mother died, when I was in the middle of my freshman year of college, my grandmother somehow procured the number of my cousin's orthodontist's nephew, a medical student at Northwestern, and for months she filled my telephone answering machine with reminders to call. *Have you talked to that Burke boy yet? I hear he's such a nice young man.* Finally, that spring I broke down and dialed the Burke boy's number, hoping for only a brief and perfunctory conversation I could later hold up as an example of my obedience as the Good Granddaughter after all. *I know this sounds ridiculous,* I said, *but I promised my grandmother I'd call.* He gave a little laugh, but he didn't hurry off the phone. We had dinner that weekend at the Magic Pan, mushroom crepes and cream sauce, and talked about Long Island, the film *Gandhi*, and the tenacity of grandmothers. *Yeah, mine's a real character,* I said. When he asked about my parents — *So what is it your father does?* — I told him my mother had recently died, and he looked genuinely pained.

This could have turned into the happy story my grandmother hoped for. If not for the part about how after we returned to his dormitory, presumably so I could visit a friend from high school, he refilled my wineglass too eagerly, and too high. If not for the part where he then pushed me down on his bed, pinning my arms with his elbows while his hips rode up and down, ignoring my pleas for release. This would have been a much more upsetting story if I hadn't remembered how my high school boyfriend once yelped in agony when I'd accidentally kneed him in the groin, and if I hadn't remembered the way back to the dorm's front door.

What made me see this as an opportunity to have the kind of honest conversation with my grandmother that we'd never had before? Or was I just hoping to force her to take responsibility for what had happened, to finally acknowledge the boundary between what was merely friendly and what was potentially unsafe? Agreeing to call the Burke boy, I understood then, had been a complicit agreement to let my grandmother play the role of sweet and meddling elder hoping to find her granddaughter a nice date. Now I needed her to be an authority, to hear what had occurred and to voice outrage, to tell me how to get the night to stop replaying in my head. To tell me it wasn't, as I feared, my fault.

"He tried to force himself on me, Grandma," I told her when she called to ask how the evening had gone. "Did you hear what I said?"

"Un-huh," she answered. We sat silently for a while, before she asked, "What do you mean?"

"He tried to have *sex* with me."

"Ohhh," she said, her voice sliding into her lap. And I understood in the uncomfortable silence that followed I had been wrong to blame her, wrong to tell her, wrong to expect her to assume, in any way, my mother's place. Yet she was the closest I could get to my mother after she'd died. My grandmother had sensed this, at times trying in her own way to compensate for some of what she believed I'd lost — buying me clothing, calling every Sunday, helping me find dates. I was just beginning, at nineteen, to realize I'd lost more than anyone could possibly replace. Yet in the years that followed, when my grandmother made these small attempts to assume a mothering role with me I let her, reducing my expectations to a level that was manageable for us both, because to me, half a relationship with my mother's mother was better than none at all.

7

Push and Pull

The greatest — and often most difficult — achievement of a female's teen years is to develop an identity independent of her mother. It's also likely to be the greatest paradox of her adolescence, since the drive to separate from one's parents at this time is just as strong as the need to feel safe within the family fold. Grandmothers, however, typically aren't involved in a granddaughter's two-steps-forward, one-step-back adolescent jig. For this reason, the grandmother–granddaughter relationship during a granddaughter's adolescence usually lacks the strong sense of identification, the antagonism, the ambivalence, the anger, and the power struggles that interactions between a teenage daughter and her mother often breed.

Even women raised by grandmothers who filled every aspect of the maternal role say they never felt the sort of extreme ambivalence and frustration toward their grandmothers during adolescence that many teenage daughters feel toward their mothers. Unless, that is, the granddaughter grew up believing her grandmother *was* her mother,[*] in which

[*]Although my sample of women in this category was

case her teen years often included the tumult that daughters raised by their biological mothers describe.

"It's hard for a mother and daughter to know where one ends and the other begins," Naomi Lowinsky explains. "A grandmother's not so entangled, she's not so enmeshed. She's not involved in a flesh-and-blood sense as directly."

My body emerged from my mother, not from my grandmother, which made my relationships with both of them qualitatively different in every way. When I first entered puberty, my grandmother was charmed. She came across me changing my shirt in the bathroom one afternoon, still young enough to be doing it with the door open but not yet developed enough to be wearing a bra. "Look at your little boobies!" she exclaimed, in a tone that was nothing short of a proclamation of joy. She grabbed me in a tight hug from the side as I quickly yanked my shirt down. "Grandma-a-a," I whined. I twisted free of her grasp and left her standing in the bathroom, still smiling, as I hurried down the hall.

My mother's signals about my sexual development were harder to read. She willingly took me to buy my first bra, sympathetic to the news that every girl in my sixth grade class was wearing one but me, but when the salesclerk in the neigh-

---

small, they all appeared to experience adolescent struggles with the grandmother similar to those reported by women who grew up with their biological mothers.

borhood children's clothing shop reached for the box marked "32 flat," she couldn't quite stifle her laugh. Two years later, she was reluctant to let me start shaving my legs or my underarms, confessing that she didn't want me to grow up too soon.

To a mother, a daughter's physical development is a constant reminder of her own advancing years. How can it not be, when a daughter's smooth skin provides such a striking contrast to a mother's emerging wrinkles, when a daughter's breasts start pushing through as a mother's lose their lift? Mothers who view aging as a natural or inevitable process can effectively guide their daughters through the physical and emotional terrain of adolescence, but mothers who associate middle age with loss and fear may unconsciously see their daughters as thieves robbing them of the youth that was once theirs, or as competitors vying for the same attention or admiring glances.

"I've seen old pictures where my grandmother had my mother all dolled up with a perm," recalls thirty-four-year-old Grace. "She admired my mother for being so beautiful, yet at the same time she constantly undermined her because of it. Mothers often do that to their daughters, brutalize them for possessing the beauty they no longer have. My mother did the same thing to me. She still does. She'll say, 'Don't you remember when you were sixteen and you were so lovely? If you'd do something about your skin, you could be that lovely again.' When I was pregnant she made some horrible comments about how I should get breast enhancement surgery. She knew I felt fat and dumpy when I was pregnant, and she said some pretty evil things. I think she picked up a lot of that from her mother, my grandmother, the one who used to tell me I was beautiful and intelligent. My mother really is beautiful, six feet tall, very slim, and I always thought it was odd that my grandmother never complimented her, but always gave strokes to me."

Grandmothers typically see granddaughters as extensions of the family line rather than as appendages of the self, as separate, precious flowers whose blossoms offer a means of immortality for their own beauty rather than a means for stealing it. The difference between a mother's "you are me" identification and a grandmother's "you are of me" affirmation may seem slight, but it's significant. It releases a grandmother from the belief that her granddaughter's appearance, actions, or behaviors are a direct reflection on her, and frees their relationship from the psychological tug-of-war associated with earning independence.

"Women don't go through the same identity formation process with the grandmother that they do with the mother," explains Evelyn Bassoff. "With the mother, there's a skin-to-skin connection, and in order to become separate beings they have to wrench themselves away from her. We don't have to constantly fight for our independence from a grandmother. We already have it."

We may, however, see our mothers still fighting for independence from their own mothers, and that's a powerful paradigm for an adolescent granddaughter to observe. Many of us were first exposed to the dance of daughterhood by watching our mothers interact with our grandmothers, giving us an early window into the mechanics of adult mother–daughter relationships. We may have accepted or questioned their apparent emotional distance, admired or criticized the degree to which they appeared to be enmeshed, but chances are we wouldn't describe their feelings toward each other — or our feelings about their relationship — as neutral.

The push–pull relationship that exists between adolescent girls and their mothers often extends well into adulthood, as a grown daughter still searches for a comfortable midpoint between remaining connected to her family of origin and standing on her own. The back-and-forth movement I observed between my mother and my grandmother was actually relatively common behavior. "Many mid-life women are reluctant or even afraid to loosen ties to their mothers," Evelyn Bassoff wrote in her 1988 book, *Mothers and Daughters: Loving and Letting Go*. "The girl-child in them clings to the illusion that Mother is endowed with absolute powers to know and protect and that only as long as they please her and conform to her standards will she be available to them." But as a teenager it never seemed to me that my mother found the right balance between her longing for maternal connection and her need to express and execute her own opinions. She was always feeling irritated by one or guilty about the other. Small wonder I grew up feeling the same way toward her, even after her death.

As my mother knew all too well, a daughter's ability to achieve any real autonomy is in large part determined by her mother's willingness to comply. It's one thing to try to declare your independence from a mother who understands the necessity of the act, quite another to try to separate from one who doesn't want to let go. I imagine that my grandmother was also frustrated by their push and pull, distressed by her inability to have the kind of closeness with her eldest daughter that she desired. Perhaps because my grandmother came from an immigrant culture and a social era when the extended family still reigned supreme, she expected my mother to grant her power based on age instead of merit. Perhaps because she remained closely connected to her own mother until her death at eighty-five, even bringing my great-grandmother into her home for thirteen years, she also expected the same type of loyalty and respect from her eldest daughter.

Responsibility for the difficulties I observed between them, however, did not lie entirely with my grandmother. If my mother had been able to remain an adult around her mother, she might have had more success at being treated like one. But she was constantly trying to prove that she was old enough, experienced enough, capable enough to make decisions on her own. Like many adult daughters, she shed her mature roles when her mother was present, sliding back into a time and place that did not yet include me. It was as close as I could get to seeing the girl who had existed before the mother I knew. I saw how she allowed my grandmother to order for her in restaurants, complained about the extra attention or gifts her sisters had received, and quickly lost patience, dissolving into frustrated submission or angry silence when my grandmother went off on a worry trip without brakes.

As an adolescent, I understood my mother at those moments better than I did at any other, because she became remarkably similar to me. How many times had I stomped around the kitchen, lamenting my position as the eldest child and a girl, when it was clear (at least to me) that she favored the youngest, the only boy? How many times had I silently glared at her until she'd stop lecturing me and then rushed off to meet my friends instead of talking back to her and getting sent to my room? Every time I gritted my teeth and warned, "Mo-*om!*" I heard the echo of her "Mo-*ther,*" both of us trying to force our mothers back onto their own turf. The distance between child and adult, I was surprised to discover, was not nearly as vast as my parents wanted me to believe. How could it be, when my behaviors could so closely resemble those of a mother twenty-six years my senior, when her voice and moods and rhetoric could so neatly overlap with mine?

Because in many families the quality and tone of one generation's mother–daughter relationship predict the quality and tone of the next's, to understand the relationships we have with our mothers we first have to understand the way they related to theirs. "Most women spend their adulthoods either sanctifying their mothers and trying to be just like her, unsure of who they are separate from her, or trying to pattern themselves as exactly the opposite, allowing their behaviors to be fueled by that strong negativity," explains Jane Warren, Ph.D., a psychologist in Omaha, Nebraska, who specializes in mothers and adolescent daughters.

My mother's fear of becoming her mother was clearly one that plagued her. My father was known to mumble, "Just like your mother. You're *just like* your mother," when other argumentative strategies failed. I tried it once as a teenager, just to see where it would lead, and she stared at me as if she'd been slapped. That was at about the same time she spent an evening at a consciousness-raising workshop with thirty other women from our synagogue, wearing a sign that read I AM NOT MY MOTHER. The other women approached her one by one, saying, "You're just like your mother. You are," while she repeated, "I am not my mother, not my mother, *not* my mother," over and over again, until it became a sweet and automatic mantra she could carry with her from the room.

Driven by this determination, my mother deliberately gave her children more physical and emotional freedom than she felt she'd had as a daughter, creating a home for them that was relatively lean on rules. I had no set bedtime, no set baths, no television shows that were forbidden. I could eat whatever I wanted — ice cream, hot dogs, even ham. We were the only kids I knew who were allowed to drink Coke with meals.

But when I entered adolescence full force my mother suddenly seemed uncertain about how to proceed. Her teenage years had been relatively family-oriented, sparse on dates, populated with girlfriends and piano lessons and constant struggles with her weight. Mine involved spending nights and weekends standing in an apartment house parking lot with twenty friends, smoking cigarettes and listening to Black Sabbath eight-track tapes, a world where parents supervised keg parties for fourteen-year-olds. My mother spent half the time inventing responsibilities designed to keep me at home, and the other half encouraging me to go to parties, meet boys, and invite friends to our house. I imagine my adolescence reminded her of all that she loved most from those years and also all that she'd missed.

I suspect she also liked thinking of herself as a parent who was clued in enough to communicate with her daughter, yet still responsible enough to impose limits when needed. She agreed to host a swimming party for my fifteenth birthday, even let my friends' garage band play in our backyard, but she drew the line at the keg. As I watched her man the clothes dryer, repeatedly loading it up with the towels and shirts of teenagers who kept throwing each other in the pool as an electric guitar blared the opening chords of Eric Clapton's "Cocaine", she might as well have been wearing her I AM NOT MY MOTHER sign around her neck. I can't imagine any scene in which my grandmother would have belonged less.

I was happy to comply with my mother's decision to give me the freedom she felt she'd never had. I'd seen what could happen when a daughter was unable to keep a mother in constant check — the upsetting morning phone calls, the "you're just like your mother" arguments in front of the kids. So I tried to keep mine at a safe distance, leaving her standing on the other side of my closed bedroom door, chewing on her bottom lip and struggling to maintain self-restraint while I did as I pleased on the other side.

I might have actually believed this was a good idea, if I hadn't discovered what my mother of course already knew. I was unprepared for the nearly overwhelming feelings of tenderness, protectiveness, rage, and guilt every time I saw the pinched eyebrows, the rapid blinks, the tiny flinches whenever I snapped at her or demanded to be left alone. Her disappointment seared through me; her pain felt like mine. I resented her for that, for reminding me that I could not stop loving people just because they angered and frustrated me, that I could not disentangle myself even from the ones who angered and frustrated me most. And at the same time I loved her passionately for it, because I knew that no matter how poorly I treated her I could always count on this connection, that because it existed she would never turn her back on me, just as her mother would never turn her back on her.

If my mother and her mother had had a smoother relationship, maybe my mother and I would have had an easier time ourselves. Maybe we would have eventually forged a different type of relationship than they'd had as adults. Chummier. Less intrusive. Exhibiting more self-control. It's hard to know what kind of balance we might have achieved over time. An adolescent's relationship with her mother offers hints to how she'll interact with her as an adult, but because my mother died when we were both so young, I don't know how our relationship might have evolved. My memories of her interactions with my grandmother are the only clues I have.

As a teenage girl takes her first tentative steps away from the family cocoon, she must find a way to integrate her self-image as a member of her family with her new self-image as an autonomous individual. Grandmothers can play an important role at this time as bearers of family history and purveyors of cultural knowledge, helping a teenager answer the questions "Who am I?" and "Who am I to be?" The information they share gives an adolescent the sense of continuity — the historical awareness reinforced by others — that she needs to develop an image of herself that is consistent over time despite the rapid external and internal changes that occur during the teen years. Grandparents are living models of continuity in that they have lived through and adjusted to more change than virtually any other generation in history.

This was the role grandparents played for twenty-six-year-old Donna, who grew up in a multigenerational Italian-American family that gathered every Sunday for dinner at her grandmother's house. During the meals, which could stretch for as long as five hours, her grandparents and great-grandparents transmitted history and culture to the younger generations, sliding in and out of their native language as they passed around platters of traditional food.

"It started with the prosciutto and the bread, and then we would go to a soup, then a pasta, then some kind of meat, then the peanuts and the fruit, and then the dessert, and then later on if we were still hungry we'd go back to the Italian cold cuts," Donna recalls. "Everyone would sit around and eat and tell stories. Sometimes my grandfather would talk about World War II and his travels all over Europe, the ideas he picked up, the people he met. He'd teach me Italian songs, and then my grandmother would interrupt and want to tell her stories. Everyone wanted to be in the limelight, and they'd go back and forth. I wasn't allowed to do anything on Sundays except go to my grandmother's house. Once I became a teenager I started to balk a little. Sometimes I'd want to be with my friends or watch something on TV instead, but once I was at my grandparents' house, eating and hanging out, I tended to forget about my friends. I loved the sense of family and the sense of history those dinners gave me. I want my children to have that too. I should start writing all the stories down for them now."

Due in large part to listening to her grandparents' stories, Donna describes herself as unquestionably Italian, an identity that provides her with both a source of pride and an enduring connection to her family of origin. Transmitting such knowledge about cultural and familial roots, says psychologist Marc Baronowski, may be the most important impact grandparents have on a teenager's search for identity by providing grandchildren with direct connections to the past and a sense of sureness about facing the future. They also make the past "real" for grandchildren, giving it color and action rather than reducing it to a faded photograph or a line in the family Bible.

Grandparents represent an especially

important tie to ethnicity and religion in families where the middle generation has assimilated into mainstream culture. Fifty-year-old Carmen says she would have grown up with a much looser connection to her ethnic heritage if not for her close relationship with her grandmother during adolescence. A third-generation Mexican-American, Carmen grew up with parents who were eager to blend into U.S. culture and rarely spoke Spanish in the home. The maternal grandmother she called "Mamacita," or "little mother," however, had emigrated to America as an adult and remained in close contact with her family back in Chihuahua. The summer Carmen was twelve and again when she was fourteen, she traveled with Mamacita to Mexico for a month to visit their extended family.

"We went in a huge circle on a Greyhound bus," Carmen remembers. "We visited some distant cousins, then some very close cousins, and then my grandmother's sister by the shore. We stayed a week here, a week there. It was such an adventure. I went to keep my grandmother company and to help her get around. I was probably more trouble than help at that age, but it was fun for both of us. And I got to meet all of my relatives, to feel a part of a much larger family than we had in California. I learned to eat tortillas and to speak Spanish. I learned the ways of the other culture, which was missing from my life in California where we were trying so hard to assimilate."

Today Carmen is the only member of her nuclear family who actively cultivates her Mexican heritage. She took ethnic studies classes in college, including one titled "La Chicana," for which she recorded her grandmother's oral history, and she's involved in several Latina organizations in her community. "My grandmother always gave me a very strong sense of who I am as a Mexican-American," she says. "Of all the roles she filled in my life, that's been one of the most important to me."

8

In My Mother's Kitchen: 1979

My grandmother has strong hands for a woman her size. Short, square nails always polished bright red, thick knuckles gnarled with arthritis. They can grip things — car keys, pocketbooks, my upper arm — much tighter than you'd expect. When I was younger, she used to clap her hands with excitement when someone delivered good news. Now she usually rests them on the table or in her lap, but her fingers are always in motion.

For as long as I've known her, my grandmother has done this thing with her hands. She drags the pad of her thumb across the tips of her other fingers, from pinky to pointer, back to pinky, back to pointer, incessantly, while other people speak. She does it when she's worried, which lately has been most of the time. She doesn't realize that she's doing it. She doesn't know how to prevent it. The motion makes a little scratching noise that irritates my mother like little else can. It grates on me, too.

We're not the kind of family that says things like "Grandma, it really bothers me when you rub your fingers together when we're talking," or

"Mother, I'm concerned about that obsessive finger action of yours." We're too normal for that. We say things like "Grandma! Stop doing that thing with your hands!" and "Mo-*ther*. You know how much that bothers the girls."

On this particular afternoon, we're all sitting in my mother's avocado kitchen, at the Formica tabletop designed to look like real wood. I'm fifteen and making a rare cameo appearance at home at 4:00 P.M. Actually, I'm expecting a phone call, so at any moment I might have to go. It's going to be from my boyfriend, whom my mother doesn't like and my grandmother hasn't met. That's deliberate, on my part. I can just see her looking at his secondhand army jacket and his long hair, asking, "Is he Jewish?" and then refusing to believe it when the answer is yes. Right now, he's the only thing on my mind. I'm drifting in and out of my mother and grandmother's conversation, something about how my sister is going to be the only one of us at sleep-away camp this summer, and will she or won't she get lonely, when my grandmother starts doing that thing with her right hand.

Scratch, scratch.

My mother's eyes immediately drop to my grandmother's fingers. Her jaw tightens. She's not going to say anything, though. That's my function. "*Grand*ma!" I say. "You're doing that thing with your hands again!" My grandmother looks up and gives a small, apologetic smile. "How about that?" she muses. "I didn't even notice." She pinches her fingers together tightly to guard against future impulse. I take her hand and squeeze it as an extra precaution. My mother's face relaxes. My grandmother squeezes my hand in return. The conversation resumes. I'm released from responsibility for at least the next five minutes, until the phone rings or the finger rubbing starts again.

Scratch, scratch.

9

Three-Generational Triangles

Once there was a world that still belonged exclusively to women, a world of chipped coffee cups and lipstick rings on cigarettes, of slips and pincushions and hairpins, of high-pitched laughs tossed around the canasta table, and low murmurs about men, always talk of men. They were friends and they were relations, mothers and grandmothers and great-aunts, held together by proximity and circumstance. And interwoven among them were the girls, holding tea parties underneath the tablecloths, bumping into knees and hips as they raced through the rooms, mimicking the older women in front of bathroom mirrors. And listening, always listening, to the talk of men.

Why is it that when I recall conversations from my childhood, the women are the only ones who speak? The men in my family — my father and my grandfather, uncles, great-uncles and cousins — obviously weren't mute, but they lived at a distance from the women, smoking cigarettes in a tight clump on the back porch, watching the basketball game on the spare television downstairs, or off doing whatever it was men did in that vague and formless place called "work." In our house that meant the family business, a six-floor manufacturing company in Manhattan that sucked up our men every morning and spit them out in time for dinner at the end of the day. The women were the ones who raised the children, ran the households, and cooked the meals that greeted the men when they walked through the doors every evening at 6:00 P.M., car keys jangling in their hands.

The men of my childhood inhabited worlds with codes and regulations I didn't comprehend. Union contracts. Golf handicaps. Mortgage interest rates. My father, I imagine, would have been happy to teach me the rules of football, but why any girl would waste time learning a game no one would allow her to play was a source of mystery to me. I was infinitely more interested in the human drama that played itself out in our kitchen each time my grandmother paid a visit, or in the car on the way to Lord & Taylor or Howard Johnson's for lunch. For one thing, in the presence of my mother and my grandmother I was encouraged — no, *expected* — to participate. For another, the rules were easy to understand.

Number One, my mother's rule: Do not make your grandmother upset.

Number Two, my grandmother's rule: Do not make your mother upset.

Number Three, my rule: Do not upset either of them, in any way.

It was remarkable early training in politics and rhetoric: Deliver what other people want to hear, then go off and do what you intended from the start. Lest anyone believe for even a moment that such behavior fooled either my grandmother or my mother, however, I am certain it did not. These were smart women. They not only knew what I was doing, they allowed it. My mother understood I was only placating my grandmother much of the time, and she was grateful for the peace it maintained. My grandmother knew I was only humoring my mother, but she preferred it over the type of disruption she was helpless to control. In much the same way, my grandmother's interjections or apparent non sequiturs — *I don't know what to do about Rea,* for example, dropped into the middle of an argument about my boyfriend — deflected attention away from any mounting tension between my mother and me. Whenever two points on our triangle started to heat up, the third immediately stepped in to cool the others down. It defused conflict rather than addressing it, but for a while, as long as there were three of us, this system of ours worked.

Every three-generational triangle has its own rules of conduct, its own patterns of interaction, and its own internal system of punishment and reward. That's because every family system communicates, distributes power, and addresses conflict in its own unique manner. The youngest members quickly learn how to behave in the presence of the others to achieve their desired goal, whether it's attention, affection, power, or peace. As Margaret Birch, the teenage narrator of Kaye Gibbons's novel *Charms for the Easy Life* who grows up with a beautiful, ethereal mother and a strong, opinionated grandmother as her co-parents, observes, "I realized fairly early into my mother's courtship that in order to live in the same house with these two women, I would need to decide whom I would defend over what issue and when. Usually I chose my grandmother, as I believed she possessed the wisdom of the ages, and when I saw my mother buck and kick against her authority, I would gently say, 'Don't you think Grandmother's probably been through this, and so she might sort of know what to do?' If my mother responded to me at all, it was to say something like, 'She's been through twenty more years than I have. That's it.' "

The word *triangle* usually inspires images of two-against-one attacks, and while it's true that in some families female allegiances shift with the wind, doing more damage than good to a granddaughter's sense of trust and emerging self-esteem, in other families three generations of women coexist peacefully and successfully, with each assuming age- and status-appropriate roles. The grandmother remains a grandmother to her granddaughter and a mother to her daughter; the mother retains her role as mother to the granddaughter without abdicating her power to the grandmother; and the granddaughter has a clear vision of who, including herself, is responsible for what.

When the grandmother and mother share a relationship of mutual trust and respect, a triangle has the best chance for smooth operation. Sandra Halperin, Ph.D., a marital and family therapist in Auburn, Alabama, recalls a childhood with a divorced mother and a maternal grandmother who raised her and her brother with minimal conflict in their home. "My brother and I perceived my grandmother as a co-parent from the get-go," she explains. "I even called my grandmother Mama and my mother Mom. Whenever we moved it was hard for the neighbors to get accustomed to who our mother was. But *we* were always real clear about who our mother was. She and my grandmother walked a fine line in terms of who had authority over what and how they negotiated it. It was clear when we were all together, from my grandmother's perspective as well as mine, that my mother called the shots. It was clear that when my mother wasn't there, my grandmother called the shots with equal authority. I give them credit for it, because it was like a dance between them. They knew exactly when to make the necessary shifts. I'm almost 100 percent positive that they never sat down and said, 'Okay, who's in charge of what and when?' I look back, especially now that I'm a parent, and I'm very impressed by that.

"The relationship they had with each other was very different from my relationship with either of them," she continues. "I wouldn't have wanted their relationship because they had their own tensions, but when it came to raising children, they kept it clean. That really tells me that no matter how many problems a family has, it may have a critical mass of health that really pulls them through. And I do think that the healthier a family is to begin with, the healthier any triangle within it will operate. The less healthy the family, the more opportunities there are for three-generational dysfunction."

By "healthy" she means a system characterized mainly by cooperation, honesty, respect, and appropriate boundaries. Whether or not a triangle includes these elements depends in large part on the type of relationship the grandmother and mother share. When their relationship is balanced — meaning it's neither overly enmeshed nor emotionally disengaged and remains relatively free of competition, conflict, and resentment — the triangle is stable enough to absorb adversity in other bonds. Thirty-two-year-old Jessica, for example, recalls how the strong relationship between her grandmother and her divorced mother helped hold all three women together during the years when arguments between Jessica and her mother were reaching a crescendo.

"My mother and my grandmother really loved each other," Jessica says. "After my grandmother divorced her second husband, she moved in with my mom for twelve years until she died. But my

140

mother and I had a horrible relationship. During adolescence, I just hated her. She's only twenty years older than me, and I think that had a lot to do with it. She was so young, and she didn't know how to handle me. My grandmother broke up a lot of our fights. If I wasn't talking to my mother, my grandmother would be on my mother's case every day to call me. She'd also call me and say I should talk to my mother. And because we both respected my grandmother so much, we'd listen to her. She'd always bring us back together. She was like our glue."

When conflict exists between a grandmother and mother, however, a granddaughter often gets caught up in a triangle beset with power struggles, shifting alliances, and jealousy. She may come to represent a new forum for competition between mother and grandmother, with her affection and attention perceived as the prize. In some of these skewed triangles, the scapegoat role, the person on whom all the triangle's problems and difficulties are projected, rotates from woman to woman, with the granddaughter constantly on the alert to be called upon as an ally or made the victim of an attack.

"In this scenario, what could have been a potentially rich situation for taking in both the grandmother and the mother as role models, for developing the awareness that you can resolve conflicts with other women and for learning to handle feelings of ambivalence, is lost," Halperin explains. "A girl in this type of family winds up having both relationships contaminated, and the triangle becomes a dangerous emotional place for her to live. She also doesn't learn how to deal with women in a free, noncompetitive but cooperative manner, and so women, to her, become more difficult to deal with or connect with than men. It's sad, because women need each other so much. We crave that connection to one another, and to have the original experience of it so contaminated is a shame."

Longstanding or dormant conflicts between a grandmother and mother are often reactivated when the women reenter a shared living environment as adults, usually when a grandmother moves in to help with child care or when a single mother brings her children back to her parents' home. Psychologist Jay Haley identifies a common example of three-generation conflict in his 1976 book *Problem-Solving Therapy*:

> The classic situation is made up of grandmother, mother, and problem child. That is the typical one-parent family situation among the poor and among the middle class when a mother has divorced and returned to her mother. In the classic example, the grandmother tends to be defined as dominating, the mother as irresponsible, and the child as a behavior problem. The typical sequence is as follows:
>
> 1. Grandmother takes care of grandchild while protesting that mother is irresponsible

and does not take care of the child properly. In this way grandmother is siding with the child in a coalition across generation lines.

2. Mother withdraws, letting grandmother care for the child.

3. The child misbehaves or expresses symptomatic behavior.

4. Grandmother protests that she should not have to take care of the child and discipline [her]. She has raised her children and mother should take care of her own child.

5. Mother begins to take care of her own child.

6. Grandmother protests that mother does not know how to take care of the child properly and is being irresponsible. She takes over the care of the grandchild to save the child from mother.

7. Mother withdraws, letting grandmother care for the child.

8. The child misbehaves or expresses symptomatic behavior. At a certain point, grandmother protests that mother should take care of her own child, and the cycle continues, for ever and ever. Included in the cycle, of course, is sufficient misbehavior or distress by the child to provoke the adults to continue the cycle.

Haley believed this scenario reflected a problem in the family power structure, with the grandmother usurping the mother's authority over her own child. In this type of family system, the grandmother assumes executive power and the mother and granddaughter exist together on a lower plane, functioning almost like siblings. Therapists work with these families to realign the hierarchy, giving each mother authority over her own child. Only when the mother assumes the parental role with the granddaughter, Haley claims, will the grandchild stop acting out. In some cases, however, a family will decide, for whatever reason, that the grandmother *should* be the one in charge of the child. If everyone agrees on this arrangement, the system can work, although it tends to become unstable as a grandmother ages.

It's important to remember that most women mentioned in psychological studies are part of a clinical population, meaning that they've either chosen to seek professional help or are currently institutionalized. In contrast, most of the women interviewed for this book came either from families or from a social era that stigmatized therapy, or from families where the effects of the grandmother–mother–granddaughter triangle were considered beneficial or benign. These women spoke of households where grandmothers and mothers split the roles that would traditionally have been divided between mother and father. The grandmother typically stepped into the role of nurturer, caring for the children in the mornings and after school, while the mother assumed the role of breadwinner, spending daytime hours at a job. In this type of family, a strong bond typically develops between the grandmother (as the primary caregiver) and the granddaughter (as the recipient of her care), which can be extremely unsettling for the mother, especially when her mother's relationship with her daughter appears to trump hers.

Forty-three-year-old Natalie, who was raised by her divorced mother and maternal grandmother after her parents divorced when she was ten, still tears up when she recalls an incident that occurred when she was three. "I was standing at the back of my grandmother's chair while she was sewing, with my arms around my grandmother's neck and my back to the door," she says, "and I told her, 'Oh, I love you more than anyone in the world.' My grandmother turned around to pat me and she saw my mother standing in the doorway. She had just gotten home from work. My grandmother saw the tears in my mother's eyes, and she tried to comfort her by saying, 'Cecile, if you could stay home with the kids they would feel that way toward you, too.'

"My grandmother told me this story when I was twelve, thinking nothing of it, but oh, the guilt I felt," Natalie continues. "I was so upset that I went off into a corner and just sobbed. I felt so bad that I had done that to my mother. When Mom came home from work that day I told her about the story. She remembered it, and she handled it extremely well. She said, 'Well, yes, that did happen, but I knew you loved me.'

When I look back on that incident now, from an adult perspective, it just feels replete with ambivalence. My mother's ambivalence about having to work but wanting to be home with her kids, my grandmother's ambivalence about wanting to be connected to us and to mother us but also wanting her daughter to be connected to us the way they were connected to each other, and of course *my* ambivalence: How do I love both of these women who are so important to me? If I can't love one more than the other, how do I manage that?"

In this scenario, a certain degree of ambivalence and envy is normal. What mother wouldn't feel dejected under such circumstances? What young granddaughter wouldn't feel confused? It's the manner in which these emotions are handled, not their existence, that matters most. In a family where the relationship between grandmother and mother lacks antagonism, a mother usually can accept the close relationship that develops between her daughter and her mother without interpreting it as a displacement of her role, and a grandmother is able to acknowledge that the child in question is her grandchild, not her child — an obvious but important distinction to be made here. But in a family where the grandmother and mother are still struggling to separate from one another or where the mother is still angry or resentful about the parenting she received, she is likely to view any bond that forms between grandmother and granddaughter as an alliance that excludes her. Especially when she sees her daughter and mother sharing the kind of intimate relationship she and her mother never had.

Angela arrives in my office on an unseasonably warm March evening wearing a long flowered skirt, laced-up boots, and a colorful narrow-brimmed hat. She settles back into the uphol-stered chair with an easy smile, hands folded in her lap, ankles crossed. Her demeanor is relaxed and casual, her manner calm. It's hard to imagine her embroiled in the kind of passionate, heated triangle she was part of for most of her adolescence, one that she extricated herself from just a few years ago.

Angela, now twenty-seven, was raised by her divorced mother with help from both grand-mothers, who lived nearby. She'd also been close to her maternal great-grandmother, who died a few months before our interview. But it was her maternal grandmother, who lived with the family for a year when Angela was sixteen, who had influenced Angela most. The two women shared an interest in art and a love for gossip, as well as similar sensibilities, tastes, styles, and methods of interaction. During the year they lived together, Angela's grandmother became her primary companion and confidante in the family.

But their close relationship soon became a source of stress for Angela's mother, who began to feel excluded from their intimacy, their passionate conversations, and their jokes. "My grandmother and I tended to take the same side on most issues, and my mother was always the odd one out," Angela explains. "Unless the issue required age and maturity, where they both had it over me." As a child Angela's mother had often felt neglected and emotionally bereft, the daughter of a mother who'd never met her needs. Even though she'd developed what appeared to be a close adult relationship with her mother, confiding in her and speaking with her nearly every day — "they've been inseparable for forty years," Angela says — the two women were often harshly critical of each other. Years later, watching her daughter and her mother share the kind of early intimacy she felt she'd been denied could throw Angela's mother into a jealous spin.

The adult relationship between Angela's mother and grandmother actually existed within a much larger family context. According to Angela, mother–daughter bonds in her maternal line tend to follow a certain pattern. Three generations of mothers, she says, have expected their children to give them the love and support they had found lacking during their own childhoods. "What you didn't get from your mother you tried to take from your child," Angela says. "And when the child couldn't provide it, because of course she was only a child, the mothers would vent their narcissistic rage on the child, who was expected to just take it. It was this vicious cycle that kept repeating itself. I could see it myself, the way my grandmother was still trying to be the child to a mother who was still cracking the whip at ninety. My mother would look at them and say, 'When is this going to end?' But I don't think she realized how the same thing was happening in her life. My mother thought that because she talked back to her mother and criticized her she was different. But on an emotional level, the same thing was definitely going on between them. And to a certain extent, she was also doing it with me.

"My mother was not available to me emotionally when I was a child," she explains. "I was very, very sensitive to what I could get from her and do with her. And so I would go to my grandmother instead of to my mother about the personal events in my life. I would tell her about the things I was going through at school, about puberty and boys. I think, looking back, that my mother would have been interested if she could have been. But she just had so many issues that weren't resolved that came from her experience with *her* mother, she couldn't be available to be *my* mother. It was like she was still a child, unable to get beyond her own resentments or losses. Whenever I would confront her about not recognizing my needs, she'd say, 'Well, what do you want? I didn't get that from my mother either' or 'Well, that's what *she* did to me.' It was almost like she was trying to get me to feel sympathy toward her, to get me on her side. I don't think she ever said to herself, 'Well, my mother did this and that to me and I'm still angry about it so I'm not going to give to my daughter.' I think it was just a matter that she couldn't, and that she didn't have the ability to figure these things out for herself. She's in her mid-forties now and is just starting to do that. It's taken a very high threshold of pain for her to get to that point, but that's just part of her personality. Which is probably the thing that my grandmother and I have complained about most all these years. She comes to me saying, 'Your *mother!*' and I say, 'I know! I know!' "

Angela's grandmother, though a much-needed confidante at the time, didn't improve the family situation by commiserating with Angela about her mother. As Evelyn Bassoff explains, the way a much-loved grandmother, especially one in a co-parenting or primary caretaking role, talks about her daughter can affect the way the granddaughter feels about that mother. "It's a terrible disservice to the child if the grandmother demeans the mother, because the child's mother is her flesh and blood," Dr. Bassoff says. "So the child who has a mother who's demeaned will hate part of herself. At the same time that the grandmother is doing a great service by stepping in and offering assistance or care to the family, part of that great service is to preserve the reputation of the mother and allow the daughter to have good feelings about her, so that she can have good feelings about herself."

In Natalie's family, the grandmother inherently understood this and resolutely refused to talk behind her daughter's back. Natalie recalls a period during her adolescence when she would approach her grandmother to complain about her mother, almost as if appealing to a mother about an annoying sibling, but instead of jumping into the fray her grandmother would gently yet forcefully guide the conversation back to neutral ground. "She would say, 'You know, you really shouldn't be talking about your mother the way you're talking about her,' " Natalie says. "She would essentially put me back in my place. It was a weird moment, because she'd be acting like the mother, but not really. It was more like the grandmother reminding me that I was my mother's daughter and I owed my mother that respect."

Alliances, connections between two or more people for mutual emotional support without regard for anyone else, are impossible to avoid in families. Mother and fathers naturally form alliances separate from their relationships with their children; siblings often ally against their parents or each other; and each parent has his or her own unique alliance with each child. To a certain extent, alliances are useful, allowing one family member the chance to discuss with another a concern or idea that can't be shared with others. They also help us feel accepted in families, especially when we feel different or alienated from other members.

An alliance can become detrimental, however,

when it turns into a coalition — two members of a triangle joining together against the third — or a triangulation, in which one family member tries to stabilize her feelings about another by confiding in a third. Thirty-eight-year-old Claudia, for example, remembers an incident when she and her husband were eating dinner in a restaurant with her grandmother and her husband forgot to pay for his beer. "Somehow, my grandmother paid for it," Claudia says. "She went insane over it, but she would never go directly insane toward me. Instead, she went to my mother, who was her minion, and then my mother told me my grandmother was upset with me." Instead of feeling angry toward her grandmother, however, Claudia found herself irritated by her mother, who had recently rejoined the family after a lengthy absence. "It can really annoy me when my mother tries to tell me something my grandmother wants, or to convey a message from her to me," Claudia explains. "I feel like, 'Who are you to talk to me about my relationship with her? I had this relationship for a long time and you were never around.' "

In a common three-generation coalition, a grandmother and granddaughter join forces against the mother. The mere existence of such a coalition isn't necessarily cause for alarm: a grandmother acting as a granddaughter's refuge from her mother is an appropriate arrangement, as long as it's temporary. It's when the coalition becomes a way of life for the family that the three-generational system suffers. Women in these families routinely turn against one another as a method of coping with discomfort in their relationships rather than exploring ways to address their problems directly. Especially when cross-generational coalitions are kept secret, the triangle is in trouble.

By allying with her grandmother against her mother, Angela earned both an adult confidante and an antidote to her feelings of maternal rejection and loss. Her grandmother, in turn, gained a close bond with her granddaughter, someone with whom she could share her anxieties about her daughter. Even Angela's mother gained something from this arrangement: continued justification for the ambivalence she felt toward her mother, without which some daughters no longer know how to define themselves. Everyone benefitted from the dynamic in this triangle, which is perhaps why it managed to persist for so long.

But the relationship Angela shared with her grandmother, which she'd thought was exclusive and confidential, turned out to be inseparable from the decades-old struggle between her mother and her grandmother, and from the difficult relationship between her mother and herself. "Later, when I started feeling closer to my mother, I would tell her about an event or a situation that had taken place during high school," Angela recalls, "and she would say, 'I already know that. My mother tells me everything. You go to her thinking you're sharing a secret, but the truth is she comes right to me. And not only does she come to me, but she says, "How could you let your daughter do this?" ' My mother would tell me this like she was throwing it in my face that I would go to my grandmother and confide in her before I would go to my own mother. She felt that was an embarrassment to her. And then, on top of that, her own mother would chide her for not bringing me up in an appropriate way.

"At first, when I learned my grandmother had told my mother these things I was like, *What?* But I'm not upset about it anymore. I realize I would have told my mother those things anyway, if we'd had a good relationship. It wasn't like I was going to my grandmother and saying, 'Don't ever tell my mother this.' I just needed someone to talk to, and my grandmother gave me a very unconditional ear. So ultimately, I was glad my mother knew about those things. I was only sorry we were never able to communicate about them at the time, instead of having to wait until I was much older."

The triangle in Angela's family actually operated something like this: Angela, feeling emotionally estranged from her mother, confided in her grandmother. The grandmother used the content of these conversations, some of which she found troubling, as ammunition against the mother, delivering them to her as an appeal to her authority, a criticism of her parenting, or both. The mother then held the conversations up to Angela as an example of inappropriate loyalty to the grandmother and criticism of Angela as a daughter. And Angela discovered she had unwittingly taken part in a family pattern that encouraged coalitions and perpetuated criticism between mothers and daughters, allowing mothers to deflect anger toward the older generation onto the younger generation instead.

Is it any wonder that not long after this discovery Angela stood up to her mother and insisted, "Enough!"?

The confrontation that took place was more a matter of serendipity than of planning, spontaneously occurring at what Angela describes as "probably the lowest point in my life." At twenty-five she had found herself pregnant, in a relationship she knew wouldn't last. Well versed in the difficulties that can arise growing up in a single-parent home, Angela chose to have an abortion. The decision left her emotionally devastated for several months. As she mourned the loss of the child she'd always hoped for but had decided not to have, she also found herself mourning for a succession of losses in her life, including her father's early departure from the family and her mother's emotional distance. And right then, at the precise moment when she most needed to receive comfort and support, her mother knocked on her door, hoping to receive the same from her.

"I hadn't been planning to go to my mother and tell her, 'You did this. You did that. How could you?' " Angela says. "She just caught me at that time when I was in immense pain. I was very depressed. I hadn't been showing it, but that's what was going on. She showed up and things weren't going well in her life. And whenever things weren't going well for her, that's when she dumped on me. I had been taking it all my life, never said anything, never fought back. But this time after a few comments from her I wasn't in a place where I could take the criticism anymore. I knew the difference. Before, I'd been living in it; I didn't know there was any other way to be. But this time, having gone through so much pain of my own, I had stepped far enough outside our situation to realize, 'This isn't right. You can't do this to me.' I looked at her and I said, 'This is it. No more.' "

The directness and the vehemence of Angela's refusal to participate in the family pattern any longer led to two unexpected results. First, her mother agreed to a truce. The two of them have been working together since then to improve their relationship as adults, often reviewing events from their past from both perspectives. And second, the confrontation started what Angela calls a "chain reaction" among the women in her family.

"When I looked at my mother and said, 'You can't do this to me anymore,' " Angela explains, "she had to turn around and look at her mother and see the things she hadn't ever communicated, either. And even my grandmother started talking about her relationship with her mother. All her life, she had been quiet about how she felt. She never confronted her mother about it, and now her mother is dead. It's funny, though, because even though my grandmother thought it wasn't the nicest thing for me to be angry at my mother, to yell at her, to be disrespectful to her, she thought the confrontation was absolutely necessary. She thought it was bound to happen. But even though she said to me, 'Well, with what your mother *did* to you it was inevitable that you were going to blow up at her one day,' I can see how she, to some degree, still denies the fact that *she* had anything to do with the reasons I blew up at my mother."

As Angela learned, a granddaughter can't heal the relationship between a mother and grand-mother, but by improving and strengthening her relationships with both women — providing they're willing to change along with her — she *can* alter the shape and content of their triangle. Acknowledging a triangle's problem and making other family members aware of it isn't enough. Talking about one's feelings or changing one's behaviors in isolation from the group usually doesn't work either. At least two people in a tri-angle need to alter their behaviors for the overall sequence of communication to change. Because Angela's mother also was willing to examine her relationship with her mother and start modifying her responses to both her mother and her daughter, the coalitions in this family could start

157

transforming into a more balanced triangle that treats all three members with equal respect.

The imbalanced triangle that once existed in Angela's family is history. The purposes it once served no longer exist. Today, Angela sees both older women for what they are: human, complicated, imperfect, yet lovable nonetheless. When the three women get together today they still debate and criticize, but they also laugh and genuinely enjoy each other's company. They swap stories. They share their opinions. They sit at a round table. No sides.

If she had been raised exclusively by her mother throughout adolescence, Angela might have come to recognize or appreciate some of her mother's strengths sooner. But with her grandmother available to offer such consistent companionship and nurturing, Angela had little incentive during her teen years to see her mother as anything but the hurt, angry daughter she recalls. When a warm, loving grandmother exists, especially as a part- or full-time caretaker, it's easy for a granddaughter to slot her mother into the role of Bad Mother and her grandmother into the role of Good Mother, without acknowledging that both women — *all* women — are a complex blend of positive and negative traits.

This impulse to project all negative qualities onto one family member and all positive qualities onto another is a process psychologists call "splitting." It often occurs when a stepparent enters a family, or when a biological parent is abusive, neglectful, or absent. Granddaughters who have close relationships with their grandmothers may also create this kind of psychological polarization in their minds, particularly when they have difficult or contentious relationships with their mothers. When Marilyn Boynton works with granddaughters who are struggling with such a split, she asks them to write down all the characteristics they admire about their mothers and all the characteristics they dislike. Then she has them make a similar list for the grandmother. "Women who have conflicted relationships with their mothers have such long lists of negatives," she says, "they can barely put down anything positive. And then inevitably the grandmother is idealized and they can't come up with anything bad to write down about her."

Splitting can be a useful short-term adaptation, especially during a stormy adolescence or periods when a mother and daughter are estranged. Then, having a Good Mother consistently exposes a granddaughter to some of the positive qualities — empathy, compassion, generosity, warmth — she needs to internalize so she can offer the same kindness both to others and to herself. It can also help equalize whatever antipathy she may feel toward the mother at that time, keeping her from being overcome by anger or feelings of diminished self-worth. But if such a psychological division between Good Mother and Bad Mother persists over time, a granddaughter never learns how to handle the natural ambivalence she feels toward her mother and, to a much lesser degree, toward her grandmother. As long as a granddaughter sees one member of the triangle as a sinner and another as a saint, she never has to acknowledge that both impulses exist in both women and, by extension, in herself.

"The saddest part of all this in the long term is not just the contamination of the mother–daughter relationship — which really *is* sad, because when a woman's in her forties and fifties it really is time to be friends and colleagues with your mother — but also what she has lost inside herself by having kept Grandmother idealized in an unhealthy way," Sandy Halperin says. She may also run into difficulties as a mother herself, creating more distance and conflict than necessary with her own daughters. Or she may carry the sinner–saint division into parenthood, labeling one of her children as all good and another as all bad.

To overcome the effects of splitting, an adult granddaughter has to challenge her perceptions of the women who raised her. That isn't always a simple task. We're deeply invested in the opinions we hold about our mothers and grandmothers, often defining ourselves in relation to them. *My mother is weak and dependent, but I am the opposite of her. My grandmother is a selfless saint, and I am blessed to have such a person in my life.* So what happens to the granddaughter who opens herself to the possibility that her mother is also likable and worthy of compassion? Or to the idea that a grandmother may not have been operating exclusively from altruism when she took on the martyr's role?

By humanizing the mother and the grandmother, bringing one up from the dungeon and knocking the other off her pedestal, a granddaughter permits all the women in her family, including herself, to be imperfect *and* lovable, to be whole as women, mothers, and wives. This is what Angela did in her story, by taking an honest, objective look at her grandmother's subversive behaviors and by interpreting her mother's in the larger context of anger and neglect. It's often painful and courageous work, to acknowledge that the perception on which we've based many of our family decisions and much of our self-concept is ephemeral, and to then dismantle it, piece by piece. Painful but useful, and often necessary. As Sandy Halperin explains, "The more real these women are to us, the more real we can be with ourselves."

Triangles are remarkably resilient, often strengthening instead of dissolving over time. In my family, my grandmother, mother, and I continued to follow our prescribed behavioral roles until the beginning of my seventeenth year, when the rules abruptly changed. In a sentence, my mother died. From breast cancer, at forty-two. She hadn't wanted to tell my grandmother about the diagnosis, and put off the conversation for as long as she could. When she finally broke the news, there were heated discussions about alternative treatments, miracle drugs, and all that processed meat, always culminating in my mother's insistence that she had the best doctors, the best hospital, the best oncologist she could find. Maybe all that was true. It didn't matter, though. Her body held out for only sixteen months, and then it declined quickly and completely, a dramatic slide from kitchen table to hospital bed in less than a week's time.

It was the most awful thing either my grandmother or I could imagine.

I don't want to make too much of what happened next between the two of us, the periodic visits, the weekly phone calls, the awareness of a shared, unspoken pain, because we never openly talked about my mother's death. From the funeral onward, we mentioned her only in the most fleeting of references. *What was it that you and Mom and I ate that night after the Scrabble game in Florida?* But even that was something. My grandmother was the only family member with whom I could insert such casual references to my mother. Everyone else either closed down, teared up, or regarded me with looks of heartbreaking pity if I mentioned her, to the point where I excised her from conversations with anyone else. But my grandmother and I shared a silent mutual acknowledgment that she had once been a natural part of our days. Sometimes I deliberately snuck references to her into our discussions just so I could say her name.

My grandmother and I each tried to fill some of the vacuum my mother's absence had created for the other, with her trying to mother me and me trying to be a sounding board for her. But I was accustomed to a more hands-on yet less intrusive form of parenting, and she just didn't have the same history with me that she and my mother had shared. They had fed off each other's frustration and concern throughout adulthood, with a relationship based on the bedrock of that early mother–daughter bond. Part of the unspoken contract between them was that my grandmother had a right as a mother to voice her concerns as often and as forcefully as she wished and that it was my mother's responsibility as a daughter to try to assuage them.

Only in my mother's absence did I see exactly how her position as both daughter and mother had bridged the space between my grandmother and me. Without my mother in the middle, I had to look at my grandmother directly for perhaps the first time. And this is what I saw: an elderly woman, still bereft from the loss of her husband, heartbroken over the loss of her daughter. Desperate to protect her surviving family members. Helpless in the face of such all-encompassing grief. She was much, well, *littler* than I'd imagined her before. I couldn't bring myself to feel genuine irritation toward her, even when she started in with me, incessantly, about the perils of underwire bras. I couldn't, even in my most exasperated moments, slam down the phone. Our bond was based on affection, not on passion. Never had that been clearer to me than after my mother died.

When one member of a triangle dies or leaves the system the two remaining members find themselves suddenly face-to-face. The old rules no longer apply, though the remaining members may try to reprise them rather than risk change. Or they may pull in a new third person and expect her to assume the absentee member's role. Ideally, though, the old triangle collapses and a new one-on-one relationship between the remaining members grows.

Thirty-five-year-old Patricia says the close adult relationship she had with her mother would never have been possible if her grandmother had remained living close by. Patricia spent her first nine years living with her grandmother and her mother, who was profoundly deaf, after her parents divorced when she was a toddler. Her grandmother stepped forward as the more capable adult in the home and became Patricia's "psychological parent," her primary emotional attachment figure during those years.

"My grandmother was my mother," Patricia states, simply. "I went to her for permission to do anything. She administered punishment, she bought my clothes, she spoke to my teachers. When I was about five, she started spending winters in Miami Beach without us and I had a terrible time with that. The separation was very traumatic for me. All I kept saying was 'I miss my mother.' I didn't really want to be with the stranger that my mother was to me."

Patricia was nine when her mother remarried and her grandmother relocated to an apartment building next door. The separation was more than Patricia could handle. She developed such an extreme fear of leaving her mother's apartment that tutors had to come teach her at home. Eventually, she moved in with her grandmother for the next two years, until her mother and stepfather bought a house an hour's drive away. This time, her mother insisted she live with them.

"When I was a kid I used to think, *If somebody has to die, let it be my mother. Don't let it be my grandmother — she's my mother,*" Patricia says. "But when we moved away and my grandmother sort of took a backseat in the family, my mother and I were able to develop a relationship and I stopped thinking that way. Especially after she and my stepfather divorced, my mother got much stronger and became her own person, like I'd never seen her before. She started movements for the handicapped, got TDD's in hotels and went to Washington to lobby for new laws. I saw her for the first time not under anyone else's control, and we became friends. She was diagnosed with cancer when I was in college, and she would let only me go with her to the hospital. We got very, very close during that time. She would say, 'I'm fighting and I'm living for you.' I feel very grateful that I mended my relationship with my mother before she died."

For twenty-seven-year-old Bari, however, a mother's death thrust her into an unwanted and complicated relationship with a grandmother she describes as "very much like an octopus. She just wraps her arms around you and doesn't let go. She wants to be in control and have you all to herself all the time. She was like that with my mother and after my mother died she transferred it right to me. There was no buffer in between."

Bari's mother, an only child, divorced when Bari, also an only child, was less than a year old. They soon after moved from Texas to Chicago into an apartment in the three-family house Bari's grandparents owned, to save money on rent. "We lived on the third floor, and my grandmother lived on the second," Bari recalls. "I can remember this happening a thousand times, where we would open the door to go downstairs and my grandmother would hear us and open her door to ask where we were going. My mother would freak out and tell her to leave us alone. After my grandparents moved to Florida, the phone became the big issue because my grandmother would call every two minutes. My mother and I would sit there and let the phone ring endlessly because we knew that it was her. It was kind of sad, actually."

Though she knew her mother and grandmother loved each other — "My grandmother really would have done anything for my mother,"

Bari explains, "and deep down I think my mother felt the same way" — her allegiance to her mother permitted only a limited emotional connection to develop with her grandmother.

"I didn't like her much when I was a kid," Bari admits. "I shied away from her in much the same way my mother did. I took advantage of the fact that because I was her only grandchild, she would do anything for me. Like there was a candy store up the street and my mother didn't want me to have candy after school, so I would go to my grandmother for money. She wanted me to like her since she didn't have that kind of close relationship with my mother. She tried with me, she really did, but I didn't respect her as a kid, probably because I didn't see anyone else respecting her, either."

Bari's mother was diagnosed with cancer when Bari was seventeen and died a year later, which left Bari to take over some of the tasks, including caring for the house in Chicago that her mother had previously addressed. As her grandparents' only living descendant, as well as the administrator of their assets, Bari found her prior relationship with her grandmother, which had left most direct contact to her mother, no longer worked in her new role. At the same time, she couldn't accept her grandmother's approach, which was to treat her in much the same way she'd treated her daughter, hoping to be kept aware of and involved in even the smallest details of Bari's day.

"When my mom first passed away," Bari says, "my grandmother called me constantly, every minute. Picture being in college with your own apartment and your own job and a telephone that's constantly ringing. If I wasn't home when she called from Florida, she would go berserk. She would even call other relatives to find out where I was."

One of those cousins, aware of Bari's dilemma, devised the winning compromise. Suspecting that what Bari's grandmother needed most was a way to alleviate her anxiety, the cousin suggested that the next time Bari's grandmother wanted to call Bari, she should call her instead. This new arrangement slowly weaned the grandmother away from calling Bari several times a day and gave Bari the breathing space she needed to start developing a more balanced relationship with her grandmother as an adult. And as both women work toward this goal, Bari has found that having a grandmother who cares so deeply about her helps make up for some of what she lost when her mother died.

"In a sense, I didn't really appreciate the love my grandmother has for me until my mother died," she explains. "I realized then that she loves me in a way similar to how a mother loves a child. She really would do anything for me. I could murder someone and she would find a way to defend me. I value that part of my relationship with my grandmother a great deal, especially now that my mother is gone."

Like Bari, I found that losing my mother allowed me to have a direct relationship with my grandmother that, difficult as it may have been at times, I might not otherwise have had. When my mother died, our triangle collapsed, and my grandmother and I had to learn how to interact only with each other, instead of with a third. I didn't always agree with what I saw and heard, and much of the time I know I wasn't the kind of granddaughter she hoped for. I did as much for her as could reasonably be expected of me, and no more. She could never understand why I chose to live so far from my family in New York. But we did share a unique type of love, and we tried to make what we were left with work.

Even so, no matter how many phone calls we placed, no matter how many visits were made, concerns expressed, requests made, expectations fulfilled, we never became two. My mother's passion and investment in both of us was what had made us complete. For all the years that followed, my grandmother and I always felt like three minus one.

10

An Unexpected Visitor: 1983

Here's my grandmother in the summer of 1983, on the boardwalk in Atlantic City with her two older sisters. They're like a mobile triptych of aging, Rea shuffling along on the left, Nell limping slightly on the right, my grandmother in the center walking a pace or two ahead of them both. She takes careful, measured steps, her low-heeled, square-toed shoes hitting the weathered boards in a steady heel-toe, heel-toe. She's seventy-six but we don't know that, on account of her flawless ability to subtract five years off her age when she met my grandfather and her family's remarkable ability not to notice. We think she's seventy-one. The temperature in Atlantic City hovers around ninety, but none of the sisters are dressed for a day at the beach. My grandmother's wearing a light wool suit and matching hat, Nell a powder-blue polyester pantsuit with nautical details, Rea a beige long-sleeved dress with a fabric belt that accentuates the bulges down her sides. They're a bit too wrinkled to be mistaken for a ladies' club, a bit too quiet to be mistaken for friends. They look like what they are: three elderly sisters who live together and stopped caring about appearances long ago.

They arrived in Atlantic City this morning doing forty-five in my grandmother's burgundy Oldsmobile sedan, taking it all in slowly as they drove into town: the bars and boarded-up store-fronts on the way to the sea, the casino towers at its shore. Atlantic City isn't as they remember, when they went to the beach as children and their parents parked umbrellas in the sand. Then families walked arm in arm along the boardwalk and rented rooms by the week. Now tour buses idle outside Harrah's and Bally's, punked-out skateboarders have taken over the boardwalk, and dead horseshoe crabs litter the shore. Every time my grandmother sees a man sleeping on a bench, one forearm carelessly draped across his eyes and a paper bag clutched to his chest, she slips a crumpled dollar bill into his hand.

The sisters will stroll on the boardwalk, stop somewhere for a lunch of soft, boiled foods, and settle back in the car. The trip here is a last-minute decision, nostalgia colliding with purpose, because they have another destination farther down the road.

I'm nineteen and living in a rented beach house an hour south of Atlantic City. You can see where this is heading. I'm here because I'm trying to figure out whether I want to go back to college in the fall. In the meantime, I've got a job waiting tables at night in an Italian restaurant. It's my first real summer job and I'm tipped well, which is a good thing since my father is about to fall on financial hard times. But I don't know that yet. My grandmother may or may not sense the trouble on its way, but that's not the reason she's heading south. I've been away at college in Chicago all winter and now I'm in New Jersey for the summer, and even though I saw her for a few hours in between seasons, she needs to see for herself that I'm managing all right.

Here I am, walking in from the beach at the end of the day, in a yellow T-shirt advertising Joe's Pizza and Clam Bar, and a pair of blue rubber thongs. I've got a beach towel wrapped around my waist like a sarong and I'm wearing red plastic heart-shaped sunglasses that have earned me the nickname Lolita. My roommate Chris is sprawled across one of the crappy orange studio beds that pass for couches in our living room, flipping through a back issue of *Mademoiselle*. "Your grandmother just called for directions," she says without looking up. "She's about twenty minutes away."

I look around the living room, at the grimy linoleum floor and the free McDonaldland Camp Snoopy glasses we use for Kahlua and cremes discarded on the end tables. I look down at myself, at my wrinkled Joe's Pizza and Clam Bar shirt and my sunburned feet.

The first thing I think: Clams aren't kosher.

The second thing I think: I can't face this alone.

It's my night off, which, in some eerie way I

don't want to think too much about, my grandmother probably senses. I run two blocks to the
ice-cream parlor where Margaret is scooping
mint chocolate chip into a waffle cone. She's tall
and blond with navy blue eyes and some connection to the *Mayflower*, and she's my best friend.

"You've got to," I tell her, "*got to* get off early
and go out for dinner with us."

Margaret was raised by her grandmother and
has met mine before. She gets it. "Give me ten
minutes," she says.

Back at the apartment, I start tossing damp
towels off the orange couches and pulling the
sheets and blanket back up over my bed. Hiding
the cigarettes. Covering the saucers of salt we've
placed in the corners to kill the land snails. Until
today, all of my encounters with my grandmother have taken place at her house, or my parents' house, or on neutral turf. This is the first
time she's stepping onto mine. I know now how
my mother must have felt all those years, that
little jolt of panic when she heard the dog start
barking to announce the arrival of the burgundy
Oldsmobile in our drive. *Uh-oh. Caught in the act
of being myself again.*

But there's something puzzling about my behavior, and it's this: My grandmother doesn't
judge. She might criticize, she might complain,
but her love has never been conditional. She
doesn't threaten to take it away, no matter how
many social or religious rules I, her brilliant,
promising, perfect-just-as-I-am first grandchild,

might break. There's no mighty arbiter of approval or disapproval here, no eternal damnation for getting caught with cigarettes on the bureau or clams in the fridge. There's just an old woman with strong opinions, but somehow, that's enough.

I'm back in my bedroom, frantically trying to towel the sand out of my hair when they arrive. I hear the screen door wheeze open and then my grandmother's familiar "How d'ya do, how d'ya do?" as she eases herself across the threshold. For as long as I've known her she's entered houses with the same greeting, first as she walked in behind my grandfather — both of them *How d'ya do*ing together with the dog barking and jumping and my mother shouting, "Candy! Down!" and all the squeals and kisses as my sister and I rummaged through the paper shopping bags filled with gifts and food — and then, after my grandfather died, walking in ahead of her sisters, who follow her single file and silently up the front walk.

By the time I get to the living room they're positioned three across on an orange couch, knees together, clutching their pocketbooks on their laps. I'm momentarily disoriented, as if three characters from one television show have unexpectedly appeared in the middle of another. When my grandmother sees me, she smiles, a sweet smile with her lips pinched together and her eyes crinkled shut.

"Grandma. What are you doing here?" I ask.

"That's some hello," Nell says.

"We were in Atlantic City," my grandmother says, even though we both know she's telling the story in reverse.

I lean down to kiss them, and they each raise a right cheek, in turn, to meet my lips. "I was thinking we could go to a nice Italian restaurant down the street," I say. "Are you hungry?"

"Can't we sit for a while?" Rea says. "We just got here."

My grandmother looks around the room, taking in the pea-green recliner, the dirty linoleum, the neighbor guys who come in to say hello wearing only Hawaiian surfing shorts and carrying their dinner in a wok, and says nothing. I'm going to hear about it in a few days later from my father, whom she'll call in a burst of concern. She'll tell him she's worried about me living like that. Like what? he'll ask, but she'll refuse to elaborate. She's worried, that's all. I'll hear this and feel annoyed and humiliated and embarrassed and everything else you feel when you're nineteen and your grandmother, who lives in a house that's in not much better shape than yours, comes checking up on you and is disappointed by what she finds. And I'll realize it's not fear of her disapproval that throws me into a cleaning frenzy but fear of her disappointment, that preserving my status as Perfect Grandchild matters to me more than I'd thought. That in the midst of the chaos that surrounds me, I find an island of security knowing someone thinks of me in those terms. And even though I'll go to bed that night still feeling annoyed at her for getting my father involved, I'll sleep just a little better remembering there's someone out there who'll drive four hours down the coast and four hours back just to see me for one hour.

Margaret and I take them to the Italian restaurant down the street. I know in advance it's not kosher and won't get away with lying if I'm asked, but nobody brings it up. We sit at a round table, me, Margaret, Nell, my grandmother, Rea, me. The table is high, or maybe the chairs are especially low, because the plates are barely level with the older women's chests. My grandmother's smile hangs almost low enough to skim the top of her empty wine glass. The waitress, who is short and cheerful with long brown bangs, brings our water and bread and deals out menus like oversized playing cards.

"How was Atlantic City?" I ask no one in particular.

"It was very nice," Rea says slowly, bobbing her head.

"We brought you some taffy," my grandmother says, reaching into her suit pocket for a small, crumpled white paper bag. Later that night I'll open it and see nine thin cylinders of colored candy wrapped in waxy white paper, with three empty wrappers lying on top. Something about those empty wrappers, the evidence of small pleasures, will speak to me of loneliness and vulnerability, and I'll rub the empty wrappers between my fingers and try hard not to cry.

My grandmother turns her attention to Margaret, who's explaining that she grew up in Rhode Island and attended boarding school in New Hampshire but now her mother lives in Texas, and since she now goes to college in Chicago she might as well call that home. My grandmother is listening intently, breaking a piece of Italian bread into small pieces and slowly slipping them into her mouth. She's met Margaret before and genuinely likes her, but she can't quite fit her into context. Margaret's father died when she was a toddler and she talks to her mother, who's remarried to a fundamentalist minister, about once a month. Only when my grandmother learns that Margaret was born in New York and was raised with help from her grandmother does she find some common ground.

The waitress returns for our order. Rea, Nell, and I immediately fall silent. It's a risk to order first in our family, to claim a culinary preference before my grandmother states hers. You can't be sure which items will be interpreted as delicious, and which as dangerous. There are few certainties. Most forms of meat cause cancer. Anything cold will make me catch a chill. Brisket is almost always a safe choice, but we're hard-pressed to find it on an Italian menu, and besides, I don't eat meat. Usually when I'm with her I just order eggs and toast.

The waitress stands with her pen poised over

the order pad. Margaret, who doesn't know any better, orders first. Chicken parmigiana. I see my grandmother's lips start moving soundlessly, as if she's struggling to hold back the words. She's too courteous to say anything to someone she hardly knows, though I did once catch her in a supermarket meat aisle trying to convince a stranger not to buy salami. I decide to order from the absolute other side of the menu. I can already feel my body tensing in expectation of the worried "Oh, no-o-o," with her eyes squinted shut and her fingers kneading each other in concern, that precedes the "Please . . . please . . . don't order *that*" which more than once provoked my father to stand up and walk out to the parking lot, leaving my grandmother to gaze around the table asking, "What? What did I do?" while everyone else sat in polite and restrained silence.

The waitress stands through another long and expectant pause. I can see my grandmother through her eyes, a small woman with a deeply lined face hunched over a menu three times the diameter of her head. Perhaps the waitress notices she wears no jewelry except a square diamond engagement ring on a simple band, or that the candy apple red polish on her short, square nails has worn away except for thin patches in their centers. Perhaps she also notices that my grandmother's hands tremble just slightly as she grips the menu, something I hadn't noticed until now. The waitress is patient with her, which speaks either to good manners and familiarity with the elderly or the desire for a very large tip. Actually, she doesn't need either. My grandmother will leave her twelve dollars on a thirty-eight-dollar bill, and when I object, telling her it's too much, she'll seek out the waitress and explain, "I'm leaving you a very large tip because my granddaughter is also waiting tables this summer." From then on, she'll have a renewed respect for servers in my presence. She'll never tip less than 30 percent.

"Ma'am?" the waitress says.

"How is the ravioli?" my grandmother asks.

"People seem to like it."

"No, how is it prepared? Is there any meat in it?"

"We can make it with meat or cheese."

"Un-huh," my grandmother says. "Okay, then. I'll have the cheese ravioli."

The waitress turns to Rea, who looks up and smiles broadly. "That sounds good," she says. "I think I'll have the cheese ravioli too."

Nell makes a big deal out of inspecting the menu. She nudges her reading glasses farther up the bridge of her nose. She pinches the left side of her mouth in what could be either a pose of concentration or a grimace. We wait. I inspect my silverware. Margaret peels the top layer of skin off her sunburned shoulder.

Finally, Nell closes the menu. "I'll have the cheese ravioli," she says brightly.

I don't like ravioli, which creates a definite dilemma. I scan my options. Any form of shellfish is out of the question. She'll tell me that anything fried is bad for my skin. The only salads listed are a dinner salad, too small for a meal, and antipasto, which includes processed meats. If I order manicotti, she won't know what it is and will grill the waitress for a list of ingredients. I choose a dinner salad and spaghetti with marinara sauce.

My grandmother peers up at the waitress. "Are there any meatballs in —"

"Without meatballs," I add firmly.

After dinner we drive back to my apartment and my grandmother steps out of the car to say goodbye. I've been trying to convince her to rent a hotel room for the night, to avoid that long drive back in the dark, but she can't be swayed. The dog needs to be fed and let out, they've already been gone all day, and Rea and Nell are tired. That last part doesn't make sense to me, but I let it go. We kiss goodbye, and when I hug her the single pearl on her hatpin slides against my cheek. She smells like she's smelled all my life, of hand cream and coffee and wool. I hold her for just a moment longer than usual, and she rubs her hand around the base of my back. Over her shoulder I see Rea and Nell waiting patiently in the car, staring straight ahead. "Digesting," they'd explain, if I asked.

Rea will live for another four years, Nell for another nine. In those intervening five years my grandmother and Nell will travel everywhere together, sisters who bickered on and off throughout their lives adjusted to a comfortable silence. They'll shuffle up our front walk together, with my grandmother in the lead, and Nell will move up to the passenger seat of the car, but something about them will always seem abbreviated to me. I don't sense this impending loss as I stand by the curb saying goodbye, but when they pull away I feel something in my chest try to follow, a thin tether connecting my heart to the rear bumper of my grandmother's car. And I know then that I should have insisted on finding her a hotel room for the night, should have offered her my room and tucked myself into a sleeping bag on the orange couch. I should have fluffed her pillows and brought her a glass of water, paused outside the door to her room several times during the night and listened to her breathe. I should have woken up early and cooked her a breakfast of eggs and toast. Instead I stand on the curb and wave, thinking I am relieved to see her drive away. She has been gone for less than a minute. I miss her already.

PART III

The Center
of the Family

11

Grandmother Power

Of all the images I have to choose from when I think of the phrase *my grandmother*, there's one that always comes to mind. She's standing on the royal blue carpet in the middle of our living room in front of the wooden upright piano, her wool coat draped over her shoulders like an oversized cape. She is, of course, wearing a hat. My grandfather is absent; her sisters are nowhere to be found. It's just her standing there silently, her bulging pocketbook trapped tight between her elbow and her side, her car keys grasped in her right hand. I can't tell if she just arrived or is about to leave. She's neither old nor young; her face has no distinct details. I can only make out her outlines. And she's huge.

I suppose what I'm describing here is my own personal twist on the grandmother archetype, my inner association of the Great Mother summoned into conscious view. I'm sure my sister would choose a different defining image of our grandmother, and my brother another one still. But this one's mine, this larger-than-life visitor who seemed to fill a room.

My grandmother may have been a tiny

woman, but when I was a child she was all-powerful to me. She seemed to win every argument she entered, and no matter how angry she made my parents, she was always welcomed back into our home. This signaled a type of omnipotence no one else in the family possessed, as well as a fortitude no one I knew could match. Though I'm sure sometimes my grandmother won because she was older and more experienced, I know that just as often she won because she refused to give in. She relied heavily on the power of persistence. That, and a very loud voice. "All right, already!" my mother, and later I, would blurt out in exasperation, agreeing to virtually anything just to get some relief.

For as long as I can remember, my grandmother had a sort of inauthentic power in my family: she could elicit compliance, but could never quite succeed in convincing us she knew best. It was a little like living in a country where the citizenry believes itself to be smarter than the king. So if you'd asked me who ran the family during those years, I wouldn't have chosen my grandmother. Especially after my grandfather died and her arguments grew wackier and more insistent, with an internal logic difficult for others to understand, the thought of her as our unquestionable leader grew increasingly bizarre. But she had a hold on us. I don't know how else to explain it. She had a hold on us. We didn't have to give in to her, but we often did. And therein lay the essence of my grandmother's power: not only in getting others to do what she wanted, but in persuading them to do what they otherwise never would.

My grandmother was a specific type of matriarch, a strong-willed woman with a need for control. I use the term *matriarch* in its broadest sense, to describe a woman who occupies a position of power in her extended family. It's not to be confused with *matriarchy*, a system in which authority resides in women and descent is traced through the female line. A true matriarchy has never existed in modern culture — the closest historical examples are probably Navajo and Hopi tribes — but it's not unusual to find families today where the eldest and most powerful member is female. Here, by *powerful* I mean able to command obedience and deference from other family members. Neither *matriarch* nor *powerful* is meant as a negative term. Though a grandmother who exercises power without benevolence can certainly do great damage to a young girl's fragile psyche, a firm and loving matriarch can offer a granddaughter structure, constancy, and a valuable example of female authority.

A grandmother is often the first woman of power that a young girl observes, especially in cultures where women have little status outside the home. Paradoxically, these are the families in which matriarchs are most likely to appear. "Take the Middle East, for example," says Lois Banner. "The Middle East is technically a very patriarchal culture, but it's filled with matriarchal families. It has to do with the separation of public and private spheres. Within the private space of the family, women develop a great deal of power. In cultures where women don't have much power in their younger years — in Classical China, in Japan to a certain extent, and in some countries in the Middle East and the Mediterranean — and young wives have to be under the thumb of a mother-in-law, their whole life becomes focused on when they'll be older and in control, and strong matriarchal patterns arise in those cultures as well. To me, theoretically, it's one of the most powerful and ironic principles that applies: the more patriarchal the culture, the more likely you are to wind up with families that have older women of power."

Matriarchs in the United States are most often associated with families at opposite ends of the class system, as the strong, regal matrons (usually, but not always, widowed) of the upper class who control the family purse strings and enforce its social code, and as the sage, resilient heads of household at the other end of the scale who hold the family together in spite of such adversities as poverty, discrimination, immigration, premature death, or divorce. Mrs. Manson Mingott, the corpulent widowed dowager of Edith Wharton's *The Age of Innocence*, who received family members while reclining in her enormous bed, is a classic example of the former; Momma in Maya Angelou's memoir, *I Know Why the Caged Bird*

Sings, the strong, proud grandmother who raised her two grandchildren and ran the town store in 1930s Stamps, Arkansas, personifies the latter. In reality, however, any family that spans several generations is capable of producing a matriarch, since their ascension to power is at least partly due to basic social psychology. Humans, compelled to create order from chaos, naturally gravitate toward structure. We form hierarchies of power and develop patterned, repetitive behaviors we can follow. Put most simply, every family is a system; every system needs organization; and every organization needs leadership.

The most straightforward family hierarchy follows the generational line, with power distributed according to age. Grandparents have the most, parents have somewhat less, and grandchildren have the least. This is a common structure in agrarian or tribal systems, where age is synonymous with the type of experience and knowledge that's vital to the community's survival. Over the past century of rapid industrial, technological, and social change, however, grandparents in Western cultures have been forced out of the position of wise and beloved elders for the first time, creating some truncated family hierarchies where parents have the most power and grandparents are moved into an advisory, or even incidental, role.

Today, the unique social, economic, and psychological makeup of an extended family determines who occupies its top seat. It may be the person with the most money or with the highest level of education. Or the first member to have emigrated to the new country, or the one with the most intimidating personality. In many families, it's still the oldest member, and because women's life expectancy exceeds men's in every racial and ethnic group in America, that elder is often a woman.

The person of most power in forty-two-year-old Joan's family was a divorced elderly grandmother with unquestioned authority over her children and more control than any man. "You know how Barbara Stanwyck ran the Big Valley?" Joan asks. "That's how my grandmother ran our family." In thirty-six-year-old Marjorie's family it was a wealthy widow who controlled her daughters' trust funds and, by extension, them. "My grandmother was always loving and generous, and we knew she was there to bail us out financially if we got into trouble," Marjorie explains. "But at the same time there was this subtle message that we couldn't do anything that would make her angry." And in thirty-eight-year-old Tamara's family, it was the maternal grandmother who raised her in a four-generation extended-family home. "My grandmother was just a human dynamo," Tamara recalls. "All of our family interactions went through her. She was the source of so much of the household's energy and direction. I think her momentum was more than my mother could handle. She didn't really know how to confront it or balance it herself, so she's still, even to this day, waiting for somebody else to direct her."

The family sequence Tamara describes — a strong, influential grandmother and a weaker, often emotionally dependent mother — is one that repeatedly appeared in other granddaughters' stories. "It's a classic pattern," explains Kathleen Moges, Ph.D., a psychologist in Beverly Hills, California, who specializes in issues surrounding intimacy and relationships. "Daughters of this kind of mother often become overly attuned and accommodating to the mother to please her, and appear to be weak people-pleasers in relation to others. Especially when a grandmother takes up all the space in a family, the mother is vulnerable to this accommodation pattern and doesn't usually have a strong sense of self."

Whereas a strong-willed mother appears able to equalize a grandmother's influence over the extended family, a mother who consistently defers to her mother starts to lose power and authority over her own daughter. "It was very obvious in my house that my grandmother had the power," explains thirty-five-year-old Patricia, who lived with her mother and maternal grandmother for her first nine years. "What she said went without question. My mother was just another daughter who had a bad relationship with her mother and was very subservient to her. In fact, when my mother was dating and I'd ask her if I could have another piece of candy or stay up late, she'd say, 'No, go to bed.' And I'd say, 'Well, if you're not nice to me, I'm gonna tell Grandma that you're seeing so-and-so, and you know she doesn't like him.' I would get what I wanted then, because my mother was afraid of my grandmother finding out."

In situations like these, Sandy Halperin explains, "The child doesn't perceive the mother as strong or as competent as the grandmother is, in the family or in life. Sometimes the mother is viewed more as a peer. In some cases, the mother really *isn't* as competent as the grandmother, and stays in the position of peer. But in healthier families, mothers aren't stuck there. They have a different kind of competence and in those particular realms they become co-parents with the grandmother. A granddaughter in this type of family vacillates between seeing the mother as weak and seeing her as having her own strengths."

The most poignant example I found of the impact a strong grandmother and submissive mother can have on a granddaughter came from fifty-one-year-old Helen. Helen grew up in a family dominated by a fiercely devoted yet extremely authoritarian maternal grandmother whose only daughter never challenged her control. "My grandmother was definitely the matriarch of our family," she says. "She always sat at the head of the table. My grandfather sat on the side. She had very strong opinions, and did whatever she wanted. Nobody else was ever consulted. She would just show up at our house on a Saturday or Sunday and say, 'We can have lunch now' or 'We can have dinner.' It was never 'Would you mind if we ate with you?' or 'Can we stay for dinner?' No. She arrived, and that was it."

Even as a small child Helen sensed her mother was afraid to contradict or anger her grandmother, and she soon absorbed that fear. She recalls an incident from her early childhood, one of the first she can remember. Her grandmother, who was a talented seamstress, had made her a beautiful romper, which four-year-old Helen accidentally ripped one morning while playing in the street. She slunk home in terror, and told her mother a man had ripped her outfit. "She knew I was lying through my teeth, but I stuck with my lie," Helen says. "I said, 'Yes, and he went that way,' even though I felt so uncomfortable doing it." But instead of reprimanding Helen for the lie, her mother threatened the child with a fate far worse. "I'm going to tell your grandmother this afternoon," she warned.

The memory of the fear she felt on that afternoon forty-seven years ago is still so visceral that Helen starts to cry quietly as she describes what happened next. "Early in the afternoon I had school and I remember being in the schoolyard with my little friend and shaking, just trembling like hell," she recalls. "Thinking that it was the last day of my life or something, because God only knew what my grandmother was going to say. I felt it so strong, the fear. I could see my body shaking and I had no control over it. At the end of the day I came home like a sheep to the slaughterhouse. My grandmother was sitting in the living room, very lovely and dainty, always very beautiful, and my mother was sitting next to her and telling on me. And actually, my grandmother said nothing. Nothing. I was expecting death, basically, some kind of awesome event, and nothing happened. But that fear of my grandmother constantly came back throughout my life, because my mother feared her mother so much. She seems to still fear her now, even though my grandmother is dead."

Helen's childhood expectation of her grandmother's anger far exceeded her grandmother's response that day, evidence of the profound psychological power the grandmother had over her, even at that young age. But this paralyzing fear might not have developed if power in Helen's family had been distributed differently. Because the family's existing power structure was such that everyone pooled together beneath her grandmother without any distinction other than Her (in the position of power) and Us (those who are powerless against her), Helen's mother became her child's equal rather than her superior. By appealing to the grandmother to determine her daughter's punishment, she acted more like a sibling who warns, "If you do that, I'm going to tell Dad," or a student who threatens to report another student to the teacher.* A person at the bottom of a hierarchy often tries to manipulate the behaviors of those beside him by threatening punishment from above. It's the threat of the powerless, trying to gain a feeling of control.

Helen's mother may also have been looking for a way to claim her daughter for herself, Sandy Halperin says. "If a mother who's afraid of the grandmother can inspire the same fear in the granddaughter, then she has an ally in her child," she explains. "At the same time, the mother is using the granddaughter so she doesn't have to deal with her feelings about her own mother. It's a very complicated triangle. The mother is going to the grandmother as an emissary, where she's the one who reports the incident and can earn the grandmother's approval. She's obviously trying to play both sides out of her own sense of terror and isolation, but it's terribly sad that she would choose to sacrifice her own daughter. And the granddaughter learns she can't trust her mother *or* her grandmother, so there's no safety for her anywhere."

Even if Helen's mother had been offered the opportunity to permanently claim a higher rung on the family ladder, there's a good chance she

---

*Patricia in the preceding anecdote acted in a similar manner when she threatened her mother with her grandmother's punishment. She sensed her mother occupied the same rung as she on the family power ladder, and used that knowledge to her advantage.

would have turned it down. Hierarchies are like little terrariums of self-governance. Participants usually work to maintain — not to change — the existing system. Those at the top act to ensure their dominance, and if they don't, those at the bottom will act in a way that forces them to stay up there rather than risk change. The same is true when someone of lesser status on the ladder tries to climb too high, too fast. Then the ones above react in a way that forces the impulsive one back down.

You can see how this plays out among grandmothers, mothers, and granddaughters, when a mother or granddaughter acts with unexpected autonomy and a grandmother tightens her control, or when a grandmother neglects to act with authority at a critical moment and a mother or granddaughter deliberately intensifies the crisis, forcing her to take charge. Or the example that perhaps most of us intuitively understand, when a grandmother starts slipping either mentally or physically and a mother or granddaughter, instead of taking steps to assume some of the grandmother's authority, tries to force it back on her by refusing to acknowledge the decline. Women are raised to define themselves in relation to others, and altering our relationships requires a corresponding adjustment in our identities. That's too destabilizing for many of us to risk. So it happens that a matriarch rules like a monarch: With tradition behind her and the family beneath her, she retains her position until death or disability takes her power away.

12

Six Weeks Before

Thanksgiving: 1987

"We're going to The Club for Thanksgiving," my grandmother says. I'm sitting on the floor of my little house in Tennessee. She's sitting somewhere in her big house in Mount Vernon. Fiber optics are as successful as they've promised us they'll be; it sounds like she's right next door. I can hear her breathing softly, waiting for a response. "We're going to The Club for Thanksgiving," she says again, softer this time.

We're. That means her and her sisters, Rea and Nell. Her two surviving daughters, my aunts. One uncle, two cousins, and possibly my great-uncle Jack. My father, my sister, and my brother. In other words, *we* means everyone, except (so far) me.

Going. That means driving, in big, heavy American cars. Everyone, again, except for me, who'll have to fly. I live six hundred miles away. That's by choice. No one is happy about this. Except me.

To The Club. That's the country club my grandparents joined nearly thirty years ago, back when

Jews were still systematically denied entry to other upper-middle-class social clubs. It's a meticulously landscaped place with a stately white clubhouse, a continuously emerald golf course, and an eerily quiet pool area. It's not a club to which my family has truly ever belonged, not to those tight circles of tanned, aging golfers or antenna-thin Westchester women with their black designer pantsuits and gold. But my grandmother automatically pays her dues every June. If nothing else, it guarantees her a place to hold Thanksgiving dinner, when her family assembles in the clubhouse dining room around a circular table whose diameter shrinks a little bit more each year.

For Thanksgiving. A day of family unity and gratitude, and thanks to God for keeping us healthy and happy this past year. Well, healthy, at least. I'm still working on happy. Earlier this year, I finally started acknowledging that my mother is dead. Which means never coming back. Which means I'm now either a few years ahead of whoever's sitting next to me at the Thanksgiving table or a few years behind. Either way, we're not all in sync. And we haven't been, for years.

The subtext of *We're going to The Club for Thanksgiving,* I know, is that I've skipped the past three Thanksgivings in a row. My father was the one who called me with those invitations, and it was easy to say no to him. *Mmm, I've just got too much work right now,* or *You know, this year*

I'm thinking about coming for New Year's instead. He doesn't argue with me. He knows the real reason I don't go is that I don't want to, and he doesn't want to have to hear it. We have an understanding there. It's not so easy for me to refuse my grandmother. I can't remember a single time when I have. But my shrink has identified assertion as one of my problem areas. We've been working on *no* for a while now.

"Did you hear me?" my grandmother asks, not unkindly. "Uh-huh," I say. And then, to myself, *Tell her. Tell her that sitting at the club reminds you too much of all those dinners at her house when your mother was still there. Tell her you can't sit and make conversation about your aunt's bulldog or your cousin's soccer game while something slowly rips from your throat down to your navel and you have to pretend it doesn't hurt. Tell her the effort is too much for you, that you know you'll be a wreck the whole week before you go and the whole week after you return.*

Only a few years ago my grandmother would have been more insistent with me about this visit. She would have questioned, argued, cajoled. "What's the matter, don't you want to come?" she would have asked, sounding forlorn. "Is it the money? I can send you a check. Are you feeling sick?" The last time I went to The Club for Thanksgiving she was still trying to micromanage the meal. But since then, her second daughter has been diagnosed with breast cancer — survivable this time, thank God, but still —

and it's pushed my grandmother to her limit. She's since taken on the unmistakable air of defeat. That and age are starting to make her crack. I can tell from the new halting, uncertain messages she leaves on my answering machine. *Hello? This is Hope's grandmother. Please have her . . . call me back. When she . . . gets in.* And from her phone calls, once made weekly and infused with simple, predictable questions — *Is it very cold there? Are you meeting any nice boys?* — which have become increasingly more erratic. In the middle of a workday. At eleven o'clock on a Tuesday night. Two messages back-to-back on a Sunday, and then no contact for several weeks. The questions, once straightforward and foreseeable, have been slowly replaced with demands. I have to convince my father to stop smoking. I have to talk to my great-uncle, to get him to see her point of view. I have to stop wearing underwire bras.

By now, my reassurances have become useless. Any attempts to change the subject are ignored. And without the dexterity to steer a conversation back to neutral ground, I realize I don't know how to talk to my grandmother at all. Most of the time, I sit on the floor with the receiver trapped between my shoulder and my ear, offering periodic *uh-huhs* while I polish my toenails or sort through the mail. For the first time, I begin trying to rush her off the phone.

Yet still I cannot say a direct *no* to her. No matter how hard I try. In her demands, I hear pleas for help, for understanding, for companionship, for me. Too many years of obedience and guilt direct me. I can't contradict her. I want to. I just can't.

Tell her no. Tell her what's happening to her destroys you. Tell her you can't go home. That home is where you live right now.

"Can you come?" she says.

No.

I slouch down farther against the wall. I close my eyes. My grandmother is sitting in the corner of her slate-blue couch, clutching the black phone to her ear. Waiting. For me.

I tell her I'll be there.

13

Matriarchs and Kinkeepers

My grandmother was a specific type of matriarch, the kind I call a Benevolent Manipulator, whose love for her family is matched only by her desire for control. Three additional types of matriarchs emerged from the granddaughters' stories collected for this book. There's the Gentle Giant, who possesses a quiet, behind-the-scenes power, the kind of elder whose very presence elicits awe and respect; the Autocrat, who rules her extended family like a despot, with members acting out of fear of her anger or loss of her affection; and the Kinkeeper, whom granddaughters often describe as the hub of the family wheel, acting as its social, cultural, or religious center and offering a sense of cohesion to the extended clan. Sometimes a grandmother fits perfectly into one category; sometimes she has characteristics of two or even three. Either way, the family's power dynamics and the granddaughter's opinion of her grandmother are closely related to the type of matriarchal power the grandmother assumes.

The Gentle Giant
   "My grandmother was a silent, gentle soul

who maintained her power through her ability to negotiate and soothe and heal," remembers forty-three-year-old Natalie, who was raised by her mother and maternal grandmother after her parents' divorce. "She was this tiny little Irishwoman in a family of big German men who would not think twice about using physical or verbal violence against women. My grandmother was the only person who could make my father cower. She would do that through speaking the truth with great, great kindness and love. I remember seeing that as a child and realizing what power kindness had. She was the strongest woman I've ever known."

The gentle matriarch runs her family from a core of inner strength, often developed after facing early adversity. She acts and speaks with confidence, rarely needing to raise her voice to command respect, and never needs to rely on control or manipulation. Margaret Mead described this type of quiet dominance when she wrote about her paternal grandmother in her autobiography, *Blackberry Winter*: "Grandma never threatened. She never raised her voice. She simply commanded respect and obedience by her complete expectation that she would be obeyed. And she never gave silly orders. She became my role model when, in later life, I tried to formulate a role for the modern parent who can no longer exact obedience merely by virtue of being a parent and yet must be able to get obedience when it is necessary. Grandma never said

'Do this because Grandma says so' or 'because Grandma wants you to do it.' She simply said 'Do it,' and I knew from her tone of voice that it was necessary."

This type of grandmother is often found in close-knit ethnic families, the older woman who sits in an armchair at holiday gatherings with younger members of the family collected around her. I had a paternal great-grandmother like this, a soft-spoken, delicate woman who was treated with a reverence that bordered on awe. Family members practically climbed over each other to fill her plate or respond to a simple request. No one ever said an unkind word about my great-grandmother because no one ever, truly, had an unkind thought in her direction.

Granddaughters typically see this type of grandmother as nurturing, supportive, and reliable. She's perceived as highly competent, capable of walking into chaotic situations where others feel fearful or endangered and knowing exactly how to achieve safety and order. These grandmothers frequently become granddaughters' preeminent models for female adulthood, teaching them by both instruction and example, and they turn to her first for emotional support or adult advice. Gentle Giants personify the crones of the ancient maiden–mother–crone trio, the wise older woman whose power is synonymous with her advanced age.

"People used to believe that when women stopped menstruating they kept that blood inside them, which made them wise," Naomi Lowinsky explains. "There was a sense that an older woman had magic power because she wasn't bleeding anymore. But contemporary American culture doesn't yet support the Wise Woman archetype, and it's the rare woman who can pull it off. It's the rare woman who can become older with a sense of her own authority and a sense of her own power and grace."

Because of the wise, gentle grandmother who served as her cultural resource, her spiritual educator, and her source of sanity and normalcy during a tumultuous childhood, fifty-two-year-old Carmen is now planning a ritual to honor her own entry into cronehood. "My grandmother represented responsibility to oneself and to society," she says. "I saw she had a greater wisdom, a kind of love and respect for other people that she passed on to me. I'd like to be that kind of person to other women, too. I have a lot of young friends, and I enjoy encouraging them and giving them support. I can see where they're at and what they're going through. When I think about getting ready to become a crone, I think, *Yes!*"

Mothers typically show great respect for these matriarchs as well, though they may depend on them heavily for emotional strength and family support, particularly when adult living quarters are shared. Tamara remembers her biological mother as a woman very dependent on her highly competent grandmother and overwhelmed by the idea of raising a child. But she recalls her grandmother, who adopted her as an infant, as a wise woman with the innate ability to effectively guide her into adulthood. "My grandmother always seemed very sensible in whatever she did," Tamara recalls. "Even when she wasn't actively directing me I felt I could still watch her example and see how her mind worked and what kinds of decisions she made. I felt I had something very stable and strong there that I could use as a frame of reference for myself." Sandy Halperin perhaps puts it most succinctly when she says, "A mother really lives in the shadow of this grandmother, but a granddaughter lives in her sun."

The Benevolent Manipulator

Stubborn, opinionated, and meddling, yet fiercely loyal and selfless, this type of matriarch claims to know what's best for all her children and grandchildren, and she doesn't hesitate to tell them. Though family members never doubt that she acts out of genuine devotion to her loved ones, this grandmother can nonetheless inspire great frustration and rebellion in those who wish to retain decision-making power for themselves. Going head-to-head with her is often pointless. The Benevolent Manipulator has more tricks up her sleeve than a seasoned magician. In the end, she always finds a way to prevail.

Think Ida Morgenstern, the mother on the old *Rhoda* shows, and you've got the right idea. Her comic manipulations and relentless persistence almost always wore her daughters down. At the same time, it never let them differentiate from her completely, which is exactly the point. The benevolent manipulator wants her children to remain dependent on her, because mothering, she believes, is the job she does best. As a grandmother, she is often loving and doting, but usually becomes even more of a nuisance to her children in the self-appointed role of child-raising educator. Family tension often grows exponentially at this time, especially when sons-in-law (or daughters-in-law, in the case of paternal grandmothers) resent the grandmother's intrusion. This type of matriarch doesn't necessarily do lasting psychological damage to a family, but she can be exceedingly disruptive. She won't ever reject the ones she loves. She will, however, give them a very hard time.

Mothers (and fathers and grandchildren) let the Benevolent Manipulator have her way more often than they're comfortable with, sometimes because arguing requires too much effort with too little payoff, sometimes because she knows exactly how to evoke their feelings of guilt. After all she's done for them, they reason, how can they say no to her? No matter how many times I dialed my grandmother's number determined to hold my own against her increasingly peculiar requests or accusations — so-and-so was trying to steal her money, or the FBI was now tapping her phone — the moment I heard her voice I slid into

207

a position of compliance. I once even agreed to call her phone company in New York from my phone in Tennessee to complain about the tap on her number. I had no intention of actually following through on this promise, and when she called me back the next day for an update, of course she caught me in my lie. I didn't like deceiving her, but I just couldn't manage a simple *no*.

Granddaughters who observe mothers backing down to these grandmothers often grow up to do the same, and never learn how to relate to strong women as their equals. They, too, may become "accommodators," quick to satisfy others' desires just to avoid confrontation or emotional distress. "Accommodators can be very easily influenced or shaken by someone else's strong or negative opinion," Kathleen Moges explains. "Their feelings and opinions are easily taken over by somebody else."

Some granddaughters who see their mothers or fathers constantly struggling with these grandmothers will adopt the role of family peacemaker. "Everyone was fighting in my family," explains forty-six-year-old Brooke, whose maternal grandmother moved in with her family for several years when Brooke was a teen, "but I was the one who entertained everyone and made them happy and smoothed everything over. I was always troubleshooting for the next argument so I could prevent it. I put myself between anyone and any form of altercation, especially where my grandmother was concerned. She would never, ever, *ever* admit to being wrong about *anything,* and she had this knack for finding the thing that would piss everybody else off. Which only added to my father's hostility. Even though he'd known my grandmother since he was ten years old, she was such a difficult, demanding person that he became really averse to her after a while. I think I could sense this in the house, and I could feel him turning away from both her and my mother. At that age and stage, as a teenager, I aligned more with my father, looking at my mother and grandmother and thinking, What's the *matter* with you? But as time went on and I saw my father more clearly, and I became very close to my mother and my grandmother, that changed."

The Benevolent Manipulator may inspire deep ambivalence in a granddaughter who loves the doting element but dislikes or resents the smothering side. Still, it's mothers, not granddaughters, who are the most likely targets for these grandmothers' manipulation and control. A granddaughter's biggest challenge with this grandmother is to avoid being used to manipulate the mother, and to resist being pulled into a coalition designed to win the mother over to their side.

Despite her success at gaining control in her family, the Benevolent Manipulator's tactics are often self-defeating. She may manage to exact compliance, but she's usually less successful in convincing others of her expertise. The result is control without authority, the inevitable outcome of being placated all the time.

The Autocrat

Unlike the manipulative matriarch, who gains control through obstinance and persistence, the autocratic matriarch earns her power through her ability to inspire fear. Parents and grandchildren follow her instructions because they're afraid of her anger, the loss of her affection, or both. Like the implacable Mrs. March in *Little Women*, the Autocrat is typically not an outwardly affectionate woman, meting out physical contact and praise in small doses. Her validation and acceptance are often contingent on her mood or on whether others follow a very specific set of behaviors that only she can determine.

Thirty-four-year-old Valerie grew up in close proximity to a maternal grandmother who was often rigid and intimidating, "the kind of woman you didn't argue with," Valerie explains. "People were afraid of her. Of her rage, of her withdrawal, of the way she lashed out. She didn't keep her anger hidden away. She wouldn't speak to my mother the whole time she was pregnant with my brother, because she thought my mother shouldn't have another baby. She had raised most of her siblings, which gave her a sense of power over them. After my grandmother died, one of my great-aunts finally told my mother she was adopted, a secret my grandmother had kept from my mother all those years. When this great-aunt later told me, 'I'm afraid to go to sleep at night now, because I'm afraid Myrtle's going to come back and get me,' there was a legitimate fear there."

Of the four types of matriarchs, the Autocrat is the one who tends to do the most psychological harm to family members. Her daughters typically suffer from low self-esteem and look to external sources for validation. Their inability when young to form secure attachments with these withholding mothers may later transform into compulsive or addictive behaviors they rely on to satisfy their longing for attachment. Or they may expect their own children to be the loving mothers they never had.

When a granddaughter sees the mother relinquishing her decision-making power to the grandmother, she begins to see the grandmother as an authority figure as well. Her mother becomes a sort of lost figure in the family, more than an appendage of the grandmother but not quite her daughter's superior, either. "The granddaughter doesn't have structure or discipline or a sense of containment from her mother," Kathleen Moges explains. "The mother may act more like a sibling and look to her daughter to be her pal. She does what she thinks she needs to do so the daughter will like her, instead of setting appropriate limits within their relationship."

Some granddaughters of autocratic grandmothers grow up resisting the powerful woman's pull on the family, acting out against her in calculated defiance. But more often they, too, are intimidated by her anger and bullying tactics. The disapproval of a powerful grandmother can mean ostracism within the family, scapegoating, or a sense of rejection or guilt so overwhelming it sends a granddaughter rushing back to apologize and set the emotional balance of the family right again. Yet granting absolute power to a grandmother neither promotes close relations between grandmothers and granddaughters nor fosters a granddaughter's independence.

Occasionally a strong father can offset an Autocrat's power, but many times he also succumbs to her control. Helen, who told the childhood story about ripping her romper earlier in this section, describes how her grandmother showed up at her parents' hotel room the morning after their wedding, asking to see what had happened to her daughter during the night. "I mean, indecency personified!" Helen says, aghast. "Didn't she have any shame? My mother once told me, 'That's when your father should have said, "Fuck you! And get the hell out!" ' But he never did, and that was the first huge mistake my parents made with my grandmother. Also, my grandparents were helping my parents financially at the time. My father had just finished medical school and money was very tight. As soon as people have you on a string like that, you hang yourself, you know? Besides, my father is so discreet, very Anglo-Saxon. He had no balls for my grandmother's kind of behavior. I absolutely think that screwed up my parents for the rest of their lives."

The autocratic grandmother often suffers from a narcissistic personality disorder, the basic inability to attach to others as separate entities. To the narcissistic character, other people are merely extensions of oneself and serve specific functions in that capacity, explains Jennifer Almouli, CSW, a psychotherapist in New York City. This type of grandmother, though she may appear independent and unshakable, actually relies heavily on the mirroring she receives from those around her. As long as they see her as important and authoritative, she can see herself that way. If their perception of her starts to shift, her perception of herself is in danger and she may fight to protect it by exercising power against them.

"Narcissistic personalities are typically powerful and ambitious, and often have a beautiful false self on the outside," Almouli says. "But they're completely vulnerable on the inside and dependent on others around them." Adds Sandy Halperin, "Many times there's a very wounded child beneath this." The autocratic grandmother may deeply love her children and grandchildren — even if only as extensions of herself — but they won't always feel they know it.

The Kinkeeper
Forty-two-year-old Janet remembers her take-

charge paternal grandmother, who died five years ago, as the nucleus of activity for more than fifty members of the four-generation African-American Roper clan. "Grandmother Roper was the main *everything* in my family," Janet says. "As a matter of fact, she ruled the world! We always lived in the same town as she, either next door or down the street, and we saw her every night for dinner. She was a short woman. You know that short person's complex? She had twelve sisters and brothers whom she raised after their mother died, and she ruled over them and their children. She's the reason that we're all so close-knit today. She made us that way. Four of her sisters also lived in town and every Sunday after church they would all sit together at her dining table with their children and grandchildren. When people talk about family reunions, I think, *I had one every week.*"

Janet's grandmother was the "kinkeeper" of her family, the one who brought members together for holidays and celebrations, remembered birthdays and anniversaries, and relayed pertinent news and information throughout the year. The typical kinkeeper is a woman in her fifties or sixties who, as in Janet's family, unifies the extended family by maintaining ties with her adult siblings after their parents die. Largely due to her efforts, the extended family branches out horizontally as well as vertically, bringing great-aunts, great-uncles, and second and third cousins together under her roof. Her influence comes not from her seat at the head of the family but from her position at its center, though she may occupy both at the same time.

Kinkeeping grandmothers often share characteristics with Gentle Giants and Benevolent Manipulators. Family is their most important asset. I think of my grandmother sharing the piano bench with her sisters at the end of her dining room table, all those great-aunts and great-uncles lining its sides. In this seat, her influence was undisputed. From the 1940s until 1976, when my grandfather died, their apartment in the Bronx, then their house in Mount Vernon and their country house at Lake Mohegan, reverberated with the sounds of her brothers, sisters, nephews, nieces, cousins, children, and grandchildren. She brought her side together for Passover and Thanksgiving every year, a clan of twenty-three if everyone in town attended. A family, my grandmother understood, is a fragile organism that needs someone to keep it from splitting apart. So she, the one with the largest house, the most money, and the most children and grandchildren, willingly took on the responsibility for keeping that sense of "family" alive in us all. It was perhaps the central irony of my childhood, that the one capable of causing the most disruption was also the one who kept us all feeling cohesive and whole.

Kinkeeping requires creativity and work, especially as younger members of the family grow up and move away. Mobility is the kinkeeper's greatest enemy. Family crisis is her motivating force. Thirty-one-year-old Marcy remembers how her maternal grandmother, the widow of a wealthy industrialist, decided fourteen years ago, after her husband's death and both of her daughters' divorces, that she would help the younger generations in her family remain close. Then in her late seventies, Marcy's grandmother took her six grandchildren along with their spouses and significant others on a week-long vacation to the Bahamas. "It was totally crazy," Marcy recalls. "We were at Club Med with my grandmother wearing a sombrero, doing beer-chugging contests with us." The trip, an unequivocal success, has since become an annual event and now includes several great-grandchildren. "It's what's given me a sense of family with all my cousins," Marcy says.

"The most important lesson I've gotten from Granny is how important it is to get the whole family together," Marcy's cousin Sheryl, thirty-four, adds. "For her, these reunions are a time when she can gather fifteen or twenty of us and give us a place where we can all be together. That's incredible. Because now that we're all spread out, we don't have meals together anymore, we don't all sit down and talk. Lately, I've been thinking that I want for everyone to have even more quality time with her. During the day at Club Med, she reads her books, the grandchildren go windsurfing and scuba diving, and the kids go to the kids' club. It's a wonderful vacation, but the only time we have with her is dinner when we sit around the table and talk. So I ran this idea by her the other day: I said, 'Look, I've never been in charge of putting together Club Med. I've never planned one reunion. But what if I do some research and find out about renting three houses on the beach in North Carolina?' It would probably be cheaper than Club Med, and it'll give us each more time to be with her. Because she just turned ninety-one, and she recently told me she feels ready to die. I think we'll be lucky if we have one more year with her."

Like the other types of matriarchs, a kinkeeper usually remains in her position for life. Her most likely replacement is her daughter, who assumes the position soon after her mother's death, though occasionally an adult granddaughter will step into a similar role. Janet's paternal grandmother had no daughters, so Janet began planning family events after her grandmother died seven years ago. The house she shares with her son now doubles as a family focal point, with aunts, uncles, and cousins often spilling onto her patio because the dining table she inherited from her grandmother seats only sixteen. As we spoke, she was preparing for the annual Roper family reunion she helped plan, with three hundred people about to arrive in her town.

But a kinkeeping matriarch does much more than plan family events. Like Baby Suggs of Toni Morrison's *Beloved*, or Mama in the movie *Soul Food*, she's the spiritual adhesive of her extended family. Age and experience are the job's prerequisites. Generational wisdom is its power source. "After my grandmother died seven years ago, nobody really filled her spot in the family," thirty-five-year-old Bettina explains. "It's sad, because I'll write to my aunts and my mother and I'll chat with people every now and then, but the family has sort of lost touch. They're not sure how to get the dynamics going again." The full power of a kinkeeper, respected and honored while she's alive, may be most evident only after she's gone.

As matriarchs age, so do their granddaughters, farther into a life cycle that grants them broader experience and deeper insight. And as this occurs, the all-powerful grandmothers of their childhood take on a more human dimension. They become women devastated by loss, hardened by adversity, limited by their own need for control. After my grandmother died I found two yellowed notes to my mother in her desk, dating back to the weeks before our 1976 trip to Florida by train.

Dear Marcia:
Eastern [Airlines] had a *standby* yesterday for 2:20 Friday. There were no train reservations until the 8th and auto train had no reservations until the 7th.
Please forgive me for not having courage to fly with the children alone.

> Good luck, good health
> and happiness to you and
> yours for many years to come.
> All my love, Mother

Please use check.

And the other, written either before, after, or as a revision of the first:

Dear Marcia:
    If you can get reservations, I will do whatever you ask.

> All my love and best wishes
> for good luck, good health and
> happiness to you and yours
> for many years to come
> Mother

Please forgive me for being afraid.

It is, perhaps, testimony to years of a sort of univision of my grandmother that I don't immediately know how to interpret these notes. They're the first tangible evidence I've seen that she wasn't as stubborn as I'd always remembered her to be, that she was even, if only for a moment, concerned about how my mother might judge her or how her fears might be perceived. The notes are a small discovery, really, but with the potential to completely alter my perception of the past. My grandmother, calling an *airline* to inquire about reservations? Asking for my mother's forgiveness? I could take these brief notes and stretch their significance like taffy, imagining my grandmother in the submissive role, my mother making the demands. Or, if I really push the image, I can almost see my grandmother in an aisle seat on an Eastern Airlines L10–11 jet, her brown wool beret securely fastened to her upswept hair, her eyes squeezed shut and her arthritic hands gripping the armrests, her ankles tightly crossed.

And then. When I close my eyes and listen far back into the past, beyond the last decade of my grandmother's life, across an entire country now, down the street where I grew up, through the front screen door of my parents' house, up the short flight of blue carpeted stairs, and into the kitchen with the flowered wallpaper and brown carpet and gurgling Crock-Pot, I can hear the avocado wall phone ring. My grandmother is on the line, her second call of the day. I can tell from my mother's response — *I know. I know. I'm fine. It's all right* — that it's an apology call, my grandmother's attempt to explain her position in the early-morning phone call that left my mother biting her lip and dialing her best friend for reassurance. My grandmother is trying to erase my mother's anger, to realign the emotional balance within the family, to soothe her own concern that she might be the cause of anyone else's emotional pain. Another form of control, maybe, but this one inspired by fear of my mother's withdrawal or distress.

Those two brief notes in my grandmother's neat, angular script ultimately bring me here.

Seeing her handwriting again after all these years, a design so personal yet so familiar — so evocative of birthday cards and signed checks and letters mailed to me in summer camp — softens something hard inside me, leading me back to a moment in my childhood where I see that chink in her armor, where I understand now (though I didn't yet then) that she may not have been the entirely invincible figure I have always imagined her to be. And forward to a time in my own life, perhaps, when I no longer gain something — *what? that's the real question* — from thinking of my grandmother so often as the difficult, stubborn figure that was only one part of the whole.

Yet there's something I have to remember: that these notes written before our trip to Florida were never sent. I don't know if my mother received a third draft instead, or an impulsive phone call, or nothing at all. The self-doubt they reveal occurred in the privacy of my grandmother's own home. A safe place, where she could be honest with herself. Not in my mother's kitchen, where she was alternately loved and feared, respected and rejected, a place where she always had to worry about how someone else perceived her. My grandmother as a matriarch may have been, in the end, a role as inauthentic to her as it felt to some of us. But granddaughters are shaped by the events they witness, not by the ones they never see. The maternal grandmother I remember may not be the woman she was, but this was the only maternal grandmother I ever knew.

14

Three Stories:

Rosie, Nora, and Marguerite

Rosie: The Education of an Activist

Thirty-four-year-old Rosie sits in the kitchen of the suburban ranch home she shares with her mother, father, maternal grandfather, and seven-year-old son. Her graduate school books are piled in a corner of the table; she's working on a thesis about rural women for her Women's Studies degree. It's a busy afternoon. The phone rings several times with calls from the local organization Rosie leads, her mother walks in loaded down with grocery bags, and her son runs in and out with a new toy. The busy extended family setup Rosie lives in now is an echo of her childhood, when she and her mother lived with her grandparents on and off throughout the Vietnam War years while her father was stationed overseas.

She remembers her maternal grandmother during these years as a hardworking, no-nonsense nurse who ministered to patients with utmost devotion and care but showed little of the same warmth to family members. "When I was a young, young child, one of our neighbors was dying of cancer, and my grandmother went to her house every day to take care of her and change her bandages," Rosie recalls. "I used to go with her, and it was always confusing for me to see her be very caring to this woman but not see that from her at home. With us, she was really aloof. I don't want to say she was 'hard,' because I don't think that's the right word for her, but I don't remember her ever being very affectionate to me or my mom. I know she loved us, because she worked long hours to provide us with material things. But she never really expressed her love for us any other way."

Rosie grew up with two models for womanhood: a grandmother who was fiercely independent and strong-willed, and a mother who was soft-spoken and avoided confrontation. "My grandmother loved my mother, but she was very harsh with her," Rosie explains. "There was a period in my grandmother's life when she drank a lot, and she would bring up things my mother had done when she was ten years old. And my mother would come home crying. My father once asked her, 'You know all you're going to do is fight if you go over to your mother's house, so why do you even bother going over there to see her?' " From her vantage point as observer, Rosie quietly witnessed how her grandmother bullied her mother, using angry silence or withdrawal as forms of manipulation, and vowed never, *never* to let anyone treat her that way as an adult.

"I always tell my mother I'm glad she's not like that, because I would never in my life put up with from her what she put up with from her mother," she says. "I ask her, 'Why didn't you fight back? Why didn't you stand up to her, or why didn't you tell her, "I don't need you"? Why did you keep going back for more and more?' She says she doesn't know why she did it. And that's when she also told me I'm a lot like my grandmother, because *she* wouldn't have put up with that kind of behavior from anyone else, either."

Rosie never spoke out against her grandmother as a child, but her resistance started germinating during those years. "When my grandmother was arguing with my mother I would be fighting back or defending my mother, but as a child I could never do that verbally, especially in her house, where children were definitely seen but not heard," she recalls. "Instead, we argued all the time in my head." Those moments when Rosie recognized acts of oppression in her family and responded with outrage, as her grandmother would have, rather than silence or submission, as her mother often did, became what psychologists call a personality "organizer," a point around which she began to develop her sense of self.

Sandy Halperin remembers having a similar response when she heard stories of her great-grandmother Gussie, a family tyrant who died before Dr. Halperin was born. "Everyone had been afraid of her, except my grandfather, her son, who was the apple of her eye," Dr. Halperin recalls. "She was a terribly controlling woman who mistreated my grandmother and my mother. When I was a child and I heard these stories I would have fantasies in which I would stand up to Grandma Gussie and protect the family." Halperin took on the psychological role of family protector as a child, marshaling her internal strength against this outside threat. "In some ways, I'm very much like Gussie," she says. "I'm forthright, and I say what I'm thinking. That must have come down to me through her, or through my reaction to the stories of her. I don't insist on always getting my way, but the truth is, if something is really important to me I'm going to make sure I get it."

Sandy Halperin's childhood response to the perceived threat of Gussie is similar to the imaginary arguments Rosie had — and still has — with her grandmother, who died twelve years ago. "Sometimes I still get very angry with my grandmother for the way she treated my mother," Rosie explains. "If I could say one thing to her now, it would be 'You had no right to treat her that way.' "

Rosie didn't have the power to stand up to her grandmother as a child, or the opportunity to go head-to-head with her as an adult, but she had enough of a fighting spirit to fantasize about the confrontation and later act it out in a public forum. Today, she's a feminist leader in her community, speaking out against oppression for women who are otherwise silenced. She has embraced the life of an independent thinker, and chosen to raise a child as a single mother. And in the process, she has discovered some startling similarities between herself and the grandmother she once alternately disliked and feared.

"My grandmother became a woman in a time when she was not a typical woman for that time," Rosie explains. "She always worked. She always kept her own checking account. She kept her own name. And we're talking the 30s, the 40s, the 50s. She was ahead of her time in many ways, and I think that was very frustrating for her. I think it was hard for her to accept the limitations that were placed on her. I can remember her coming home from work all the time saying she could do anything the doctors could do, but she just wasn't allowed to. I think I knew she was frustrated when I was a child, but I couldn't name it. It wasn't until I started experiencing some of those same frustrations in my life that I recognized them in hers. When she was dying she came to live with us, and one day she said to me, 'You are too much like me.' We were not at that particular point getting along very well, and she didn't mean that as a compliment. I think she was talking about stubbornness, that determination to the point where you block out important things in your life, like family, to reach that ultimate goal, success, however you define it. Sometimes I think she was right. I see it more and more as I get older."

Rosie has put together a life for herself based on conviction and compassion, but she also describes herself as stubborn and combative, occasionally "antagonistic for the sake of being antagonistic," very much the opposite of her soft-spoken mother. Whereas many women on an identity quest put their mothers under a microscope, Rosie believes that to fully understand the qualities she admires most and least in herself she needs to understand how those same qualities developed in her grandmother instead. Behind her grandmother's actions was a philosophy, she knows, and behind the philosophy lay a woman shaped by personal experience. And this was a woman Rosie never got to know.

The stories leak out slowly, like drips from a reluctant faucet. Family members, afraid of her grandmother's posthumous wrath, have been slow to comply. Rosie knows her grandmother had a brief, early first marriage to a much older man who died, and among the papers her grandmother left behind she found a photo of another young man whom no one can identify. She's also heard veiled references to a woman who moved into her grandmother's room when her mother was a teenager, while her grandfather retreated to the guest room down the hall.

"I'm slowly finding out the answers to these questions I would have liked to ask her myself, like who is that man in the photo? What was this woman to you? What was your relationship to your first husband? I'm really trying to understand who my grandmother was," Rosie says. "Because I truly believe that knowing these facts might help me answer, Why am I as independent as I am? Why am I as strong-willed as I am? To a detriment sometimes, I think. Why do I perceive certain situations the way I do? As I get closer to the age my grandmother was in my memories of her — she was fortysomething when I was born — and I'm making important choices in my life, I've started thinking about the choices she could and couldn't make in hers. It's helped me feel a little more tolerant toward her.

"My mom asked me this morning how I feel about my grandmother, and I realize I'm very ambivalent about her. I don't want to say that I absolutely loved her, because I didn't. I didn't absolutely hate her, either. But I do realize as I get older what a huge influence she was on me."

Nora: Assuming the Mother's Role

Throughout her childhood and adolescence, Nora, now twenty-seven, was her paternal grandmother's "shining star." She spent weekends at her grandmother's house, and when her parents went on vacation they'd drop her off there for as long as a week. "She'd take me to the circus, take me out to buy toys," Nora recalls. "We really had a wonderful relationship. When I was in high school, the minute I had a boyfriend I would want him to meet my nana. The night of my prom she was at my house taking pictures. When I went off to college I spoke with her every week. She comes to visit me for the weekend now, and we go shopping and to a show. Everyone in my apartment building knows my nana. They always want to know when she'll visit next, so they can stop by and say hello."

But Nora's depiction of family unity lasts only until her parents enter the tale. Nora's mother, who died four years ago, and father had very separate and very different relationships with the grandmother Nora recalls with such affection, and as she fills in the details of those interactions a more complicated and tumultuous story starts to emerge.

"I should tell you that my father is an only child and my grandmother was very protective of him," she begins. "When my mother came into the picture and married him, my grandmother was so possessive that she made it very difficult for my mother. Both my mother *and* my grandmother had a difficult time. I think my grandmother felt that she was losing her only child, and felt in competition with my mother in many ways. My mother once told me, 'Within the first two months of our marriage I told your father that I wouldn't live the rest of my life with him constantly battling between his mother and his wife, so we needed to figure out a way for us all to live in harmony,' " Nora says. "My father told my grandmother that my mother was his wife and he respected her opinions and judgments and would stand behind her. He loved his mother so much, but he didn't want her to become a constant source of stress in his marriage. However, I think it was inevitable that she would be.

"And to throw another wrench into the story, both of my mother's parents died when she was a girl. I think my grandmother thought she could embrace my mother and become the mother that my mother never had. But my mother basically said, 'Hold on. I'm not looking for that. You're my *mother-in-law*.' My grandmother is also very opinionated and controlling. She tried to put her two cents into everything. The minute I was born, she wanted to come over and give my mother advice on how to change a diaper. I think if my grandmother had been a little less controlling my mother would have been a little more willing to try, but my grandmother didn't know how to be a friend to my mother. She knew how to be a mother, which my mother didn't want, or how to totally back off. There was no middle ground. My mother opted for the backing off because she couldn't take what my grandmother wanted to give her. There were terrible arguments over it for a long time.

"When my grandfather died in 1978 my grandmother became even more difficult, because she didn't have him around to balance her out," Nora continues. "She and my father were arguing constantly. At that point, my father suggested trying family therapy. He thought someone else could offer some insight into the situation. After a year, the therapist said, 'I don't know what to tell you anymore. She's a very

strong-willed person and she has certain opinions. She makes it very difficult for people.' The
therapist basically said, 'It's useless. Nothing I
can do is going to matter.' "

Throughout Nora's childhood and adolescence, her mother and grandmother remained
locked in an ongoing struggle for control.
"Trivial things that didn't seem like they would
be the source of a problem would become a
problem," Nora recalls. "Like whose house we
would go to for the holidays, and who would
cook dinner. My grandmother and my mother
would fight over whose house we would eat at
and who would bring what. It was this never-
ending source of conflict. I know that it wasn't
all my grandmother's fault, either. My mother
also wasn't willing to give in. She felt that if she
let my grandmother take control everything
would start revolving around my grandmother,
and she would become the family matriarch. To
some degree she already is, because she's so
opinionated and strong-willed. People are afraid
to say no to her or do things she wouldn't want
them to do. But my mother's fear was that my
grandmother would become this Almighty in the
family, and then where would that leave *her?*"

As a child Nora didn't understand the intrica-
cies of the struggle between her mother and
grandmother; this is an insight she developed
only during the past few years. "I used to get
mad at my mother," Nora recalls. "I would say to
her, 'Why do you and Nana fight? She's my

231

grandmother and I love her. Why can't you just get along?' My mother would throw her arms up in the air when she was on the phone with her, saying she couldn't take it anymore. But I never saw that side of my grandmother. To me, she was loving and caring and giving. I would spend time alone with her and I loved her so much, I could never understand what there was to fight about."

Until four years ago, that is, when Nora's mother died after a yearlong struggle with cancer. Then twenty-three, Nora stepped in to assume some of her mother's role in the family, and became the person to whom her grandmother now presented suggestions or concerns about family matters.

"I remember the first time it happened," she recalls. "I was on the phone with my grandmother, who was going on and on about something, and I threw my hands up in the air. I finally understood what my mother had gone through all those years, rolling her eyes. My grandmother really doesn't listen to reason, and her opinion is the only one she wants to hear."

When Nora's father started dating a year after her mother's death and became engaged a few months later, the relationship between him and his mother became particularly rocky. "My grandmother kept calling my father and saying, 'I hope you know what you're getting yourself into. I hope you're not making a mistake,' " Nora recalls. "She nagged him and nagged him about it. My father would tell her it was his business and to stay out of it. He would tell her not to call me and try to put these thoughts into my head, because she was trying to win me over to her side. For a while, I would listen to her because I'm so sympathetic, and I could see where she was coming from. But after a year or so of dealing with it, I finally said I didn't want to be in the middle. Whatever their differences are, let them work it out between the two of them. Sometimes it still bothers me, though. I was never in the middle of it before, only since my mother died."

Nora soon realized that standing up to her grandmother would become a virtual necessity if she wanted to maintain a peaceful relationship with her as an adult. Still, she wanted to do this with love and respect. Her recent engagement offered her the opportunity to try.

"Right after we got engaged, I called my father and my fiancé called his parents," Nora says. "Then I called my grandmother. She was crying on the phone, she was so ecstatic. She kept saying she knew my mother could see what was going on and that she was very proud. The next time we talked, she told me we have to go to Kleinfeld's [a wedding-dress emporium in Brooklyn] to look for my wedding dress. I told her that Kleinfeld's isn't my style, that I'd rather go to a small, quieter store where I'm going to get a little more attention. She told me I don't know what I'm talking about. 'Everyone needs to go to Kleinfeld's!' she said. Before, I would have given in immediately and said, 'Okay, do you want to come with me?' but this time I held my ground. You know, I love my grandmother a lot and I trust her opinion, because I really believe that the older you get the wiser you are from all your accumulated experiences. There's truth to a lot of what she says, but I have to stand up to her when I disagree. Otherwise, she'll run right over me like a freight train and keep on going. I've recently started to say to her, 'Listen, this is why I feel this way,' or 'You need to take a step back.' Instead of immediately agreeing with her or accepting her opinion, I'm trying to take each thing she says with a grain of salt and decide for myself what I want to take out of it and what I don't."

Nora's mother showed her daughter the necessity of standing up to the family matriarch, giving Nora a model for dissent when her turn in the family hot seat arrived. She also relayed the message that women are strong but not invincible, that holding on to one's own power is preferable to always giving in. As many granddaughters like Nora have found, standing up to a matriarch doesn't always lead to annihilation. Sometimes the matriarch, whose love for her family may ultimately surpass her need for control, even backs down.

Marguerite: Making Peace With an Autocrat
Marguerite stands outside her mountain

home, wrapped in a bulky wool sweater. She spreads her arms wide, ready to welcome a visitor. Inside, through a living room filled with decorative blankets, pottery, and the soft strains of classical music, she has carefully arranged on top of her kitchen table several dozen artifacts of her maternal grandmother's life. Photographs, music books, pieces of linen, a tin of candy, a can opener, a metronome, all labeled with handwritten explanatory notes in both English and her native French. She picks up a photo album and leafs through the pages, pointing out a portrait of her grandmother at age four; a snapshot of her grandmother as an adult, supervising the construction of the mountain château she built with her own savings; and a photograph of Marguerite as a toddler with her grandmother, who was then fifty, the age Marguerite is now.

"This is to show you what my grandmother looked like," she explains. "I think she was very beautiful. Nobody else got her features, but apparently I got her character" — she pauses to laugh — "according to my mom, and to some degree it's true. I just recently starting appreciating that instead of dreading it, because when I was a teenager and my mother would say, 'You're just like your grandmother,' that would be the most awful thing she could say to me, because I really didn't like this lady who was so tough on me and on most of the family."

She's talking mainly about the weekly piano lessons she had to endure as a child and a teen.

Marguerite's grandmother was a concert pianist-turned-professor at a prestigious European music conservatory who was determined to mold her granddaughter into a world-class musician. Unlike her mother, who had small, delicate hands, Marguerite had long, strong fingers that would grow to easily span an octave. Noticing this when Marguerite was very young, her grandmother began their lessons when the child was only four. Marguerite became her grandmother's special project, the student whose failures and mistakes would cast her grandmother in a negative light and whose successes were evidence of her grandmother's superior tutelage.

Marguerite summarized the years as her grandmother's pupil in a letter she sent a few weeks before our interview, explaining, "My grandmother was very temperamental — a real prima donna, and quite domineering. As a matter of fact, she imposed her will on the entire family. Her ambitious hands took me out of my crib to perch me on a piano stool and started modeling me into her phantasmagoric dream: to make me the pianist of the century! Nothing seemed to matter to my self-centered grandmother if it didn't involve music. . . . I grew to intensely dislike this woman who had so much ambition for me. I felt quite isolated in the midst of her adoring students. I even secretly contemplated suicide to escape her.

"Nobody ever asked me if I wanted to play the piano," Marguerite recalls. "I had to do it, because that was the decision. It was my destiny. My grandmother had absolute weight in the family, and an almost pathological expectation of my musical life. I must have sensed that, because after a certain point I started to put up some resistance to her, in my own way. Whereas she had once studied twice as much as a normal child would, I would deliberately not do enough, or I would daydream during the two hours a day that I had to practice. I'm a great daydreamer to this day, to escape whatever I don't want to do. When my grandmother saw that I was not as dedicated as she'd been as a child, she started coming to our house on weekends, as well as on Thursdays, which were a day off from school, just to make me work, because by God, she was going to turn me into a pianist."

Whatever small amounts of power Marguerite's acts of subversion earned her hardly compared to the amount of grief the additional lessons caused. "Our lessons generally ended up in a scene, because she would try to make me do something and I wouldn't do it right," Marguerite says, displaying a yellowed book of sheet music with her grandmother's angry red notations scrawled across the pages. "She would shout, 'How could you not have this tempo already? I showed you last week. I'm going to come back tomorrow to make you work more, and by God, we're going to get it right.' Then she would say how stupid I was or she would flick my fingers because they were in the wrong position.

And yell. Lots of yelling. The neighbors could hear, and I would dread it. I would cry, and I would resent her. Mostly resent her. Often she had my classes in the conservatory. I was always the last in the schedule so she could spend a longer time with me and really bawl me out, probably. She probably didn't look forward to bawling me out, but it was like she couldn't control herself. My grandfather would be waiting in the car for both of us, to take me home, and he saw me in tears so often. It must really have upset him."

The lessons' emotional toll on Marguerite was obvious to the entire family, but no one stepped forth to object. Not her grandfather, who patiently endured his wife's rages; not anyone at the conservatory, where her grandmother was held in such high esteem; and not her parents, whose silence spoke volumes at the time.

"Only since five years ago have I been able to say the words 'They abandoned me,' " Marguerite explains, "and I guess that's why I was so terrified. Because I had nowhere to go. That's why I thought of suicide. Although this was a family that talked a lot and made huge scenes, it was a family that was pretty emotionally repressed. I couldn't imagine going to my dad and saying, 'Look, this is horrible. And I expect you to do something about it.' You just didn't talk about those kinds of things. You didn't complain. And besides, my grandmother would have killed me if I had gone and complained about her. At least that's how I felt. She had that kind of psychological power over me."

But then in 1961, during Marguerite's sixteenth year, the completely unexpected occurred: Her grandfather suffered a painful death from cancer, and her grandmother, the family's pillar of fortitude and strength, collapsed. She even left the country as her husband's health failed, lamenting, " 'How could he do this to me?'

"Anyone who understood psychology probably would have expected that after knowing her," Marguerite says, "but nobody in our family expected that from her. And we especially didn't anticipate what happened next. She completely fell apart." The matriarch who ruled her family, who could not tolerate anyone acting without first seeking her permission, found herself helpless against death, and unable to function without her steady, patient husband at her side.

Just after her grandfather's funeral, Marguerite accompanied her grandmother and another student to a music festival in Europe. They traveled by train, and "my grandmother was just *nuts,* like a fruitcake," Marguerite recalls. "She spent most of her time counting her money, wouldn't let me go to the bathroom without her, and if she went to the bathroom I had to stand right outside the door. If I got up in the train and looked out the window, she would panic and ask, 'Where are you going?' *Nuts!*"

A matriarch's power often relies upon a fragile

emotional balance within the family. Remove any one of her supports — a husband, a daughter, a son — through death or disability and the hierarchy can come tumbling down. Marguerite believes her soft-spoken grandfather may actually have been her grandmother's source of power. "After my grandmother became a widow, I realized how much he had given her strength," she explains. "Without him in her shadow, her strength just crumbled."

This can easily happen when a grandmother has narcissistic tendencies, Jennifer Almouli explains. That's because these grandmothers don't exactly attach to people; they attach instead to the functions those people serve in their lives. Losing someone who fulfilled an important function — whether it was as an unequivocal supporter, an alter ego, an inferior, an admirer, or any other role that bolstered the grandmother's self-image — can lead to the collapse of the constructed false self, Almouli says. The change in Marguerite's grandmother may have been the result of having to come face-to-face with her true self, she explains.

The death of her husband heralded the end of Marguerite's grandmother's psychological regime. As her granddaughter watched her obsessively counting her money in a train compartment, the great and almighty Oz vanished, replaced by the little woman behind the curtain. Dependent. Vulnerable. Confused.

"The way I saw it, my grandmother completely lost her power upon my grandfather's death," Marguerite says. "So I seized upon her weakness, and that's how I made my escape." She terminated her piano lessons soon after her grandfather's death, and two years later made plans to finish school in the United States. She never returned to France to live.

Once removed from her family environment and from the teacher–pupil power structure she had previously known, Marguerite's vision of her grandmother as an ultimate authority began to erode. During her periodic travels back to France the two women visited briefly and began a correspondence that lasted for more than ten years. In her letters, Marguerite began asking her grandmother questions about her past, and in a series of lengthy, handwritten responses throughout the 1970s, the older woman eloquently recounted her ascent from a humble coachman's family to a professorship at the conservatory, and shared with her granddaughter some of the wisdom she had accumulated over the years.

Marguerite picks up a letter from 1976 in which her grandmother encouraged her to enjoy these years with her husband. *It's evident how as time passes the couple will better understand and tolerate each other,* Marguerite translates from the French. *You and Michael enjoy this time together, because afterward the solitude is great.* In another letter, her grandmother described a recent concert given by a famous pianist who had cancer and knew this would be his last public performance. "She described it in such a powerful way, this guy fighting to give his last passion in a huge symphony concert," Marguerite says. "She really understood both the tragedy and the beauty of that scene."

In 1986, Marguerite returned to France for a year to help nurse her younger sister through the final stages of a terminal illness. This trip marked the first time she had ongoing interaction with her grandmother as an adult. "It was an opportunity for great healing to occur between us, because there was no piano involved," Marguerite explains, "and I was able to see my grandmother in a very different light. I recognized she had a very wide curiosity. Even in her retirement, her mind was always working. When she knit she was listening to programs on the radio. She studied Russian literature in a special class for retirees. If one of her grandchildren or great-grandchildren was interested in car mechanics, she would ask, 'So, what is it about?' When presented with a totally unknown subject, she would try to educate herself a little bit by listening to that person. And that really is admirable. I think she was the best listener in the family."

Thirty additional years of life experience as a mother, stepmother, and now a step-grandmother have given Marguerite a more mature perspective with regard to her grandmother's earlier behaviors. "I reflected for many years about how people demonize a person," she explains, "and when I started the long process of demystifying my grandmother, I could better understand some of the dynamics of my family. I eventually made peace with my grandmother, and I also understand enough now to forgive myself for having had such an intense dislike for her." Instead of seeing her grandmother purely as the tyrant of her childhood, Marguerite now views her as a woman with multiple skills — music, gardening, cooking, needlework — but one who'd had to accept her limitations at a young age. "I think she aspired to perform, to tell you the truth, and that's why I think she tried to make me into a great performer," Marguerite says. "When I asked her about this in a letter, she claimed that wasn't the case, but I know enough about life now, knowing that maybe we don't always want to say what's true. Because she lived such passion through me when I performed in public, that I just knew . . . I think maybe she herself didn't have what it took."

Marguerite's earlier fear of resembling her grandmother has been replaced by the acceptance that they share certain traits but not others. "Turning into her stopped frightening me a long time ago," she explains, "because I realize I have surpassed her in other ways. Not as a musician, ever, and not in terms of the innumerable talents she had that I will never have, but as a human being. I definitely have stretched myself. I've been interested in the human connection for so long because of my experiences with her. She gave me that gift through this trauma. I now actually enjoy thinking that I am somehow like her. I grow the raspberries she had in her garden, and I make some of her recipes. She became a true inspiration to me before she died, because she had no more grasp on me. The type of relationship where my life depended on her mood was finished."

PART IV

Mother of My Mother

15

Woman to Woman

Because maternal grandmothers are typically the grandparent who lives longest, it's not at all unusual to find adult women still active in the granddaughtering role. Staying in touch by telephone. Mailing photographs of the great-grandchildren. Driving home on weekends to take her shopping or to the hair salon. Sixty-one percent of the women surveyed for this book had a maternal grandmother living until they were in their twenties. Twenty-five percent were older than thirty when she died. And nearly one-third of them said they'd helped care for a maternal grandmother as she aged.

Still, very little research has been done on what Lynne Gershenson Hodgson, Ph.D., a professor of sociology at Quinnipiac College in Hamden, Connecticut, calls the "graying grandchild." Surprised by this oversight, Hodgson, who had all four grandparents living until she was in her mid-thirties, conducted a national survey of 208 adult grandchildren in 1990 and found what she'd anticipated: that the bonds between adults and their grandparents are strong and enduring, even as the relationship changes steadily over time. "When I was a young child, my grandmother held my hand crossing the street," Hodgson explains. "Just before her death she was holding my hand so I could help her across. It didn't change the fact that we were emotionally close all along, but ours became a very different relationship." One that involved a certain degree of caretaking, she means, but also one that started to approximate interaction between equals.

Just as the mother–daughter relationship levels out during a daughter's early adulthood when her experiences — career, marriage, motherhood — start to resemble her mother's, so too can the relationship between grandmothers and granddaughters. "During adolescence, you usually say, 'Yes, my grandparents are very important, but I don't see them very much and I don't know if I'd go to them in particular if I had a problem,' " Hodgson says. "Then, when you become an adult, you come full circle. You realize, 'Whoa, I'm getting to the age where my grandmother already had my mother, and I'm having a child. My goodness. Think about this.' At around that time, granddaughters and grandmothers start relating more as adults."

This is particularly true when younger women reach the developmental point, usually in their early- to mid-twenties, where they're ready to have a woman-to-woman relationship with an older female. Most women achieve this with their mothers, but those without mothers, or those raised by a grandmother, may develop this type of relationship with the grandmother instead. "When a guy comes on to me I can tell my grandmother about it, and she'll come right back and tell me stories of when she was young," explains twenty-eight-year-old Janelle, who had been raised by her maternal grandmother since birth. "We sit there and laugh. It's that kind of ability to converse and bond with an adult woman that I don't have with my mother. We're working on it, but we're not there yet. My grandmother is like my sister and my friend and my mentor. I completely trust her. I feel like I can talk with her about anything."

In families where a mother is present and emotionally close to her daughter, the grandmother is more likely to act as a supplemental adult figure, one who represents heritage and continuity. Physical proximity continues to play an important role in the relationship: Young adult granddaughters who live in the same state as their maternal grandmothers tend to be emotionally closer to her, more compatible with her, and consider the relationship to be more personally significant than do young adults whose grandmothers live in different states.

Assuming the grandmother is both mentally and emotionally available at this time, a granddaughter may find these years together to be the most rewarding of all. After all, how many eight-year-olds can fully appreciate a grandmother's ability to hold a family together? How many ten-year-olds are willing to listen to stories of the adversities she overcame? If you scratch beneath the surface of any grandmother's life you'll find tales of hardship and triumph, of learning how to cope with change and loss. But who would think at twelve that these stories set in distant countries or different social eras might relate to us in any way?

"Like most kids, I blotted out my grandmothers' stories when I was young," Joy Horowitz says. "I thought they were boring. I loved Pearlie's food, her French toast and her laughter, but her stories were never something that appealed to me until I was an adult. I think it's not until you reach a certain age that you're willing to deal with some emotional truths about life. For most women, it's not until you reach your thirties or your forties that you start to deal with loss, and how you deal with loss is really how you get defined in life. That's what my grandmothers, to me, represent. These women have lost so much that's important to them — both of them have lost the love of their life; their first-born sons; all of their siblings; countless friends — and still they have this life force that's so remarkable and inspiring to me. Especially in middle age now, I'm finding that I'm wildly obsessive about the ephemeras of life. I'm so aware of the fleeting nature of everything. And my grandmothers become that much more important to me."

Adult granddaughters tend to expect little

from grandmothers other than some gift-giving and sharing of family history. They don't expect to turn to grandmothers for personal advice, to act as a liaison with their parents, to support them financially, or to act as role models. That doesn't mean, however, that grandmothers never fill these roles. Active, mentally vibrant grandmothers who historically had close relationships with their granddaughters often remain sources of emotional sustenance as both women age. The unconditional love a grandmother gave a granddaughter when she was young may take on a renewed importance during the granddaughter's adulthood, especially when her decisions have more serious consequences and unqualified support is harder to find.

Thirty-three-year-old Joyce, a single mother, remembers how reluctant she was to reveal her unplanned pregnancy to the grandmother she adored and how relieved she was to receive her grandmother's blessing and support — the only family member who offered this to her. "I visited my grandmother when I was about six months pregnant and I was really showing," Joyce recalls. "She could tell something was going on, but I didn't discuss it with her because I was worried she'd be distressed. It was a scandal in the family. I wasn't married and I was pregnant. Somebody finally told her, and she called me and said, 'Why didn't you tell me you were expecting? I just thought you had put on an awful lot of weight.' She didn't care. It wasn't a scandal to her at all.

She grew up in such incredibly hard times — she was orphaned, saw her siblings get split up then reunited, lost a child, lived through four wars. I think she's seen so much in her life that she knows not to make a huge issue out of a pregnancy without the benefit of marriage. She has such a good perspective. I really feel that if we'd been born in the same year we could be best friends, because she has this very free spirit and a tough attitude and she doesn't exhibit fear. I feel she's a kindred spirit. I want to be just like my grandmother when I grow up. I want to be old and live by the ocean and be content with a very simple life."

Thirty-eight-year-old Claudia also remembers how her maternal grandmother stepped forth at a moment of family crisis and confusion to offer constancy and support, and became a surprising source of comfort to a granddaughter who hadn't felt particularly close to this grandmother before. Claudia grew up mostly in Europe, thousands of miles from her maternal grandmother, whom Claudia and her siblings visited once every few years. She recalls her grandmother during those years as a proud and dignified woman from whom she always felt a certain emotional distance. "She lived in a great ranch house, and when you walked into the kitchen there was always the smell of applesauce cookies," Claudia remembers. "She had two silver pheasants on the dining room table, very elegant. And a little buzzer at her foot under the table so she could buzz the help to come in, even though she didn't have any help. Her home was very formal, and I guess I thought of her that way." She pauses, absorbed in thought, and then looks down at her hands. "I must have loved her, because she had veins sticking out of her hands and I wished I could grow some, too, to be like her. That to me conveys I did feel love for her during those years."

Claudia's family returned to the United States about the time she began college, and her parents separated soon after. Her mother partnered off with another man and left to sail around the world for the next eighteen years — "It's great fiction, I know," Claudia admits — and her father soon remarried. The following summer, in a state of numbness and anger, Claudia flew to Florida to visit her grandmother, the only adult member of her family with whom she had any desire for contact at the time.

"That's where our relationship began, as far as I'm concerned," Claudia says. "We'd lie in the sun together slathered with baby oil and iodine — it was her recommendation — and we talked about everything. I found someone I could talk to about my mother and how I thought her and my father's behavior was terrible. Grammy didn't say anything, but she listened. When I got home, I told all my siblings, and they went, too. Then we all started going regularly to see her. We told her about everything, even sex, and she loved it. I think that's what isolates grandparents, that they start being treated as outsiders. When I was a child, my relationship with her was mostly obligatory, 'Thank you, blah, blah, blah.' But then I started to get to know her because my mother wasn't around. It sounds really unremarkable to describe what she offered me at that time, but it was the only consistent thing I had. She replaced the absent mother."

Claudia's younger sister, Sheryl, thirty-three, had quite a different relationship with their grandmother during childhood and, not surprisingly, has a very different relationship with her today. Sheryl had to undergo several surgeries during her childhood, and while her family was moving from one European country to another she was often moving from one American hospital to the next. She remembers little about this time, but has been told that her grandmother became extremely protective of her during those years, visiting her daily and even sneaking in after hospital hours to make sure she was recuperating properly. "I'm sure that part of Grammy felt I'd been abandoned," Sheryl says. "Even though I don't feel I was, I was left alone at a really tough time when children should not be left alone. My grandmother wanted to fill in the gap, and I think that was valuable for me to have." Though she's always felt what she describes as a spiritual connection with her grandmother, probably dating back to those years, Sheryl says she, like her sisters, didn't develop a full emotional relationship with their grandmother until adulthood.

Sheryl was fifteen when her parents divorced, the only child still living at home. She remembers those years as chaotic. After brief periods living with her mother and her mother's boyfriend, then with her father and stepmother, she moved in with a boyfriend until she left for college. Four years later, when she was starting to launch a career as an artist, Sheryl invited her grandmother to come to Boston for a visit. As they continued to visit back and forth over the next few years, the two women began an adult dialogue that continues to this day, providing Sheryl with a source of inspiration at times of confusion or stress.

"Claudia bonded with my grandmother when things were not good between her and my parents," Sheryl says. "The same with my other sister. They felt their relationships with our grandmother were extremely valuable because she filled the void my mother and father left behind. The role I feel my grandmother has in my life is more of a constant pillar of strength, courage, and fairness. She's also levelheaded, humorous, and witty in her own way, incredibly intelligent and driven, but beyond that she's always remained happy. How many people are really happy, especially someone who's ninety? She fell in the supermarket one day and broke her knee, and had to go to the hospital and get physical therapy. It was a little bit frightening. But she surprised us all — the physical therapy they use on ninety-year-olds was too easy for her, and in the middle of all this she wanted to sneak her girlfriends into the hospital so they could all play bridge. She's got this unbelievable drive and spirit. I wish I'd learned that a while back. It might have helped me in my more troubled times. But I know it now, and it's become very important for me to keep in touch with her, to write her letters, call her on the phone. I'm hoping I have another four or five years with her, now that I'm able to realize how valuable and unique she is."

Over the past few years, Sheryl has gone through a divorce, a health scare, and the initial disorientation of living alone for the first time in ten years. She's had to cope with a series of losses, real and threatened, that have made her intimate connection with her ninety-year-old grandmother all the more important to her.

"I have an incredibly hard time with death," she explains. "I lost my grandfathers when I was young. I knew it was their time, but I also lost a man I loved, a boyfriend, when I was eighteen, and it wasn't his time. I have a terrible fear of losing people now, and I've come to a time in my life when I've lost a lot of friends to AIDS. I think my way of dealing with the fear of the inevitable is by getting everything I want from Grammy and giving her everything that I can give. I want to give her a side of me that she might not have known. I want to learn everything about her that I didn't know. In talking with her about my experiences of this past year, we've created our own language, which is what I always wanted. Even though she was my grandmother, I wanted us to be just two friends talking. I'm getting that now. I talk to her about feelings, directions, and fear. Sometimes I hang up the phone with her and think, 'She's ninety years old, and she's incredible.' "

Grandmother as Role Model is a theme that appears spontaneously and often in adult granddaughters' stories. As the younger women begin to face the challenges and responsibilities of adulthood, they start to develop a deeper appreciation for grandmothers who faced similar and often more adverse challenges in the past. Even women who barely knew their maternal grandmother spoke of referring to stories they'd heard about her for inspiration at critical junctures in their own lives. And other women spoke of the ongoing relationships they have with grandmothers who died years ago, continuing to refer to them as moral guides or as barometers for acceptable behavior.

"To this day, I regularly think of my grandmother," says thirty-year-old Pamela, who was eighteen when she lost the paternal grandmother who had helped raise her for several years during her childhood. "She was a devout Catholic, and her Catholicism was dominant in our relationship. She took me to church every Sunday, and we'd stop in there during the week and light candles and pray. Her 'struggle, struggle, survive, you'll get to your final destination one day' philosophy had a huge impact on my life. And I'm driven by the concept of the Seven Deadly Sins. I don't mean sin in the contemporary, paranoid sense, but in the spiritual sense of trying to become better and avoid sin in your soul. Whenever I'm doing something new or questionable, I wonder, What would she think? Would this be something she'd approve of? It's like she's been internalized as a guide. She's definitely the person in my mind whom I sort things out with." Sometimes Pamela believes her grandmother approves of her choices, and sometimes she's not so sure, she says. It often matters less to a granddaughter that she and her grandmother are in sync than it does that she has this internal standard against which she can measure her actions or behaviors.

Yet despite a granddaughter's ability to converse with her grandmother as an adult, at most their relationship only approximates, never becomes, interaction between peers. Peers are equals, sitting side by side. Grandmother and granddaughters are not. The generational ladder that mandates respect and deference to elders and offers emotional protection and guidance toward younger members may relax a bit as granddaughter ages, but its basic framework remains intact. At the same time, a type of role reversal starts to take place, where the granddaughter who was once dependent finds herself turning into the one who's now depended on.

The inversion occurs slowly, in stages. It begins with an elbow grip as you cross the street. A correction when she calls you by your mother's name. A menu she hands you because her eyes can't read fine print. And then one day you realize you're the one who picks up the phone now to ask how she's doing, instead of the other way around.

My grandmother's slowdown elicited an unexpected surge of protectiveness in me each time I saw her. It was almost an animal reaction that I felt, a fierce impulse to physically stand between her and any source of pain, emotional or physical. At my brother's bar mitzvah, when I was twenty years old, the whole family stood to say the mourner's prayer for my mother. My grandmother was sitting next to me in a dark wool suit, and when we stood she stooped over slightly, gripping the back of the seat in front of her. I put my arm around her and held her tight. I could feel the sharp edge of her shoulder inside my right palm. She was so narrow, her left shoulder didn't quite reach my side and I wound up partially crushing her against my chest. She reached up and patted my right hand. This urge I felt to protect her was so wildly inconsistent with the impatience I felt during our long-distance phone calls that I didn't know how both sentiments could exist inside me without canceling each other out.

Most young adult grandchildren start to feel definite responsibilities toward their aging grandparents during their late teen years. A 1976 study of eighty-six grandchildren between the ages of eighteen and twenty-six found that two-thirds of the respondents agreed grandchildren should help grandparents who need it, and more than half felt a grandparent was someone they should visit and to whom they should give emotional comfort. More recent studies have confirmed the same: Most adult granddaughters see themselves as their grandmothers' helpers and protectors, and are willing to assume a portion of that family role.

I wasn't a primary caretaker for my grandmother as she aged; she had two surviving daughters who arranged for her care, and their position in the lineage indisputably superseded mine. If my mother had been an only child, however, my grandmother's elder care would most likely have fallen to my siblings and me, and I would be telling a very different story here.

The degree to which a granddaughter participates in an aging grandmother's care is closely related to three factors: her mother's degree of involvement, the quality of her relationship with her grandmother, and her physical proximity to the grandmother during those years. Of the thirty percent of women interviewed for this book who said they were responsible for some of a maternal grandmother's care as she aged, nearly three-quarters reported they'd been "extremely close" or "very close" to their grandmothers during childhood. More than half of the women who lost their mothers at an early age also reported having taken some responsibility for their maternal grandmother's care as an adult.

Thirty-six-year-old Marion, for example, was raised by her maternal grandmother from the age of eight, after both her parents died. She was in her twenties, working as a school guidance counselor, and starting a family of her own when her grandmother's health started to fail, and she and her brother divided the caretaking duties between them. "I had someone come in to help my grandmother during the day, and then I would come over after school," Marion recalls. "I'd pick up my kids and bring them over, put them in the playpen there. Then I'd give her dinner, bring the kids home, put them to bed, go back to my grandmother's house, put her to bed. It was a lot of work. My brother lived an hour away but he managed to come three or four times a week to help, just to give me a break. Eventually he bought a house with my grandmother in mind, a ranch house she could get around in with her walker, and she moved in with him and lived there until she died."

Marion represents a different twist on the sandwich generation: Instead of a woman at midlife caring for both teenage children and elderly parents, she was a new mother in her mid-twenties caring for infants and an eighty-three-year-old grandmother, trying to meet the needs of both life span extremes at a relatively young age herself. Those years of dual caretaking were difficult for her, Marion says, but she wouldn't have chosen to spend them any other way. "I'd been married for about two years when my grandmother was first diagnosed with cancer," she explains. "I wanted to have a child but I didn't at that point. I didn't feel I could while I was taking care of my grandmother. Then a friend of mine asked, 'What are you waiting for, for her to die?' and I realized that I really wanted her to see my children. So that summer I got pregnant. It was hard to take care of her in addition to my son, but I felt I owed it to her because she had taken care of me for all those years. If her mind was gone and I couldn't take care of her, it would have been a different story. But I never felt like, 'God, I don't want to do this anymore. I'm gonna just put her in a home.' Never. Never. I knew how much she had given to me. I was an orphan, and she was a sixty-year-old woman who took me in. I just want to thank her for the rest of my life."

When a mother is living, most granddaughters serve as a backup caregiver, filling in when she's temporarily unavailable or offering supplemental support. Unless, that is, the mother isn't emotionally or physically able to assume the caregiving role. Few mothers expect a teenage granddaughter to help care for the grandmother, but many will rely on a granddaughter who's an adult.

"My mother cannot deal with her mother getting older," says thirty-three-year-old Sarah. "Cannot deal with it. My grandmother has an aide who comes in five mornings a week, so there isn't even really that much that my mother needs to do. But still, she leans very heavily on me whenever my grandmother needs help. Last Christmas my husband and I were visiting his parents and my grandmother contracted the flu. They admitted her to the hospital for observation. I spoke with her on the phone and she said she felt she was going to be fine. But my mother called us at my in-laws' house and asked me to come home because she didn't think she could handle it herself. I said, 'Are you kidding? We'll be home in three days. You can manage until then.' She insisted she needed me there. We were going back and forth like this for twenty minutes. Finally, my husband got so fed up listening to this he got on the phone and told her it didn't make sense for us to fly home early if the doctors thought my grandmother was going to be all right. We wound up not changing our flight, but as soon as we got back I drove to the hospital and started talking with the doctors and the insurance company. It's not like I'm in that role every day, but if someone needs to help out with my grandmother, I'm usually the one who winds up doing it."

Sarah's mother, frightened by her mother's vulnerability, tried to decrease her anxiety by foisting responsibility for the grandmother's care onto Sarah. We all carry the childhood fear of being alone and unprotected right into adulthood, and a mother watching her mother's health fail cannot help having two unconscious responses: How will I survive without her? and Who will stand between me and my own mortality when she's gone?

These are the fears of a daughter, not of a granddaughter. Whereas a mother is likely to see the grandmother's advancing maturity as symbolic of the passage of her own youth, a granddaughter is far enough removed from the process to view it as a natural and inevitable progression. She doesn't perceive a grandmother's aging as a threat. From her position as the youngest member of the female trinity, the granddaughter looks at her grandmother realistically with acceptance, as the crone who will introduce the maiden to the mysteries of aging rather than as the crone whose role she will inherit before long.

"Always with the jokes, they can get on my nerves," Joy Horowitz writes about her grandmothers. "They can even drive me crazy with their Neanderthal attitudes about a range of issues. And yet, they are my gurus. Just as striking as their longevity is the sense of utter constancy they offer in a world that seems to speed along faster and faster. Like it or not, they are my personal guides into old age and the existential dilemma."

We count on our grandmothers to remain static throughout our adulthood, to offer us, through their permanence, the opportunity to revisit our childhood whenever nostalgia or desire strikes. We search out our baby pictures on their walls and mantels. We're disconcerted when they redecorate. We crave their foods. The beauty of being an adult granddaughter is that you're relied on as a woman yet still embraced as a child. With no one else are you ever so comfortable being both at the same time.

16

The Grandmother in Me —
1975–1993

It is 1975. I am eleven years old. The phone in our house is ringing. I pick it up, just in time to hear my mother say "Hello?" on the extension upstairs. I can tell it's my grandmother by the response: "I'm worried about Hope." I put my hand over the receiver so they can't hear me breathing. "Nothing's wrong with her, Mother," my mother says. "It's only strep throat. I've got her on penicillin." My grandmother is not convinced. "Ooo-ooh," she says, her voice unsteady with concern. "I just hope she's going to be okay. I just want her to be healthy. Please God, let everyone be healthy." I gently hang up the phone before I can hear my mother's exasperated sigh. I already know how the rest of the conversation will go. I've had strep throat four times already this year, and it's only October. I've learned to dread the Q-Tip the doctor swipes against my tonsils, the nurse's matter-of-fact tone on the telephone announcing the positive result, and these calls from my grandmother. They start with her concern about me, expand to a generalized worry about the health of everyone she knows, and retreat back to her fears for other, specific family members. I'm only the starting point.

Perhaps it is because my grandmother has witnessed several legitimate medical disasters in her family that she expends so much energy worrying about illnesses that never occur. Her sister-in-law's colon cancer, diagnosed too late. Her husband's colon cancer, discovered in time but with a surprise recurrence more than twenty years later that cost him his life. And although she doesn't know it yet, breast cancer is gathering microscopic momentum in my mother's cells. My grandmother refuses to feel helpless. Worrying is an action; it provides her with something to do. When she spends the weekend at our house, I often find her sitting at the kitchen table at dawn, drinking cup after cup of coffee, her forehead knotted in anxiety. I'll give her this much, though: She's proactive about her concerns. She'll ask for feedback on late-night radio call-in shows (unfortunately, the same ones my father falls asleep to) and devour everything she can find about new treatments and miracle cures. Even at eleven, I know that once the process begins, we're powerless to stop it. But if I stay quiet and hang up the phone, eventually she'll stop worrying about my throat and start urging my mother to keep my sister out of public swimming pools.

It is 1980. I am sixteen years old. All my

friends have tickets for a rock concert thirty miles away, but my mother won't let me go. No amount of persistence can sway her. She doesn't know the driver of the car, and besides, who knows what could happen to me at a concert without an adult as chaperon? Her catalog of possible calamity is endless: I could get lost, kidnapped, molested, maimed in a crash. I could wind up on drugs. But Ma-a-a, I whine. Everybody's going. She purses the corners of her mouth and rolls her eyes in an I've-heard-that-one-before response. If everybody jumped off the Brooklyn Bridge, would you jump off, too? I cross my arms and shift my hips to the left. Yes, I tell her. Probably I would.

What does she expect? I'm sixteen. Hypotheticals don't scare me. Since that dreadful year of strep I've never even been ill, though oddly enough, considering my grandmother, my mother doesn't worry about my health. When I run a fever or come down with the flu, she pops a thermometer in my mouth, pours me a glass of juice, turns on the TV. Nothing excessive. Internal chaos does not scare her. Random acts of crime are her speciality. She worries I will innocently accept a date with a sociopath, or that my sister will get abducted by a pedophile while on a field trip in New York. She is convinced our house will get robbed when we go away for a night.

Because she will not let me drive with anyone newly licensed, I make plans one afternoon to take the bus to go shopping with friends. Don't sit next to strangers! she calls after me as I head for the door. And when you get on, right away tell the driver which stop is yours!

Ma-a-a, I say, deliberately slamming the screen door behind me. I pretend not to hear the instructions that follow me down the front path. I am sixteen, and I am going to the mall.

It is 1993. I am twenty-nine years old, and I live in New York. Even though this is, according to my mother, Crime Capital of America, after ten years of wandering I've chosen it as my home. I never feel unsafe. I often ride the subway alone at midnight and walk the quarter-mile back to my apartment on nearly deserted streets. My friends say I take foolish risks, but I say it's important to live as you choose without giving in to fear. Last year, when I lived in Iowa City, I used to run by myself along the river after dark, and before that, in Tennessee, I almost never locked my doors.

The threat of physical danger doesn't scare me. It's the body that I fear. Too much goes on at the cellular level I can't see. I monitor my skin and breasts for indicators of even the slightest abnormalities, call my doctors with news of every minor change. At least twice a year I am convinced I am seriously ill. Last year, I had jaw cancer and lymphoma. This year, I have already had Epstein-Barr and diverticulitis, and I am very worried about HIV.

When I can't glean a satisfactory answer from a doctor or a toll-free hotline, or when I am too embarrassed to ask (for even I know this kind of worry is not completely normal), I opt for self-education. They know me at Barnes and Noble as the woman who sits on the floor in the Health section with copies of *The Mayo Clinic Family Health Book* and *Our Bodies, Ourselves* lying open in her lap. Once, when I had an abnormal Pap smear and was convinced I was dying of cervical cancer, I spent three hours in a university medical library reading everything I could find on the human papilloma virus. At my next visit, my doctor raised an eyebrow and said I knew more about the current research than she did.

I used to think my fear of disease was a result of my mother's death from breast cancer when I was seventeen, but the roots for such behavior started growing in my family long ago. (A real-life image: my grandmother, in 1963, sitting in a New York City medical library reading everything she can find on endometriosis, the apparent cause of my mother's temporary infertility.) My mother didn't want to adopt her mother's obsessions, but she couldn't completely escape the generalized fear of calamity with which she was raised. I've made a deliberate choice to reject my mother's specific anxieties, but I can't figure out how to leave behind the expectation of disaster (or the belief I can somehow control it). Whenever I get started on another worry trip, I see how my friends regard me with expressions of sympathy, or confusion, or concern. It's not insanity, I try to tell them. It's just the grandmother in me.

17

One Woman Leads to Another

The differences between my grandmother and me were easily distinguished: she had red hair, I had brown. She was short, I was tall. She drove slowly, I loved speed. For many years, the similarities were harder to find. These were the small behaviors and mannerisms that only family members familiar with us both would notice, and sometimes not even then. Such as the Barnes and Noble outings that I deliberately kept hidden from view, fearing that whatever obsessions percolated in her brain had begun to noticeably bubble up in mine.

It's amusing to me now that I once considered hair color to be a significant difference between us, as if the essence of a person were so visible or simply defined. A similar superficial logic inspired me to spend nearly all of adolescence trying to pattern myself in opposition to my mother, believing that if only I could be thinner than her, braver than her, more career-focused and independent than her, I could somehow avoid whatever forms of unhappiness or restlessness seemed to plague her as an adult. I would concentrate on education and writing before marriage and children, I vowed (not exactly a renegade's decision in 1980, but one that forced me to deny I wanted all with equal passion), and I kept that promise to myself, through my first entry-level editorial job paying $15,000 a year, through three years of graduate school, through most of my friends' weddings and baby showers, and through the publication of my first book, eventually becoming a wife at thirty-two (eleven years older than my mother had been) and a mother at thirty-three (the age she was when she had her third), with my own investment account and a third book contract in my hand. It did not even occur to me until I finally stopped to pause for breath that in running so swiftly away from my mother's example I had landed squarely in my grandmother's lap.

Faye Weitzman Rosenberg, working woman for fifteen years, married at age thirty, a mother at thirty-one. (That's according to the birth certificate I finally dug up in a Boston vital records office just before she died.) The Depression was as much a factor in her timing as adolescent rebellion and the women's movement had been in mine. She was twenty-two when the stock market crashed in 1929, already working as a legal secretary to help support her family and not at all unhappy with the job. Long after she'd traded work for marriage to a businessman, she still referred to her office years as a sort of intellectual Eden.

It's not a coincidence that my grandmother

and I both worked throughout our twenties, holding off on marriage and motherhood until our thirties, unlike my mother, who married straight out of college and started trying to get pregnant within two years. My mother's generation was the aberrant one, coming of age in the plentiful 1950s and eager to trade schoolbooks for Tupperware and Enfamil. My peers actually brought the female demographic curve back closer to its prewar shape, when women were marrying and bearing children at later ages. The result is now a generation of adult women with life trajectories that look considerably more like their grandmothers' than their mothers'.

"I grew up listening to my grandmother's stories about working as a buyer for Saks Fifth Avenue, all these glamorous stories about leaving Ohio and being a single career woman in New York in 1941," recalls twenty-eight-year-old Becky. "She met my grandfather in the store and after a six-month courtship, they married. I always thought of her as brave and daring to have left her family in Ohio and set out on her own, to achieve her dream of having a more challenging job than the farmwife existence her parents had in mind for her. I could never figure out why my mother didn't see her mother the same way. She seemed to pattern herself in exactly the opposite direction, leaving college to marry my father, settling in the suburbs, devoting herself completely to her children. She's never had a job outside the house. I never, not even for a moment, considered that for myself. I knew from the time I was ten that I was going to finish school and move to New York. And that I was going to have a career there, and meet the man I would marry. Which was exactly what happened. But I never really connected that with my grandmother's story until I went back home for Christmas a few years ago and we got into a long conversation about my life here, about how much New York has changed since she lived here in the 40s. And I realized then that she had been my model for adulthood. We were sitting around the dinner table as we talked, and my mother just sat there with this look on her face. My grandmother and I have a whole history in common now, and you can tell my mother feels left out."

Author Anita Harris found similar family sequences among many of the adult women she interviewed for her 1995 book, *Broken Patterns: Professional Women and the Quest for a New Feminine Identity*. Grandmothers, not mothers, were the family members these women identified with most, although it was the desire to choose a path other than the mother's — not necessarily to choose the same path as the grandmother — that appeared to be their leading motivation.

"I would ask women about their grandmothers, and they would start telling stories and say, 'Oh, I never thought about that before. But you know, you're right. My grandmother was a doctor. My grandmother was a lawyer. My grandmother was this amazing powerhouse,' "

Harris explains. "The mothers of the women my age [forties] and of those I interviewed really fell into a kind of docile mode the daughters didn't want to emulate, but whether they liked their grandmothers or not, they thought of them as powerful. The question I then have to ask is 'How much of that is projected and how much of that is real?' " In other words, how much of that perception is an outgrowth of a woman's need to have an older female in the family with whom she can identify if she doesn't view her mother as an adequate role model or if — especially among late adolescents and young adults — resembling the mother is still perceived as a threat?

I have much more in common with my grand-mother than I do with my mother. I feel much closer to my grandmother than either of us feels to my mother. My grandmother and I have nearly identical interests and personalities, but it's like my mother is from another planet. These are the words of women interviewed for this book, who say in their families a grandmother's values, philosophies, passions, temperament, achievements, goals, and opinions seem to be suppressed in her daughter but then resurface in her granddaughter, often leading to a strong adult grandmother–granddaughter bond that exists independent of the middle generation's involvement. "I don't know if it's genetics or whatever," says thirty-four-year-old Lucy, "but I'm very different from my mother and very much like my grandmother. We just had a special understanding, she and I."

Behavioral geneticists now believe that about half of our personality traits, including extroversion, introversion, nervousness, and anxiety, can be attributed to heredity. The other half is assumed to be shaped by our environment, probably a combination of our parents' behaviors, our peer group's influence, and the random events we're exposed to throughout childhood and adolescence. No one knows — least of all the mother — exactly how granddaughters turn out to be little replicas of their grandmothers, only that it happens. "Did I turn out like my grandmother because of my mother or in spite of my mother?" wonders thirty-four-year-old Rosie. "I'm still not sure."

It's not unusual to find families where mother–daughter relations are so impaired that the only possibility for female alliance is between grandmothers and granddaughters, or families where grandmothers have historically raised granddaughters and form bonds with them that resemble parent–child unions. Or where a grandmother's and granddaughter's personalities really do seem to mirror each other's. It's equally common — sometimes even in the same families — to find certain traits and behaviors shared by each member of the maternal line. "It's amazing, how many characteristics are identical from my grandmother to my mother to myself," says Helie Lee, thirty-two, the author of *Still Life With Rice: A Young American Woman Discovers the*

Life and Legacy of Her Korean Grandmother. "When the three of us walk together, anyone walking behind us knows we're related, because we walk exactly the same way. We have the mother, the daughter, the grandmother walk, and it's very distinctive. You can't get away from those genes."

Helie is talking here about an actual walk down the street, but she's also flirting with metaphor. The way a woman moves through her world is based, in large part, on how the women before her move through theirs. Women raise women who raise women, each generation of females shaping the next. Even when a woman makes a deliberate effort to pattern herself differently from her mother, she often finds she can't easily shrug off a core set of behaviors that generations of women before her passed down. Perhaps in no arena is this quite as evident as motherhood. How many women startle themselves by uttering the same words or by relying on the same techniques they remember hearing and seeing their own mother use from their childhood? How many of their mothers are startled by exactly the same thing?

Women in a family pass their mothering practices from one generation to the next, like stations in a bucket brigade. Mention this to any women positioned between two generations and the anecdotes will flow. Most scientific studies of this phenomenon, however, rely on clinical populations for data, examining mothers who are either institutionalized or have serious psychological problems, in an attempt to uncover the origin of abuse. From these studies, we know that mistreatment of children, harsh parenting practices, and hostility toward children are often passed down from generation to generation, and those of us whose mothers grew up in extremely repressive or abusive households have felt the trickle-down effects of our grandmothers' behaviors, sometimes suffering at the hands of mothers who never received the nurturing they needed. The death or divorce of one's parents also appears to be linked to later parenting difficulties when severe family disruption follows the event.

But what about the rest of us, who come from families that may be idiosyncratic but fall far short of psychologically troubled?

In the average family of women, certain behaviors and characteristics appear to repeat more often than others. These include the amount of affection shown toward children; the degree of mother–daughter autonomy;* the ability to promote structure among children; disciplinary practices; the tendency toward neurotic behaviors; and the capacity for empathy. In addition, nearly all these studies indicate what may seem obvious: that affectionate mothers usually raise

*This refers to the degree to which mother and daughter are able to see and respond to each other as separate individuals rather than as one "merged" unit.

279

psychologically sound daughters. Similarly, mothers who are anger-prone, irritable, nervous, depressed, anxious, or unable to form emotional connections with their children are more likely to raise daughters who are less capable of supporting and responding to their children when they become parents themselves.

This doesn't always mean, however, that a woman who received deficient mothering is doomed to be a deficient mother herself. As British psychoanalyst Michael Rutter has pointed out, generational discontinuities are just as common as similarities. Two key factors appear to be critical for interrupting a negative parenting pattern. The first is the ability to express anger and resentment toward the rejecting mother during childhood and forgive her as an adult. The other is the early presence of a nurturing, supportive adult who compensates for a mother's shortcomings and helps a child develop the empathy and self-esteem she needs to one day be an attentive mother herself.

In some families, this supportive adult is the grandmother, in an example of second-chance mothering. Once unable to give affection or support to a daughter, a grandmother may at a later stage in life be able to offer it to her granddaughter and undo some of the long-term emotional distance or damage she helped perpetuate years before.

A grandmother's effectiveness as a mother isn't necessarily an accurate predictor of the kind of grandmother she'll be. Lucy, now a single parent to a seven-year-old son, grew up in a highly volatile relationship with her own mother and left home at seventeen. After a relationship with a boyfriend turned physically violent, she went to live with her grandmother for several years and found the stability and security there that had been lacking in her childhood home. Today she's deeply committed to raising her son with structure and respect. "I learned my mothering ability to a great extent from the mothering my grandmother gave me, the solid, stable meal-on-the-table nurturing," she explains, "but I got to miss out on a lot of the really negative stuff she went through when she was developing herself in her thirties and forties and raising her own children. By the time I got her, she was solidly who she was and comfortable with that. She was able to be a much better mother to me than she was to my mother, who often felt — and had been — neglected while my grandmother pursued her career. If I'd been my grandmother's daughter back then, our relationship would have been just as screwed up as my mother's relationship with her was, no doubt."

By all accounts, my grandmother was a devoted and responsive mother to my mother. Setting aside her tendency toward hyperinvolvement, I recognize her ability to respond to my mother's distress as a child most likely gave my mother the ability to respond to her own children, which helped give me the ability to respond to my daughter's cues today. I didn't know a thing about babies when Maya was born, never had much interest in them at all, but as soon as my daughter emerged from my body a kind of empathy and patience I'd never experienced before began to flow. I spent the first few hours after her birth sitting in a plastic chair outside our hospital room, holding Maya while she inexplicably screamed her way through sunrise and my husband snored from his makeshift bed on the tile floor. It must have been excruciating to be sitting on all those stitches without a pillow as the anesthesia wore off, but what I remember about that morning isn't the physical pain but the concern I felt for Maya as she outcried — by far — all the other newborns on the ward. Before that morning, three hours of relentless, piercing screams would have driven me to near madness, or at least to hand over the baby and flee, but instead I felt only empathy for this little wailing bundle with a conehead and a splotchy face. That response had to come from somewhere, and I don't believe hormones were the only source.

Psychoanalyst Nancy Chodorow, in her landmark 1978 volume *The Reproduction of Mothering*, makes a convincing case for the grandmother–mother–granddaughter mothering sequence when she claims every infant internalizes her earliest memories of child care, which lie dormant for decades until she needs to pull them up and refer to them — completely at the unconscious level — when she has a child of her own. A poignant example in support of this theory comes from a 1950s study involving a child named Monica, who was born with an incomplete esophagus. For her first two years, Monica had to be fed through a tube while lying on her back, across her mother's thighs. Years later, when her first child was born, Monica laid the baby across her thighs to bottle-feed her, even though she had no conscious memory of having been fed that way herself, indicating that some of what we commonly refer to as "maternal instinct" may instead be residual imprints our mothers and grandmothers left behind.

Some days this is a great comfort to me, knowing that both I and my daughter are securely rooted in a distinct behavioral line, and that my mother and my grandmother join us in every diaper change or bedtime story in the rocking chair. But on other days it's easy for me to apply this generational theory to other practices, and I start to feel a creeping sense of the inevitable, worried that the specific anxieties and obsessions that plagued my grandmother and my mother will soon torment me, too.

Charlene, a thirty-one-year-old mother of three, is struggling with this concern right now. As a teenager, she watched her grandmother, once a vibrant, happy woman who'd been involved in church and community, sink deeper into depression and self-imposed isolation after Charlene's grandfather died. Charlene's mother, the oldest daughter in her family, became her mother's part-time caretaker, an arrangement that exposed the whole family to ongoing conflict and frustration.

"My grandmother lived for five years after my grandfather died, and those five years were brutal for all of us," Charlene recalls. "We tried to do whatever we could to cheer her up, but if anyone tried to reach out and get help for her, she pushed them away. It seemed she always looked on the dark side of everything, and she incessantly talked about her own death. It was especially hard for my mother. They were constantly arguing. Constantly. My mother was really quite harsh with her mother, and in turn my grandmother really made my mother's life miserable. It caused a lot of turmoil between my parents, too. When I was a kid, the majority of their arguments were about my grandmother — why couldn't my mother get her to do this, why was she acting like that, why couldn't my mother's sister take more responsibility, etcetera."

Charlene remembers how, in moments of exasperation, her mother would turn to the family and say, "If I ever get like my mother, just take me out and shoot me. I don't ever want to be like her." This became a running joke among the four siblings in Charlene's family, provoking behind-the-scenes whispers of "Let's take her — it's time" whenever one of them felt their mother was getting out of hand. But recently, eight years after her grandmother's death, Charlene has started noticing tiny nuances in her mother's behavior that remind her of her grandmother, and these similarities no longer feel like a joke.

"My mother made a comment around Christmas this past year that really alarmed me," she explains. "She's usually pretty stressed out around holiday times, and she was launching into some kind of tirade about my youngest brother spending the week with his girlfriend's Unitarian family instead of at home. She was talking about what she's taught my brothers and sister and me about the family traditions, everything she's done for us over the years, and whether we'll do these things for ourselves after she's gone. And she made a comment like 'Next year — if I'm even here next year.' Where was that coming from? It sounded exactly like the kind of comment my grandmother made that would drive us all crazy. What do you mean, 'If you're here next year'? My mother has had some health problems recently, but nothing to warrant that kind of comment. That night I called up my other brother because I was so upset by it. I said, 'She's turning into Grandma. What do we do? I think we need to do — what is it called when you confront someone who's an alcoholic? an intervention? — I think we need to do an intervention. I think we all need to show up and say, "Look what you're becoming. You're becoming her. And you said you didn't want to." ' "

Charlene's concern about her mother's behavior stems not just from the fear that her mother, like her grandmother, will succumb to a long and difficult episode of depression, but that she, like her mother, will be thrust into the caretaking role. She saw what being in that position did to her mother — and to the whole family system — and doesn't want her husband and children to be subjected to the same stress she experienced as a teenager and young adult.

"If God forbid anything happened to my dad, I hope that my mother wouldn't turn into the same unhappy kind of person my grandmother did," she says. "I'm very afraid that could happen, and I'd probably be the child who would end up in my mother's old role. Because I seem to be the family member who'd be suited to that situation. I'm the oldest one, and the only one who's stable, with my own family and own home. So I'm just as concerned about my mother turning into her mother as she is, in that respect."

The psychological separation needed to perceive ourselves as fully distinct from our mothers and their mothers, and therefore immune to repeating their lives, goes exactly against the manner in which those women raised us to live. Connected. Loyal. Of them. How can we fully separate from our mothers and grandmothers when the way we hold our children, the lilt in our speech, the shape of our hands, so closely resembles theirs? It's a question not one of the seventy women interviewed for this book could answer.

In the movie version of *The Joy Luck Club*, there's a scene where the sweet, submissive Rose awaits the arrival of her American husband to discuss the terms of their impending divorce. She's just spent the afternoon with her mother, An-Mei, who's deeply troubled by Rose's lingering desire to please a husband who's been unfaithful to her. She recognizes her daughter's dilemma as a crisis of self-worth, and in a last-minute attempt to help her recognize her value, An-Mei tells Rose the story of her own mother's death, which occurred in China sixty years before.

An-Mei's mother, widowed young, had brought shame upon her family and herself when a wealthy man in need of a male heir raped her and then brought her to Tientsin as his Fourth Wife. Beautiful and proud, she lived in misery as a woman in China who was forbidden to either speak out or run away. As a Fourth Wife, she was little more than a concubine whose son, when she bore him, was taken from her and given to a wife of higher stature. Believing her own life to be worth little, she poisoned herself with opium in the hope that by killing her weak spirit she could help her daughter An-Mei's spirit grow strong.

Cut back to the present. Ruth's husband arrives, and she's waiting for him outside, sitting in their garden in the rain. He's known her as the type of wife who lets him make all their decisions and adjusts herself accordingly, and he expects little resistance to his plan to sell their house or share custody of their young daughter. But instead in the garden he finds a woman who's newly righteous in her anger, and no longer willing to sacrifice her needs to those of a man. With rain streaming in rivulets down her face, she stares straight ahead, toward a distant point in the yard. "You're not . . . taking . . . my house," she says, through clenched teeth. "You're not taking my daughter. You're not taking any part of me. Because you don't know who I am. I died sixty years ago. I ate opium, and I died. For my daughter's sake."

It's a chilling, pivotal moment in the film, and afterward I couldn't shake the memory of that scene. That absolute collapse of boundaries between the generations, granddaughter and grandmother merged. That certainty; that access to ancestral power. Rose's message — I Am My Grandmother — quite literally haunted me for months with its simplicity and exactitude.

Because as much as I have tried to shrug off the implications of this very basic truth, I know my grandmother is in me, too. She's there every time I knock on wood to ward off evil spirits; she's there whenever I see a homeless person huddled on the sidewalk and slip money into his hand. She's there every time I stubbornly insist a doctor give me the time and explanation I deserve.

I can't pretend to know my grandmother as a

mother, sister, wife, or friend. But I won't pretend that because I knew her only as a grandmother that I barely knew her at all. The more I live, the more I realize that in some respects I know her better than I knew my mother, even as well as I know myself. She had red hair, I have brown, which has turned out to mean nothing at all. We are both writers, both worriers, both hungry for intellectual growth. Stubborn in our own ways, both quick to take on other people's pain. Can anyone tell me, definitively, where does one woman end and the next begin?

If Barnes and Noble superstores had existed in my grandmother's heyday, I do not doubt she would have routinely been escorted from the Health section at closing time. I know this with a certainty that transcends generations and time. And from there it is not difficult to imagine extending my own need for reassurance one more step away from the center, into the zone where my grandmother spent much of her time. Because of her, I understand there is a delicate and permeable line between obsessions that are manageable and obsessions that spiral out of control. Perhaps that is the only authentic line that separates my grandmother from me.

18

Reclaiming a Culture:

Helie's Story

Helie Lee was twelve years old when her maternal grandmother emigrated from Korea to southern California, and she barely remembered the woman she called *halmoni*. Helie had last seen her grandmother in 1967 when she waved goodbye at Seoul's Kimpo airport, leaving Korea for good at the age of three. "My mother kept saying, 'Say goodbye to Grandma, say goodbye to Grandma,' but at that point I didn't really understand the connection we had to her," explains Helie, now thirty-two. "I knew she was my mother's mother and that she'd been nice to me, but that was it."

Helie and her family settled in the San Fernando Valley, where she attended public school and spoke perfect English, secretly envious of the light-eyed girls in her class. Then in 1976 her grandmother arrived, greeting her in a language Helie barely understood. "My grandmother . . . God. She was so different," Helie recalls. "And back then, *different* meant in a bad way. Because we had come to America, I thought, to be American. And being a perfect family meant being the perfect American family. My grandmother was so far from that. She didn't know how to drive a car or use a toaster. She didn't even know how to turn on the television set. We had to do everything for her, even dial the phone. I'd come home from school and find her squatting in the backyard, picking weeds to cook us for dinner. It was a war mentality, but back then I didn't even know there had been a Korean War. I never knew my grandmother had been involved in it. Or my mother. My parents pretty much protected us. That's the whole thing with Asians, especially Asian women — you don't want to burden the younger generation with your grief, because if you do they'll be loaded down and won't be able to think about the future."

Though Helie grew to respect and love her grandmother, her desire to blend in with the surrounding culture was a more powerful force than either her grandmother's or mother's model of Asian pride. During her teen years, Helie bleached her hair and tanned her skin. She joined the cheerleading squad. In college, she lived in a rowdy coed dormitory and pledged little sister to a fraternity. The traditional Korean woman's path as she saw it, with its emphasis on assessing a woman's worth by her marital status and number of sons, held no appeal for a budding feminist raised outside L.A.

Just before her senior year of high school,

Helie, on her parents' urging, accompanied a group of other teenage Korean-Americans and Korean-Europeans on a tour of the homeland. The timing, she says with a laugh, was all wrong. She was more upset at the thought of having to leave cheerleading camp in the middle of the session than she was excited about returning to the country of her birth. "They took us to the DMZ, and I was so ignorant about my own culture and history that my friends and I kept calling it the DMV," she recalls. "We saw the North Korean soldier on the other side, but it just didn't register that this was anything significant. And it didn't register that my grandmother had said she was from North Korea, which was basically the only story about her past that I'd heard."

It would be almost another decade before curiosity began to replace Helie's lack of interest. In a pivotal scene she re-creates in the introduction to her 1996 book, *Still Life With Rice*, Helie sits uncomfortably at a restaurant table while her mother and grandmother revisit a subject they've gone over many times before: Helie's unmarried state. They want her to marry before she becomes the equivalent of "rotten fruit"; she insists that in America she still has time to enjoy being a single woman, to focus on her career before taking on the responsibility of a family.

"I am who I am," she tells them. "I'm not like you."

"You Korean, you always be Korean," her grandmother says. "Our people so good."

"Why did you bring us to America if you didn't want us to be American?" Helie asks her mother defiantly.

Her mother's answer surprises her. "Your father and me give up everything, our home, our life, to bring you kids to America, not to be American people, but so you can be Korean," she says. "Here, there is no Cold War, no hunger, no losses. I know you tired me tell you eat more, do nice hairstyle, change lipstick color, wear nice dress, but I do because when others see your Oriental face I want them to say, 'Ah, she Korean lady, they so proud people.' "

Months after this conversation, Helie still heard the echo of her mother's words. *Your father and me give up everything . . . so you can be Korean.* For months, she tried to reconcile the Korea of her imagination, where the men were selfish lovers (or so she'd been told) and the women reproduced copiously and too young, with the Korea that sustained her mother and grandmother's ethnic pride. "My grandmother loves her family, and everyone who knows her knows she has made so many sacrifices for them," Helie says, "but her love for her country was even bigger than the love for her children." Nonetheless, the silence surrounding her family's past had created a deep rift between Then and Now, making Helie's task of connecting the terms *Korean* and *American* a difficult one, at best. So she took an impulsive next step: She bought a one-way ticket into Kimpo airport and, without any solid plans, returned alone to the country of her birth.

In Korea, she worked as an English instructor and lodged at the home of her mother's cousin. There, she was surrounded by family members who remembered her grandmother as a woman of "unshakable conviction and great heart" who'd built up an opium empire during the war to support her family. She'd lost all her money and land to Communist insurgents, they told Helie, as well as her husband and first son, and had been imprisoned as a traitor. These were stories Helie had never heard before, tales of heroism that were difficult to imagine when she thought of the grandmother back in California worrying her granddaughter might turn into "rotten fruit."

Back in Los Angeles the following year, Helie began asking her grandmother direct questions about her past. What was your childhood like? Who was my grandfather? What happened in North Korea? "It wasn't until I made my own journey [to Korea] that I finally started paying attention to my grandmother's history," Helie says. "And also, my Korean had improved. It was the first time in my life that I was able to talk to my grandmother in her native language, not quite at her level but close enough that I could hear how she knit her words together. And I realized, God, she's incredible. Not only is she witty, but she's also intelligent. She can really tell a story. And she's funny as hell."

Sometimes grandmothers are reluctant to re-visit episodes from the past, particularly an immigrant's past, but more often they're only waiting for the opportunity to arise. Late in life the impulse to create a coherent narrative out of one's life often emerges, a phase that's commonly referred to as the "life review process." It's the psychological equivalent of putting one's house in order, and for grandmothers part of that process involves giving away pieces of their stories to younger generations, in much the same way they also might start giving away jewelry or furniture before they die.

When Helie arrived at her grandmother's house with her tape recorder, she found a woman who was eager to share her stories. "When we first started talking, she would speak very fast, because she was afraid my interest level would recede to its prior state," Helie recalls. "She started taking me seriously when I would show up pretty consistently at the same hour every day. Eventually I wound up getting fired from my job because I was so passionate about spending time with my grandmother that I kept calling in sick. The first couple of tapes we made are so loaded with tears and wailing that you can't understand a lot. As the stories progressed, there were times when we'd be laughing together, or my father would be translating in the background and his voice was shaking. Or my mother was there and you could just hear the emotion between my grandmother and her."

A remarkable story of wartime survival began to emerge, the transformation of a young, sheltered North Korean girl into a clever, resourceful woman who supported her family after they fled to China and who, after their return to Korea, kept her children from starving by traveling from town to town practicing *chiryo,* an ancient form of healing, for which she was ultimately banished from the country. "Each story my grandmother told me made me think how much more incredible she was," Helie recalls. "If she'd been born in today's time, she would be a powerhouse. She would do the same type of things as the women I look at and think, *That's a woman I really admire* do. She would be one of them."

As Helie gathered her grandmother's anecdotes and started weaving them together into a book, she made an unorthodox literary choice: to tell her grandmother's story in the first person, from her grandmother's point of view, so that most of *Still Life With Rice* is a biography written in autobiographical form. It's risky to assume inner knowledge of someone else's character, but some experts believe that the natural connection between a grandmother and granddaughter gives the younger woman unique access to some of her grandmother's actions, responses, and fears.

"Eric Erickson talks about the long-term family memories that people carry," Anita Harris says. "It doesn't necessarily depend on having a direct relationship. It's really based more on what people have been led to believe about their grandparents, the sort of family myth. And remarkable unconscious things can happen. People find out many years later that they've chosen a line of work similar to a grandmother's, or they find themselves in a relationship or a space that's similar to one their grandmother experienced. That actually happened to me. When I was teaching at Simmons College, I was telling my students about my book and my findings, and I realized here I was teaching at this women's college, and that my grandmother had run a girls' camp and had been a teacher. I don't think it was just coincidence. I never would have said I modeled myself after my grandmother, but the impulse or desire was in me, and it felt comfortable for me to be doing it. The pathways are somehow in us."

Some therapists also believe that the displacement of the emigration experience and the horrors of war result in certain behavioral cues that get passed down from generation to generation in a family. Some studies on grandchildren of Holocaust survivors, for example, reveal these children to have a heightened sensitivity to trauma, though other studies have been inconclusive. In the workshops Valerie Kack-Brice leads on healing early childhood wounds, she regularly asks participants to indicate how many generations their families have been in this country. "Very, very often you will see emotions from the experience of being picked up and moved somewhere else recur in subsequent generations," she explains. "I've seen men and women who've carried generations of pain or rage for a family that had to leave their home as a result of war, or had to flee their country for one reason or another. I also see carried fear, where people are walking around in a state of paranoia or anxiety, or having panic attacks. I worked with a woman in one of my workshops whose grandmother was a first-generation Jewish immigrant who'd had a tremendous amount of fear about leaving her home and coming here. She also had a tremendous amount of shame because when she arrived there was a lot of discrimination against Jews, as well as discrimination among Jews toward women. Two generations later, her granddaughter showed evidence of what we would call a shame core that prevented her from seeing her value and reinforced over and over again, 'You're a woman. You can't be anything in this culture. You're only good for getting married and making babies, and if you can't do that then you're not good for anything.' If you're able to identify this connection and work on it, you can start peeling away the layers and discover that some of the shame you're carrying isn't yours. It's your grandmother's."

If all of this is true, then who better to tell a grandmother's story than one of her direct female descendants? When Helie sat down to write her book, she says, her voice and her grandmother's smoothly merged into one, and she felt she truly understood her grandmother for the first time. The passion, the silence, the pride, the emphasis on marriage and family, all of it — in the context of a complete life, each of these elements, even those that had puzzled or irritated Helie before — fell into place. In her grandmother's stories she discovered evidence of the type of determined, self-assured woman she'd always hoped to become. And to her genuine surprise, Helie found herself longing to take her place in line behind the women — the strong, proud Korean women — who'd raised her.

"Even though I still strive for literary success and to improve as a writer," she says, "my purpose in this life will be to become a good mother and wife. I'm actually not ashamed to say that. I fought that idea so much before, because I thought if I fought against marriage and motherhood, I was fighting against my culture and the restrictions of my culture. Now that I've to a great degree accepted who I am, where I come from, and who my grandmother and mother are, I realize that the things they strived for — family, freedom, security — are exactly the same things that I want." To Helie, being Korean-American now means not to collapse one culture inside the other but to accept and celebrate both.

19

Saying Goodbye

A grandmother is often an adult granddaughter's escort to the border of the unknown, introducing her to the awesome certainty of death. It is the work of the crone to demystify this final passage for the maiden, and to then complete the journey alone. "During her dying I felt as if, as always, she had taken me to the edge of a territory that she herself had not been able or willing to enter: but she could show it to me," writes Suzannah Lessard about the death of her ninety-six-year-old grandmother in her memoir, *The Architect of Desire*. "It was as if out of a concealing darkness that was right there in the light she had slipped me a golden apple, without a word, without a look."

While Lessard's grandmother drifted painlessly into death, dying can be messy business, especially when it occurs to the oldest of the old. Grandmothers in their eighties and nineties are likely to be suffering from multiple physical ailments, or from years of mental decline. Nursing homes, bedpans, and the loss of bodily functions may factor in, and an adult granddaughter is long past the point where such details go unnoticed. In the case of Alzheimer's or dementia, a grandmother may no longer recognize her granddaughter, a separate and often overlooked form of loss.

My grandmother's descent into senility meant the narrowing, and then the closing off, of any one-to-one relationship between us. The geographical distance I put between my family and myself meant communication had to occur mainly by telephone or by mail, neither of which my grandmother could manage after a certain point. This reduction in contact between us happened so gradually, and so quietly, that I eased into the loss bit by bit. One year there were no letters; the next year no cards. Then the telephone calls dwindled away, replaced by ones initiated by me, until she could no longer talk by phone. Finally, she lost hold of her memories of me. Long before my grandmother died physically I had to start letting go of our emotional connection, allowing her to start sliding into story, into myth. Without even realizing it, I began alternating between the present and past tenses when writing about her, confused about whether my grandmother still existed outside of me or had made the transition to exclusively within.

Losing a grandmother to mental deterioration is an ambiguous form of loss. She's neither here nor there, neither accessible nor completely out of touch. Families have to make hard decisions about care, often opting for nursing homes or institutions, and granddaughters find it can take years before memories of happier times push through the traumatic images of the final few. I've heard stories from adult granddaughters who can still become profoundly upset when recalling stories about retrieving Nanas from police stations because they'd wandered into unfamiliar neighborhoods, who went to visit Grandmas in nursing homes and saw them tied into their chairs, who sat by the bedsides of Mimis they'd once lived with but who no longer knew their names.

"It feels like the most violent act in which I have ever participated," writer Cynthia Kaplan has said about admitting her grandmother, who suffers from Alzheimer's, to a nursing home. "I would take it back if I could."

Yet even at its worst moments, a grandmother's dying has the potential to open new emotional vistas for an adult granddaughter, who, from her unique position of emotional connection without intense psychological fusion, is ideally suited to receive such knowledge. Though she may know she'll miss her grandmother profoundly, the threat of losing her usually doesn't make her feel as vulnerable or emotionally bereft as the threat of losing her mother might, and she can focus more on the abstract profundity of the event.

"My grandmother's death was the event that made me wish I could accept and deal with death better," says fifty-two-year-old Carmen, who is now involved with organizing a traditional Mexican Day of the Dead celebration in her community after losing her grandmother to complications of diabetes last year. "It was hard for me to see her become debilitated. She had always been someone who loved to read, crochet, cook, and watch TV. She liked to run around all over the place. She had to have one of her legs amputated, and then the other one below the knee. Then her eyesight started going, then her strength. She couldn't even eat much at the end, just pureed foods because her system was so delicate. She was miserable, but even in the middle of all that I would go stay with her and we would have good times and crack jokes. I really felt that by being there with her I was there to observe and learn. I could ask myself, How does this person I've admired all my life experience this? The answer was sometimes well, and sometimes badly: she was a normal person. At the end she lost control of her bowels. It was so real. It made me say, 'This is life. This is okay.' But it was also so heavy. It took me about two years to recover. I felt like I was carrying a burden on my shoulders, and then one day it wasn't there anymore. But I knew I had made the decision to go through with it, because I wanted to meet my obligation to my grandmother. Also, I recognized that I could make a choice between being the kind of person who hides and the kind of person who deals with important things."

Thirty-four-year-old Lucy also found that her

grandmother's impending death offered her an opportunity to transcend cultural discomfort and personal fear, and face the finality of the event. Lucy had lost her father when she was eight, and never formed a close emotional connection with her mother. Her grandmother had been her only constant during childhood and adolescence, even taking Lucy in for three years in the midst of a turbulent adolescence. Matter-of-fact and honest, Lucy's grandmother represented a forthright, hardworking example to the troubled teenager, whose life slowly started to turn around. So when she got the news that her grandmother was in the final stages of her disease, Lucy immediately flew to Wisconsin for a three-week visit. During that time, she helped with her grandmother's care, bringing avocadoes and sourdough bread to her bedside, trying to coax her to build strength even as she grew visibly more frail.

"The last night I was there was the most profound experience I've ever had in my life," Lucy remembers. "I was leaving for the airport, and I gave my grandmother a hug and a kiss and said I'd give her a call soon. I was halfway through the door when I realized I couldn't do it like that. I turned around and said, 'Nana, let's face it. I'm never going to see you again. You know it, and I know it, and I can't walk out of here and pretend this is just another goodbye.' I said there were some things I had to tell her. So I sat on the edge of the bed and thanked her for all the input she'd given me all my life, and I told her I loved her a lot and that her life had meant so much to me. I said, 'If it weren't for you, I don't know where I'd be. I don't even know if I'd be alive.' I hugged her and kissed her and told her she was the best thing in my life. She said I was the most beautiful thing in her life, too, and she thanked me for being me.

"Saying goodbye to her was the most excruciating thing I've ever done, but having lost my father in a freak accident, I realized it was the most important thing I could do," she continues. "And how could I walk away without acknowledging the obvious? We'd acknowledged everything else. My grandmother knew everything about me, every abortion I had, the first time I had sex, all the intimate details of my life. And death is the most intimate of all — you can't beat that one.

"It was the cleanest relationship I ever had with anybody in my life. She loved me from the time I was born. She had her life, I had mine, she gave me the most positive parts of herself with a few exceptions, and we finished it, we said goodbye when it was time to say goodbye. Truly, it was the most beautiful thing I think I could have done, to sit there and be honest with her. She died exactly a month after that goodbye."

Like Lucy, many adult granddaughters intuitively feel that after a grandmother has given all she can emotionally give to the granddaughter during her childhood, and after the granddaughter has given back all she can as an adult, the relationship is complete. I expected adult granddaughters raised by grandmothers to have a more extreme emotional response, assuming they would feel the same devastation that young granddaughters in this situation felt upon their grandmothers' deaths, but this was not always the case. These granddaughters often had a very practical, matter-of-fact view of the relationship, perhaps a result of having been brought up by an older woman from whom they'd always had psychological autonomy, or who'd raised them with a quiet expectation of their eventual death.

Thirty-eight-year-old Tamara, for example, who was raised as her maternal grandmother's child, says her biological mother had a much harder time adjusting to the grandmother's death seven years ago than she did. "My mother was really devastated," Tamara explains. "She still hasn't completely recovered. To me, the loss meant missing a person that I loved very much, but that level of 'What am I going to do without her?' wasn't there for me. I felt as if the relationship had done everything it could have done in terms of preparing me and supporting me. It finished that job. I was at a point where I saw my grandmother as a wonderful, loving, important person in my life, but not as somebody I had to have to help me get through things. I felt I was able to come to terms with letting go of her a lot easier than my mother has been."

One notable exception here involves granddaughters for whom the loss of a maternal grandmother triggers incomplete mourning for a mother who died when they were young. When grief feels too threatening or disorienting for a child or teenager, or when they have no stable adults to lean on at the time, the child may suppress her feelings of loss, sadness, confusion, or rage, allowing them to surface only through smaller or later losses — the death of a pet, the breakup of a romantic relationship, or the loss of another family member in subsequent years.

Thirty-two-year-old Roberta was sixteen when her mother died after a lengthy illness, and her coping mechanism at the time was to assume a stoic and brave public facade. "I always had to be the strong one in my family," Roberta explains. "I actually went to school the day my mother died. I didn't cry once, and I said to a friend as we were walking down the stairs, 'Will you get the assignments for me tomorrow? My mother died and I won't be in school.' The look of horror on her face! She couldn't believe I would come to school. No one realized that all the time my mother was sick, I had gone through years of hiding my feelings, of putting up a screen in order to function every day. Then I would go home and cry in my sleep every night." For sixteen years, Roberta suppressed the pain of her mother's death, until just a month ago, when her maternal grandmother suffered heart failure in the middle of an afternoon.

"When I got the phone call at work from my

cousin, I immediately thought I would respond the same way I had with my mom," Roberta says. Stoic. Strong. "But when I went in to tell my boss I would be leaving early, I burst into tears. It shocked me, because I'd always been so good at controlling my emotions. Then I told a co-worker that I was going to be out for a few days, and it was like the floodgates opened. I cried and cried. I didn't even say goodbye to anyone, I just left and cried the whole way on the subway out to my aunt's house. I'm doing better now, but it still hits me from time to time. I can't predict when it's going to happen. It seems to come especially when I go to bed at night, because that was the time when I cried about my mother."

My grandmother lived until she was 104, and she'd been sick off and on for two months, Roberta told me. These are the words of explanation a granddaughter reaches for, seeking to justify and make sense of the death. Common sense tells us that the loss of a grandmother is a timely event, occurring to a woman of advanced age who's physically frail and has lived a full life. Yet when the actual phone call comes, we're often unprepared for the powerful emotion we feel. As the novelist and award-winning columnist Anna Quindlen wrote about the loss of her grandmother, "I accepted the inevitable disintegration of age without realizing how bereaved her death would leave me."

Even when a grandmother has been disabled or mentally absent for years, the sorrow at the moment of loss can extend deep — not the type of acute pain that pierces your chest but the kind that leaves an aching hole inside you. It feels, truly, as if a piece of oneself has been irretrievably lost. One of my friends who recently lost her ninety-three-year-old grandmother perhaps explained it best: "I can't imagine not missing her," she said.

A granddaughter's grief is a grief without a forum. It's not typically considered the kind of death that should rearrange her world, or the sort that warrants bereavement services of any kind. Without social validation or recognition for her loss, a granddaughter often finds herself in what psychologists call a state of "disenfranchised grief." She knows the loss is legitimate, but her emotional needs and reactions don't fit into a category others can easily identify, appropriately respond to, or adequately understand. She may get sympathetic smiles, even some generic condolence cards, but after only a few days others expect her to be "over" the loss. It's only a grandmother who died, after all. Or so the prevailing sentiment goes.

So the granddaughter also tells herself that she should recover soon. That this was a logical loss, a not entirely unexpected loss. That she's an adult, and that losing loved ones is an inevitable part of adulthood. She mourns for her grandmother in the manner most appropriate for her family, or her religion, or her personal philosophy about death. And maybe, after a few months or even just a few weeks, she does start to feel more emotionally centered again. But something remains out of sorts, out of sync, and that confuses her. If the relationship filled its purpose in her life, if she's at peace with the loss, if she said her goodbyes, why does she still feel imbalanced, and her mourning incomplete?

Most granddaughters fail to recognize what psychologists call "secondary losses" after a grandmother dies. They're the symbolic losses that occur after the death of a loved one. Whether the actual loss of a grandmother was a devastating event or not, whether the grandmother died after a short physical illness or after years of mental decline, most granddaughters — especially those who had distant relationships with their grandmothers toward the end of their lives — are surprised by how destabilizing and profound the following secondary losses can be.

The Loss of the Granddaughter Role
Because maternal grandmothers tend to be the longest-lived grandparent, for many women her death means the loss of the last surviving grandparent. Even women who were no longer active in the granddaughtering role speak of the significance of this transition. A piece of their identity disappears when no one can call them "granddaughter" anymore. Women who were highly involved with their grandmother lose

whatever sense of definition they received from interacting with her, whether it was the gratification of helping someone in need, the pride of acting responsibly, or the satisfaction of caring for someone who'd once cared for them. On the other hand, women who felt that caring for an infirm grandmother was a burden or granddaughters who felt guilty for not helping their grandmother more may initially experience the loss as a relief, and begin to mourn only months later.

The Loss of a Multifaceted Relationship

A grandmother may fill several roles in an adult granddaughter's life: grandmother, adviser, confidante, great-grandmother to her children. These are all separate roles, and need to be individually recognized and mourned. Lucy remembers how the friendship component of her relationship with her grandmother was the one hardest for her to let go of. "I remember waking up the morning after my grandmother died and going outside," she recalls. "It was one of those really interesting spring days where it was warm and breezy, just beautiful. Those were the kind of days when I would call up my nana and we would chitchat for a while. I thought about calling her, and then I thought about how I couldn't do that anymore. That was one of the most profound things I remember about the first few months after her death, not having that long-distance relationship with her anymore. Most of our bond was based upon it. It's been six years now, and I still go out on spring days and think about calling my nana, and I have to remind myself I can't."

The Realignment of the Female Line

When the eldest member of the lineage dies, those beneath her all get bumped up a seat. The mother, accustomed to being in the middle of two generations, now sits at the top; the granddaughter who once sat underneath two generations may sense, for the first time, the significance of the spot beneath her. Some granddaughters who are not yet mothers speak of the desire to have a child at this time. It's a purely psychological realignment, subtly urging a woman to reconsider her slot in the family and adjust her expectations and self-perception accordingly. Disorientation and acting out can occur when she's not emotionally ready for this change. If her mother predeceased her grandmother, the disappearance of what previously felt like a sturdy roof above a granddaughter may now leave her feeling vulnerable and exposed.

The Loss of a Direct Connection to One's Childhood

The loss of a beloved grandmother, to either death or mental disability, brings an adult granddaughter face-to-face with her emotional tie to her childhood and her ever-loosening grip on the girl she was then. When a grandmother dies, her memories of the granddaughter as a child go with her. Who else now will remember her as a girl who could never do wrong? Who else in the world will ever find such delight in merely serving her food? With whom else, unless she becomes a grandmother one day, will she ever share that pure, safe spiritual bond that she once had with her grandmother? The subsequent sale of a grandmother's house may also be emotionally difficult for a granddaughter, marking the living end of an association with a place that was familiar, safe, and warm. "My grandmother's house in the Bronx was exactly the same when she moved three years ago as it was thirty years before," says twenty-six-year-old Donna. "The furniture . . . you'd walk in and you'd feel like you were in the forties. I didn't want her to sell it. When I was a kid, I'd be surrounded by all this chaos outside in the city and I'd walk into her house and feel like I was home. I miss the place so much."

The Passing of an Era

For many granddaughters, the maternal grandmother represents a source of family heritage, a tie to the country of origin, or a link to religious tradition. My grandmother's death meant the passing of the last Orthodox Jew in the family, the last member who could speak fluent Yiddish, and the first woman among us who'd been born in the United States. We're no longer made up of Polish-Americans or Americanized Poles. We're now just simply Americans.

Like Helie Lee earlier in this section, granddaughters who see their grandmothers aging often run a mad race to collect their stories, knowing that the time between the moment they recognize the value of their grandmother's experience and the moment they lose living access to it may not last long. Though other family members may be able to recount dates and names and places for us when called upon to do so, no one else can explain exactly what a grandmother thought the moment she first saw her husband, or what the flowers outside the church smelled like on her wedding day, or how she reacted when she received news that her son was coming home from war.

I've met granddaughters who've made audiotapes of their grandmothers' stories, who've put them on film, even written short stories and poems inspired by their grandmothers' lives, attempting to capture the essence of the woman in artifacts and mediums that will live on. It's not a completely selfless act. A grandmother's history is a granddaughter's history too. "Mother of my mother" is just another way of saying "the source of me."

"Granddaughters who go looking for their grandmothers' stories are looking for a way of seeing life, a philosophy of life, one could say, that's intrinsically theirs, that doesn't belong to the culture," Naomi Lowinsky explains. "Once you reach back to the grandmother level, and the great-grandmother level, you're getting into the soul of the family. You really don't know your own soul until you can place it in the soul of your family. And that requires knowing history."

When I finally accepted, in 1989, that my grandmother's mind had begun an irreversible retreat, I tried to preserve some of her stories on tape. Under the pretext that I was collecting family anecdotes for a graduate school project — because my grandmother would not have thought her childhood stories otherwise worth telling to me as an adult — I dialed her number in Mount Vernon, reciting the antiquated letters-and-numbers prefix, MO 4, to myself as I pressed the corresponding buttons on my Touch-Tone phone.

"Do you remember," I asked, partway into our conversation, "telling me the story about your doll when I was a little girl? About how you cut the hair off your doll?"

"Yes. I told you that?"

"You told me that story several times. Can you tell it to me again?"

"Well, the hair got messed up. You know, how a doll's hair gets messed up and you can't comb it. So I wanted to comb it and I cut it and I messed it all up. But I didn't even remember that. I can't imagine telling it to you so many times when I barely remember it now."

"You told me you did it because you thought the hair would grow back."

"I did? Well, I don't remember that."

"You told me your parents didn't have money to buy a new doll."

"No, we didn't have money for a new doll," she said thoughtfully. "I thought it would grow back? That was cute." We sat quietly then, both breathing into our phones. I could imagine her sitting in her darkened living room, perched on the edge of the couch, working her lips in between her teeth. When she spoke again, it was with a tone of bemused resignation. "Hm," she says. "I didn't remember that about the doll. You remember better than I."

Grandma, your memories live inside me now. The imaginative little girl in Newark, the sixteen-year-old legal secretary with dark red hair. They superimpose upon my memories of you. Reading me *The Poky Little Puppy*, banging on our front door, clutching the steering wheel and staring straight ahead. Ah-beh-cuh-duh. Heh-heh-heh. I no longer know which stories are yours and which are mine. Here is my secret: Now I tell them all for you.

20

Mount Vernon: 1996

It's a Thursday afternoon, and the drive from my apartment in Greenwich Village to my grandmother's house in Mount Vernon takes only forty minutes. My red Jeep emerges from the city's honking, swarming hive and plunges into the leafy, bright canvas of an October Westchester afternoon. Quicker than I can adjust, I've crossed into another dimension, of Tudor houses and expansive front lawns and stately maple trees arcing out over the road. When I turn left onto my grandmother's street, my tiny brownstone apartment in New York feels not so much twenty miles behind me as twenty-five years ahead. What am I doing, driving this car? I'm only six years old.

There I am, playing a makeshift game of hop-scotch on the front-path flagstones with my sister, using maple-seed boomerangs as place-holders. My new black patent leather shoes slip and slide against the blue and gray planes. "Look, I'm a tightrope walker!" I tell my sister, trying to balance along the border between path and grass. The house vibrates and hums behind us. My grandmother leans out beyond the front screen door and calls, "Gi-irls! Din-ner!" in her high, sweet voice. In the background we hear my mother calling a distant singsong "Ju-lee-an!" toward my father, who's smoking a cigarette on the back porch. My sister and I trip over our shoes, always purchased a half size too big, as we head for the door. My grandmother, smiling impishly, grabs both of us at the threshold, one under each arm, and pulls us into a tight hug. "Oooh-*ooh!*" she exclaims, squeezing us one notch tighter with her voice. "Grandma, I can't breathe!" I shout into the wool of her waist, but she's caught up in her rapture, oblivious to my sister's squealing "Let me go! Let me go!"

Today in 1996 the yard is unnaturally quiet, like an abandoned movie set. As I park the car and stride across the lawn, a distant dog barks once, then three times. My black cowboy boots make a few dull thuds against the flagstones, a path I've walked on hundreds of times before. I breathe in and out evenly before I step up to the closed door. The round bell doesn't work, and the screen on the screen door has been missing for years. I reach inside and knock on wood and wait for Rita, the home aide, to answer.

It's the fifth time I've come to see my grandmother since I moved back to New York in 1992. The first time was a few weeks after I returned. On that particular weekday afternoon, I was driving east on the Cross-County Expressway on my way to New Rochelle to do an interview for my first book when the roadside landmarks started looking unexpectedly familiar. On my right, the old J. Wanamaker's department store building, where I was periodically steered through the children's department in search of a party dress. The Tudor-style apartment building up on a hill to the left, the one I used to gaze at from the backseat of my parents' station wagon and wonder what it might be like to have friends my age living right down the hall. And then the exit onto Columbus Avenue, the one that led us beneath the freeway underpass, around four corners, and down the street to my grandmother's house. *Over the hill and through the woods, to grandmother's house we go,* the echo of my mother's wavering soprano chimed from the passenger seat beside me.

My grandmother's house. I knew I should go to see her. When we'd talked by phone three weeks earlier — a halting conversation punctuated by her shouts of "Wha?" — she'd had to be reminded who I was. I knew I should go.

So on the way to New Rochelle I dialed her number. When she was living with her sisters, you had to let the phone ring twenty times before someone heard it and made her way across the room to pick it up. This time it was answered on the fourth ring. I didn't expect it to be my grandmother, and it wasn't. It was Rita, the aide who had moved in to care for either Rea or Nell, I don't remember which, and stayed, nursing each of the three elderly women through their final days. (Rita! Was there ever a kinder woman?)

319

"Al-LO?" she said, in a lilting Jamaican accent. She also couldn't place me right away. "Hope!" I shouted, even though my grandmother, not Rita, was the one who couldn't hear. "I'm Mrs. Rosenberg's oldest grandchild!" Rita scanned her memory and landed on a Thanksgiving dinner three years past. "Ah, Hope!" she said. "Yes, come! Come!"

When I arrived, my grandmother seemed to know who I was. Her hearing still worked within close range, and she could see objects if they weren't too far away. So I sat up close next to her on the slate-blue couch. She rested the palms of her hands on her knees and perched expectantly at the couch's edge, staring straight ahead.

"How are you feeling, Grandma?" I asked her after we'd settled on the couch, enunciating my words so clearly you could insert a period after each one.

Seeing her this sedate, and having to project all my words directly into her ear, made me slide right into the authoritative and patronizing speech pattern I'd adopted around her as an adult. I would automatically dumb down to the simplest language possible, with the kind of loud, brash tone that would prompt someone who's hard-of-hearing to protest "I'm deaf, not *stupid*." I hated the way I sounded, but I couldn't control it. Ever since my grandmother's hearing started to fail a few years before, my voice had started taking on the steely edge I remembered hearing in my mother's, as I tried to keep my speech as clear and straightforward as possible, with little room for confusion or dissent. There was nothing natural about these exchanges. On my end, at least, they were deliberate and self-conscious and not very reciprocal at all.

"Not bad," she said. "How about you?"

"I'm working hard on the book now."

"That's good. A book about what?"

"A book about my mother."

"Your mother was a wonderful woman," she said.

There was a long pause, during which I tried to think of something else to say, and then she asked about the baby. "What baby?" I said.

"The baby," she repeated. Possibly she was mistaking me for my aunt, who had a two-year-old? "No, Grandma," I told her. "I'm Hope."

"Hope is your granDOTTer!" Rita shouted from the corner. My grandmother looked genu-inely confused. "Wha?" she said, gazing from side to side. "Your granDOTTer!" Rita shouted again. The room was warm and dim, and particles of dust swirled in the thin stripes of sunlight that pushed through the lowered Venetian blinds. Watching them made me dizzy. "The *baby*," my grandmother repeated, a little desperately this time, and I couldn't find the energy to contradict.

I once met a woman whose grandmother had had Alzheimer's disease and believed she was in Israel as she lay dying in a hospital bed in Queens. I must have winced in sympathy when I heard this story, because the granddaughter immediately tried to clarify her point of view. "I never thought of it as tragic," she explained, "because my grandmother was happy. She'd always wanted to die in Israel, and she got her wish."

I aimed my mouth toward my grandmother's ear. "The baby's doing fine," I shouted. "Growing up so fast. She's very healthy!"

"That's good," she said, and relaxed into the sofa. Her youngest grandchild. Happy and healthy. What more could she want? Recent snapshots of her grandchildren, my cousins, sat propped up on the marble and mahogany coffee table in front of us, their smiles directed toward the couch. There was one of my cousin Meri at a sorority formal with her boyfriend. Meri, who in the photo must have been . . . twenty? Twenty-one?

Impossible. Meri is only . . . two. And I'm nine. My sister is six. There we are, sitting on the floor in front of the mahogany desk strumming the Autoharp my grandmother keeps in one of the spare bedrooms. My two-year-old brother is crawling on the carpet, his head dangerously close to the underside of the coffee table. My mother, grandmother, and aunt are looking through some papers in the dining room, trying to keep us all in view. "Where's Glenn?" my mother calls, craning her neck in our direction. Meri is standing by the coffee table, watching him crawl underneath. "He's here!" she says, pointing down at him.

There's a moment of silence and then an explosion of activity. My grandmother comes rushing into the room — *Oh! Oh!* — with her arms stretched out. My mother and my aunt are close behind. "Did you hear that? Did you hear that?" my grandmother calls out. "What happened?" my sister asks, in a sudden panic. "He's here!" Meri says again, grinning. It's her first full sentence. My grandmother hugs her and my mother claps her hands. We all applaud. *Yay, Meri! Yay!*

Rita coughed and the memory popped like a soap bubble. I was back in my grandmother's living room, where applause emanated from the television droning alongside us, an afternoon talk show with people lined up in chairs onstage. Someone was accusing someone else of something. It didn't look promising. The voices escalated to a thin screech. I stood and walked around the living room purposefully, taking in the cluttered desk, the twenty-year-old family pictures crowded on top of the mantel, the portrait of my mother as a toddler banging on a piano keyboard, my grandfather's empty leather recliner, and the rabbit ears balanced on top of the old sixteen-inch TV. Something about the flimsy TV stand made me feel irrepressibly sad. I had the sudden urge to rush out to my car, but at the same time I felt drawn to the room, to the couch, to my grandmother in this state, and I knew I would remain there as long as I could, until her eyelids started drooping and Rita politely informed me it was time for her to get some sleep.

Within a few weeks, my grandmother lost the ability to talk on the phone. Despite a new hearing aid, she couldn't hear what I was saying, even when I shouted my name so loudly that my neighbor started banging on the wall. And I couldn't bear to hear her asking "Wha? Wha? Who is it?" before giving up and handing over the phone. So I started asking Rita for updates, and keeping track of her progress with one of my aunts. But I didn't visit again. *I'm busy,* I told myself. *I've got a book to write, and besides, just the other month when I started running out of money I had to sell my car. I'm hardly ever in town. And most of the time she doesn't even know who I am.* I had more excuses than a cornered politician. *My aunts are making sure she's well taken care of. It's my mother's job, damn it; not mine. I'm too emotionally fragile for this. I'm too young.*

It's awful to watch someone you love slip into dementia. There's no other way to say it. It's awful. I'd always imagined that the day my grandmother stopped arguing with me, the day she stopped endlessly pressing her point, would be a day of victory, a deep exhalation of relief. But the only relief I felt as my grandmother deteriorated was the kind that came from knowing that my aunts were taking care of my grandmother and that I, as just a granddaughter, could easily disappear.

And then. Meri's wedding in June of this year, an elegant, beautiful affair. I hadn't expected my grandmother to be able to attend, but when I walked in through the country club's doors I saw Rita in the vestibule, with my grandmother in a wheelchair at her side. She looked so vulnerable. So small. When I shouted "Hello, Grandma. It's Hope!" into her ear, and bent down to kiss her soft, sagging cheek, expecting no recognition, no response, she said, *"I want* you *to get married,"* into my ear. I tried to keep my face composed, but I failed.

So now it's October and I'm standing here in my black cowboy boots, waiting for Rita to answer the door. I don't know what to call the way I'm feeling right now. Edgy, but it's more than that. Apprehensive? Reluctant? Sorrowful? Guilty? Ashamed? Emotions are situational, not literal: adjectives fail me here. It's the same way I felt whenever I returned to my father's house after my mother died. I didn't want to be there, but I didn't want to be anywhere else, either. Pulled in two equally forceful directions at once, I had no choice but to stand still.

Rita greets me at the door and together we help my grandmother from her bed to the couch. Her walk is more of a shuffle, with her arms held directly in front of her, like a caricature of a hesitant sleepwalker. Her breathing sounds more labored than it did a month ago. Around the time of the wedding, I found out she'd recently been diagnosed with breast cancer at the age of eighty-nine. When my forty-one-year-old mother was first diagnosed in 1980, my grandmother had asked, "Why couldn't God have given it to *me?*" Surgery is out of the question for her at this point; tamoxifen and monitoring are the kindest options.

I don't know how much my grandmother enjoys my visits, if at all. Last time I hugged her hard just before I left. "I enjoyed that," she said, so I hugged her again. Sometimes she seems more agitated as I'm leaving than she was when I arrived. But I keep coming back. I'm not sure at this point if it's for her or for me. Usually we have two simultaneous conversations, with me relaying news I can't tell if she hears and her asking questions I can't understand. Last time I visited, she spent an hour asking, "Where is the house? What should I do about the house?" I didn't know how to respond. "What do you mean, 'Where is the house?'" I shouted into her right ear. "You're *in* the house! The house is right here!" I lifted her foot and placed it firmly down on the hardwood floor. "Here! See? You're *in* the house." And then, after a brief pause, she asked, "Where is the house?"

Finally, after the sixth or seventh round of this, I relented. "All right, Grandma," I said, exasperated. "You want advice about what to do with the house? I'll tell you what to do with the house. *Don't do anything with the house.* Tom left you the house. You keep the house. All right? *That's* what I think you should do with the house."

And then, after another pause, "Where is the house?"

I had the distinct feeling I was out of my league

here, trying to apply ordinary reasoning to a disease with a complex illogic of its own. Three hours later, when I stood up to leave, I kissed her on the cheek and told her I'd be back in a few weeks.

"You're leaving already?" she said. "But you didn't even give me any advice."

"I *did* give you advice," I said, an automatic protest.

"You told me to keep the house," she said. "What kind of advice is that?"

This is what I try to convey to people about my grandmother: that she's always been more complicated than she seems. Whenever I felt I'd finally gotten a handle on her, just when I'd finally convinced myself that she was either mentally intact or not, she'd go and act in a manner so diametrically opposed to my assessment that it would call all of her prior behaviors — and my powers of evaluation — into question. It was a tricky and effective mind game: Instead of doubting her, I started to doubt my own judgment about her. I existed in a state of constant uncertainty with my grandmother, never quite sure how to perceive her and therefore how to act.

Even now, when I'm otherwise convinced of her dementia, she'll have moments of startling clarity that make me stop and reconsider. They happen without warning, and often with unsettling prescience. Driving over this morning I was thinking about my mother's old bedroom in my grandmother's house, and how I'd love to have her dresser, then immediately felt ashamed for having even thought of such a thing while my grandmother was still alive. When I first arrived at the house that day she was upset by my presence at first. "You've come to take away my furniture," she kept insisting, rubbing her fingers together and turning her head away. Coincidence? Telepathy? Or a border where intuition and insanity intersect?

Something else is bothering her now, but I can't determine what it is. "I'm so afraid," she began saying shortly after the furniture episode, but my repeated inquiries — *Of what, Grandma? Can you tell me what you're afraid of?* — don't elicit a response. "I don't know." Rita shrugs. "She's been saying that all week, but I don't know what she means." After a while I'm frustrated too, helplessly watching my grandmother try to communicate a thought that keeps getting stuck on the way. I'm debating whether I should stay or go when Rita walks back to the kitchen to get a drink and my grandmother says it again: "I'm so afraid."

"Afraid of what, Grandma?" I say, expecting nothing. It's like a routine, by now.

And then, very simply, she spits it out. "Of *death*."

Oh. *Oh*. I open my mouth to tell her she's not dying, that there's nothing to be afraid of, but all that comes out is a little *ah*. My impulse, as always, is to calm her down, but this time pacifying her feels like a dreadfully wrong response. Yet the kind of emotional connection my grandmother is asking for requires a kind of honesty that's never existed between us before. At least not from me.

It occurs to me in that moment as the television drones on in the background and Rita's glass makes a distant clink against the kitchen counter, that maybe my grandmother wants me, or whoever she thinks I am, to give it to her straight. Not to placate her, and not to force her back behind the safest fence. For the first time, I sense how lonely it must have been for her to keep trying, month after month, year after year, to have a dialogue with a granddaughter who never let a conversation exceed a certain boundary. I know how isolating it's been to be a granddaughter who never felt safe enough to share anything real.

All those years of placating my grandmother, all those times when I sacrificed the possibility of honest conversation for the sake of peace, now deliver me here: to this one moment where the turmoil of my grandmother's mind has quieted long enough for her to reach out with one extremely lucid and primal fear. I can join her in this temporary zone or I can let her disappear back in there alone. Either way, I know this instance of clarity won't last long.

I take my grandmother's hand. It's misshapen by arthritis, the knuckles wider than the nail beds. My mother's knuckles were just as wide, but she didn't live long enough for arthritis to resculpt her.

"I know, Grandma," I tell her. "I'm afraid of dying too."

She relaxes a little, and I take that as a signal that I'm in. Death's a scary concept, I tell her, and it's impossible sometimes to live without knowing what, if anything, comes next. Judaism doesn't help us out much here, I say. We've got to take it on faith. I can't tell if she understands me, but I keep going. I tell her I hope there's such a thing as an afterlife, and if there is, she'll be reunited with everyone she loved and lost: Rea and Nell, her sisters; Murray, her older brother; Tom, her husband; Marcia, my mother; and her parents, Max and Ida.

"Max and Ida?" she interrupts me. "How do you know about Max and Ida?"

"*You* told me about them. When I was little."

"I did?"

Max was a religious man, I tell her, who sold junk for a living. Ida was a wonderful cook. They came from Russia to Boston, where she was born, I explain, and she grew up in Newark with two brothers and two sisters. They lived in an apartment with three bedrooms, one for the boys and one for the girls. I tell her that when she was a child she once cut the hair off her doll.

I hand my grandmother's history back to her like my penance, the wayward granddaughter come to make amends. I reconstruct her past through stories I've heard and photographs I've seen. She sits quietly and listens; she doesn't argue or contradict. I tell her how she worked as a legal secretary, that she once wanted to become a lawyer herself. I tell her how she met my grandfather at a hotel in the Catskills, and how he used to drive from the Bronx to Newark every weekend for their dates. The sun starts its descent, and Rita walks over to an end table and switches on a lamp. She turns down the volume on the television. I tell my grandmother about her honeymoon in Cuba, about how every night at dinner my grandfather wore a white suit. And on this quiet autumn afternoon, which is to be the last time I will see my grandmother alive, I think perhaps this is what it all comes down to: these few precious memories and a hand to hold at the end. It is nothing, and it is everything, and in these waning moments of my grandmother's life, it is the only meaningful gift I can think of to give.

Epilogue

My daughter was born on October 13, 1997, pulled out into a dim birthing room in the presence of five adults who badly needed some sleep. I hadn't spent those surreal gray hours in a hospital since I was seventeen years old, and I hadn't planned to spend them there again. But this time, instead of the muffled sobs of relatives and the background hum of institutional machines, there was screaming and sweating and swearing and nobody, thankfully, was thinking about death. The first words my daughter heard from her mother were "Is it a girl?" and from her father "I can't tell." I lifted my head as the doctor propped Maya into a sitting position, her mouth stretched into an angry howl, the slimy, ropy umbilical cord stretching like a purple leash from her stomach back to the birth canal, and I saw the unmistakable crease of skin between her legs. I had the sudden urge to grab the cord and yank the placenta free. The nurse wiped the baby dry and placed her on my chest; I traced the outline of her tiny shoulder blades with my index fingers and tasted her forehead with my tongue. She raised her head and blinked. And at that unforgettable moment, when I might have been awed by the miracle of birth, or apologizing to my husband for punching him in the chest and yelling "I *am* pushing!" as I forced the baby out, or wondering how the hell a newborn could lift its head like that, I was thinking this instead: that my daughter's time of birth missed my mother's time of death by exactly ten minutes on the clock, and thank God my grandmother never knew her first great-grandchild was born on the thirteenth.

They appear like this without warning, my grandmother and my mother, speaking to me in unexpected ways. They act as my domestic Greek chorus, reminding me to light the menorah, make my house presentable for guests, and keep my husband and child well fed. Some would call them my conscience. Yet, occasionally they're discordant, continuing to disagree even after death. "Isn't it too chilly in the house to bathe the baby?" my grandmother asks, wringing her hands as I start to fill the tub. "Oh, for God's sake, Mother," my mother says, hands resting on her hips. "The child needs a bath and it's the middle of December. We can't postpone baths all winter." And so I, still trying to be the peacemaker, drag the space heater into the bathroom so Maya can be warm *and* clean, which is, I realize as she splashes happily in the tub, exactly the right compromise to have made.

According to Louise Kaplan, Ph.D., a psychologist in New York City and the author of *No Voice Is Ever Wholly Lost*, when a loved one dies, a mourner restores that person in the form of an

333

inner presence — if not precisely a spirit or a ghost, she says, then an aspect of ego or conscience, an ideal, a passion. "Over the course of time, these inner presences may undergo further development and revision, but they will never leave us," she writes. "We can call on our inner presences to join us in the morning over coffee and rolls, to help us fold the laundry properly, to guide us in planting a garden, to inspire a painting, to give us the courage to protest social injustice. The human dialogue — that which makes living a life worthwhile — goes on. In the absence of this dialogue, we are lost."

Without any older women in my family to guide me as a mother, I rely on this inner dialogue as well as on instinct and memory and the residual advice my grandmother and mother left behind. During Maya's first year I pored over the baby books my grandmother kept for my mother and my mother kept for me, searching for clues about normal development, secure only when I found precursors of Maya's late achievements, early teething behaviors, or growth plateaus in my grandmother's or mother's comforting script. True to form, my grandmother kept extensive records of my mother's childhood illnesses and vaccines; my mother catalogued every car trip I made and every gift I received for my entire first year. I ink in every measurement, every milestone, adopting the same child-centered voice my grandmother and mother used, as if the baby were writing each entry —

First tooth: March 20, 1998. After we visited Stacey and Gabrielle, Mommy noticed one of my front bottom teeth had pushed through the gum. No wonder I was so cranky the night before!!! — just in case one day Maya has to refer to her book for guidance in lieu of me.

It was there, in the book my grandmother kept of my mother's first year, that I found a possible explanation for Maya's surprising nine-and-a-half-pound birth weight. (My mother, according to my grandmother's notation, was a large newborn as well.) And though infant-care practices have changed considerably over the years, there is a certain uniformity to the three books' details. My mother, myself, and my daughter: all early talkers and average walkers, all unusually tall throughout our toddler years. We all liked carrots and egg yolks, all cut our bottom right teeth first. I keep the three books stacked together in a drawer, like a trinity of early female development. When I lay them open side by side, they blend into one another, one daughter taking on characteristics of the next, each mother assuming the previous one's voice.

Do I see connections where there are none, trying to place my daughter and me in the security of a family line? It's possible. But then, how do I explain the way boundaries between us blur even without my involvement? Above the living room fireplace in my home hangs the photograph of my mother as a toddler banging on a piano. The child in the photo is pale-skinned, chubby-fingered, a round face framed by short, dark curls. Everyone who walks through my door thinks it's Maya. The resemblance is that striking. Lately, while I answer e-mails in the morning, Maya has taken to sorting through the bag of family photos in my office and separating out the ones of me as a small child. *"Maya,"* she proclaims, pressing her little index finger against each tiny face. *"Maya."*

I would be lying if I said I didn't feel a small twinge of satisfaction when this happens — doesn't every mother hope her daughter will identify with her in some way? — but I fight the impulse to encourage it. Mothering a daughter is a tremendous challenge already, trying to find the proper balance between remaining separate and allowing a natural and inevitable merging to occur. My grandmother and my mother struggled with this for my mother's whole life, establishing the model for my mother's relationship with me. I find myself wondering what Maya will lose (or gain) by not having the chance to observe such interaction between my mother and me. On the one hand, she will grow up without an ongoing model for the adult mother–daughter relationship. On the other hand, especially because I never had an adult relationship with my mother, my daughter and I will be freer to create a relationship of our own.

For Maya, I believe, the more pressing issue will be to grow up without a maternal grandmother to visit, admire, listen to, learn from, push against, or love. Knowing my mother's mother taught me about empathy and compassion, about exhibiting patience and managing ambivalence, about the virtues and the dangers of loving selflessly and without restraint. Yes, she could be difficult and stubborn and exasperating, but she was also the most powerful source of unconditional acceptance and the strongest promoter of family unity I have ever known. What might I have missed if I hadn't known her? How differently might I have turned out?

My daughter is fortunate to have a paternal grandmother who adores her, but the connection just isn't the same. Maternal grandmothers and granddaughters are part of the same direct physical and psychic line through which feminine identification flows without the interruption of a male "other." "There's something so profound about your daughter having a child," Naomi Lowinsky says, "that if the channels are open for a good connection it's a revolution in the grandmother's life and the mother's life. And the granddaughter feels that. She feels that charge." I'm reminded of a story my friend Carin told me a few years ago when she gave birth to twins. Carin and her mother had never had an emotionally close relationship, but toward the end of Carin's pregnancy her mother was adamant about flying eight hundred miles to help with the babies, as eager as any prospective new grandmother would be. "The thing was," Carin said, "my mother had already been a grandmother for more than a dozen years to my brother's kids. When I pointed that out to her, she got very serious and said, 'Yes, but they're not my *daughter's* children.' "

Women are born twice, the poet Anne Sexton wrote, and I once interpreted that to mean first from their mothers and again through their daughters. But now I think women are born many more times than that, three times, four times, for as long as their maternal lines remain intact. When my husband and I first saw the blurry physical evidence on the ultrasound screen that Maya was a girl, he said, "I don't mean to scare you, but that's where your grandchildren are going to come from." It was both an overwhelming and a comforting thought. We are all inside one another, like the painted wooden Russian matrushka dolls my grandmother bought for me when I was six. I see this with startling clarity now as I watch Maya sitting at her toy piano. She bangs on the keys with her tiny hands and we tunnel together through time. She is a child and I am her mother, she is me and I am my mother, she is my mother and I am my grandmother. This is our family album. My grandmother and my mother live on through my daughter as surely as they live on in me. Listen to her play. They are her inspiration. She is their song.

Bibliography

Alcott, Louisa May. *Little Women*. New York: Tor Books, 1994.

Allison, Dorothy. *Bastard Out of Carolina*. New York: Dutton, 1992.

Angelou, Maya. *I Know Why the Caged Bird Sings*. New York: Bantam Books, 1971.

Atwood, Margaret. *Selected Poems II*. Boston: Houghton Mifflin, 1987.

Banner, Lois W. *In Full Flower*. New York: Vintage Books, 1993.

Barker, Philip. *Basic Family Therapy*. Baltimore: University Park Press, 1981.

————. *Basic Family Therapy. 3rd ed.* New York: Oxford University Press, 1992.

Bassoff, Evelyn. *Mothers and Daughters*. New York: Plume, 1989.

Bengtson, Vern L., and Joan F. Robertson. *Grandparenthood*. Beverly Hills, Calif.: Sage Publications, 1985.

————, and W. Andrew Achenbaum. *The Changing Contract Across Generations*. New York: Aldine de Gruyter, 1993.

Bowlby, John. *A Secure Base*. New York: Basic Books, 1990.

Boynton, Marilyn Irwin, and Mary Dell. *Goodbye Mother, Hello Woman*. Oakland,

Calif.: New Harbinger Publications, 1995.

Chodorow, Nancy. *The Reproduction of Mothering.* Berkeley: University of California Press, 1978.

Cohler, Bertram J., and Henry U. Grunebaum. *Mothers, Grandmothers, and Daughters.* New York: John Wily & Sons, 1981.

Cournos, Francine. *City of One.* New York: W. W. Norton & Co., 1999.

De Beauvoir, Simone. *The Coming of Age.* New York: W. W. Norton & Co., 1996.

Deutsch, Helene. *The Psychology of Women.* Vols. I and II. New York: Grune & Stratton, 1944.

Framo, James. *Family-of-Origin Therapy.* New York: Brunner/Mazel, 1992.

Freeman, David S. *Multigenerational Family Therapy.* New York: Haworth Press, 1992.

Gibbons, Kaye. *Charms for the Easy Life.* New York: Avon Books, 1994.

Haley, Jay. *Problem-Solving Therapy.* San Francisco: Jossey-Bass, 1978.

Harris, Anita M. *Broken Patterns.* Detroit: Wayne State University Press, 1995.

Heilbrun, Carolyn G. *Reinventing Womanhood.* New York: W. W. Norton & Co., 1979.

Hendricks, Jon, ed. *The Ties of Later Life.* Amityville, N.Y.: Baywood Publishing, 1995.

Horowitz, Joy. *Tessie and Pearlie.* New York: Scribner, 1996.

Ione, Carole. *Pride of Family.* New York: Avon Books, 1991.

Jonas, Susan, and Marilyn Nissenson. *Friends for

Life. New York: William Morrow & Company, 1997.

Kack-Brice, Valerie. *For She Is the Tree of Life*. Emeryville, Calif.: Conari Press, 1994.

Kornhaber, Arthur. *Grandparents/Grandchildren*. New Brunswick, N.J.: Transaction Publishers, 1985.

————. *Grandparent Power!* New York: Crown Publishers, 1994.

————. *Contemporary Grandparenting*. Thousand Oaks, Calif.: Sage, 1996.

Lee, Helie. *Still Life With Rice*. New York: Scribner, 1996.

Lessard, Suzannah. *The Architect of Desire*. New York: The Dial Press, 1996.

Lowinsky, Naomi Ruth. *The Motherline*. Tarcher/Perigee, 1992.

Mead, Margaret. *Blackberry Winter*. New York: Kodansha America, 1995.

Morrison, Toni. *Beloved*. New York: Plume, 1998.

Niethammer, Carolyn. *Daughters of the Earth*. New York: Touchstone, 1977.

Quindlen, Anna. *Living Out Loud*. New York: Ivy Books, 1988.

Rando, Therese A. *How to Go on Living When Someone You Love Dies*. New York: Bantam, 1991.

————. *Treatment of Complicated Mourning*. Champaign, Ill.: Research Press, 1993.

Sexton, Anne. *The Complete Poems*. Boston: Houghton Mifflin, 1981.

Smith, Peter K., ed. *The Psychology of Grand-parenthood*. London: Routledge, 1991.

Tan, Amy. *The Joy Luck Club*. New York: Ivy Books, 1989.

Walker, Barbara. *The Crone*. San Francisco: HarperCollins, 1985.

Wharton, Edith. *The Age of Innocence*. New York: Tor, 1998.

Notes

"Sons branch out, but/one woman leads to another . . .": Margaret Atwood, "Five Poems for Grandmothers," *Selected Poems II* (Boston: Houghton Mifflin, 1987), 14.

Introduction

13 . . . part of the magic between . . . : Arthur Kornhaber, *Grandparents/Grandchildren* (New Brunswick, N.J.: Transaction Publishers, 1985), 15.

15 As Carole Ione writes . . . : Carole Ione, *Pride of Family* (New York: Avon Books, 1991), 114.

17 "the familiar dance of . . .": Anna Quindlen, *Living Out Loud* (New York: Ivy Books, 1988), 214.

18 Particularly when a grandmother functions . . . : personal interview with Sandra Halperin, Ph.D., psychologist in Auburn, Alabama, January 31, 1997.

18 . . . between 1970 and 1993 . . . : Arlene F. Saluter, Marital Status and Living Arrangements: March 1993, U.S. Bureau of the Census, Current Population Reports, Series P20–478. U.S. Govern-

ment Printing Office, Washington, D.C., 1994, Table H., xiv.

19 Today at least 1.6 million children ... ibid.

19 An additional one million children ... ibid.

19 ... that women are more likely to have ... : Ann R. Eisenberg, "Grandchildren's Perspectives on Relationships with Grandparents: The Influence of Gender Across Generations," *Sex Roles* 19 (1988): 205; Boaz Kahana and Eva Kahana, "Grandparenthood from the Perspective of the Developing Grandchild," *Developmental Psychology* 3 (1970); Timothy S. Hartshorne and Guy J. Manaster, "The Relationship with Grandparents: Contact, Importance, Role Conception," *International Journal of Aging and Human Development* 15 (1982); Gregory E. Kennedy, "College Students' Expectations of Grandparent and Grandchild Role Behaviors," *The Gerontologist* 30 (1990); Valerie Hyde and Ian Gibbs, "A Very Special Relationship: Granddaughters' Perceptions of Grandmothers," *Ageing and Society* 13 (1993).

20 *... women from Asian families ... : Kumiko fujimura-Fanselow and Atsuko Kameda, eds. *Japanese Women: New Feminist Perspectives on the Past, Present, and Future* (New York: The Feminist Press, 1995), 213–228. ...

and rural children raised on farms . . . : Valarie King and Glen H. Elder, Jr., "American Children View Their Grandparents: Linked Lives Across Three Rural Generations," *Journal of Marriage and the Family* 57 (February 1995): 168.

PART I: Grandma and Me
1. Through a Child's Eyes

41 More than anyone else in a family . . . : Kornhaber, *Grandparents/Grandchildren*, xxiv.

41 "I edged forward until . . .": Dorothy Allison, *Bastard Out of Carolina*. (New York: Dutton, 1992), 20–21.

44 Instead, she goes about her ordinary . . . : ibid., 133.

45 Very young children . . . : Kahana and Kahana, 100–3.

45 By age eight . . . : ibid.

46 A few years later . . . : ibid.

46 By age twelve . . . : ibid.

48 . . . . an older child's feelings of closeness . . . : Sarah H. Matthews and Jetse Sprey, "Adolescents' Relationships with Grandparents: An Empirical Contribution to Conceptual Clarification," *Journal of Gerontology* 40 (1985): 624; Chrystal Carol Barranti, "The Maternal Grandmother/Grandchild Rela-

tionship: Relationship Quality as Perceived by the Young Adult Grandchild," diss., University of Georgia, 1985, 90; Marc D. Baronowski, "Grandparent-Adolescent Relations: Beyond the Nuclear Family," *Adolescence* 17 (1982): 578.

48 *Matthews and Sprey, 624–25.

48 ". . . three-quarters of the women interviewed . . .": *Mother of My Mother* 1996–1998 survey of 187 women in 29 U.S. states, Britain, and Canada (81 percent Caucasian; 11 percent African-American; 4 percent Asian-American; 2 percent Hispanic-American; 2 percent other) between the ages of 19 and 70, cross-reference of questions 15 and 27.

49 A 1987 study of 126 triads . . . : L. Thompson and A. Walker, "Mothers as Mediators of Intimacy Between Grandmothers and their Young Adult Granddaughters," *Family Relations* 36 (1987): 72–76.

50 The importance of physical contact . . . : personal interviews with Dr. Arthur Kornhaber, October 28, 1996, and Dr. Vern Bengtson, February 12, 1997.

51 Seventy-eight percent of the women . . . : *Mother of My Mother* survey, cross-reference of questions 15 and 19.

3. The Eternal Grandmother

58 "Perhaps nothing is more valuable . . .":
Margaret Mead, *Blackberry Winter*
(New York: Kodansha America, 1995),
45, 54.

59 Marion's grandmother became the . . . :
John Bowlby, *A Secure Base* (New York:
Basic Books, 1998), 11–12.

68 Most children don't have what's called . . . :
Maria Nagy, "The Child's Theories
Concerning Death," *Journal of Genetic
Psychology* 73 (1948): 3–27; Richard A.
Jenkins and John C. Cavanaugh, "Examining the Relationship Between the
Development of the Concept of Death
and Overall Cognitive Development,"
Omega 16 (1985–86): 193–94; Sandra
E. Candy-Gibbs, Kay Colby Sharp, and
Craig J. Petrun, "The Effects of Age,
Object, and Cultural/Religious Background on Children's Concepts of
Death," *Omega* 15 (1984–85): 329–32.

68 This adultlike concept of death . . . : Jenkins
and Cavanaugh, 194.

68 Those are roughly the same years . . . :
See Sol Altschul and Helen Beiser,
"The Effect of Early Parent Loss on Future Parenthood," in *Parenthood: A
Psychodynamic Perspective*, Rebecca S.
Cohen, ed. (New York: Guilford Press,
1984), 175.

69 Although many bereavement centers . . . : personal communication, JoAnn Zimmerman, director, Amanda the Panda, Des Moines, Iowa; Donna Schurmann, executive director, The Dougy Center, Portland, Oregon.

4. Conflict and the Emerging Self

75 "Then, when Grandma was mad . . .": Francine Cournos, *City of One* (New York: W. W. Norton & Co., 1999), 75.

PART II: The Three of Us
6. Adolescence

97 Ten- to twelve-year-olds still . . . : Edward Hoffman, "Young Adults' Relations with Their Grandparents: An Exploratory Study," *International Journal of Aging and Human Development* 10 (1979–80); A. Marcoen, "Children's Perceptions of Aged Persons and Grandparents," *International Journal of Behavioral Development* 2 (1979): 87–105, in Barranti, 6.

97 Grandmothers who felt adept . . . : Marcoen, in Barranti, 6.

97 . . . occasionally treating them with . . . : Lillian H. Robinson, "Grandparenting: Intergenerational Love and Hate," *Journal of the American Academy of Psychoanalysis* 17 (1989): 484–85.

97 As young teenagers make the shift . . . :
Baronowski, 576.

101 . . . the developmental stage when alienation . . . : Marcoen, in Barranti, 6

101 Granddaughters ages sixteen to eighteen
. . . : Baronowski, 579.

101 . . . and treat them with more consideration
and indulgence . . . : Marcoen, in Barranti, 6.

102 A 1976 survey of 920 girls . . . : G. Ko-
nopka, *Young Girls: A Portrait of Adolescence* (Englewood Cliffs, N.J.:
Prentice-Hall, 1976), in Mary Dellmann-
Jenkins, Diane Papalia, and Martha
Lopez, et. al., "Teenagers' Reported Interactions with Grandparents: Exploring the Extent of Alienation,"
Lifestyles 8 (1987): 37.

102 . . . and that their interactions with grandparents . . . : J. F. Robertson, "Interaction in Three-Generational Families,
Parents as Mediators: Toward a Theo-
retical Perspective," *International
Journal of Aging and Human Development* 6, 103–10.

7. Push and Pull

121 "Many mid-life women are reluctant . . .":
Evelyn Bassoff, *Mothers and Daughters:
Loving and Letting Go* (New York:
Plume, 1988), 215.

128 Grandmothers can play an important . . . : M. D. Baronowski, "Grandparent Adolescent Relations: Beyond the Nuclear Family," *Adolescence* 17 (1982): 580–81.

128 The information they share . . . : ibid.

128 Grandparents are living models of . . . : ibid.

129 Transmitting such knowledge about cultural . . . : ibid.

9. Three-Generational Triangles

138 "As Margaret Birch, the teenage narrator . . .": Kaye Gibbons, *Charms for the Easy Life* (New York: Avon Books, 1993), 104–5.

142 Psychologist Jay Haley identifies . . . : Jay Haley, *Problem-Solving Therapy* (San Francisco: Jossey-Bass, 1978), 110–11.

144 In this type of family system . . . : S. Minuchin et al., *Families of the Slums* (New York: Basic Books, 1967), in Haley, 110 fn.

144 If everyone agrees on this . . . : Haley, 132–33.

151 Alliances, connections between two . . . : David Freeman, *Multigenerational Family Therapy* (New York: Haworth Press, 1992), 44; Philip Barker, *Basic Family Therapy* (Baltimore: University Park Press, 1981), 47.

151 To a certain extent, alliances . . . : Freeman, 42–44.

151 They also help us . . . : ibid.

151 An alliance can become detrimental . . . : ibid.

152 In a common three-generation . . . : Haley, 109.

152 It's when the coalition becomes . . . : ibid.

153 Women in these families . . . : Freeman, 42–44.

153 Especially when cross-generational . . . : Haley, 104.

157 At least two people in a triangle . . . : Haley, 107; 118–19.

160 She may also run into difficulties . . . : personal communication, Halperin.

160 Or she may carry . . . : personal communication, Marilyn Boynton, R.N., M.Ed., psychotherapist in Toronto, Ontario, February 8, 1997.

PART III: The Center of the Family
11. Grandmother Power

185 I suppose what I'm describing . . . : See C. G. Jung, *The Archetypes and the Collective Unconscious* (Princeton, N.J.: Princeton University Press, 1969).

187 A true matriarchy has never . . . : Carolyn Niethammer, *Daughters of the Earth* (New York: Touchstone, 1977), xii.

187 . . . the closest historical examples . . . :

ibid., 3, 15, 24–25, 129.

189 Humans, compelled to create . . . : Haley, 101.

189 We form hierarchies . . . : ibid.

189 The most straightforward family . . . : ibid., 103.

189 . . . grandparents in Western cultures . . . : Kornhaber, *Grandparent Power!*, 37.

196 Participants usually work to maintain . . . one back down: Haley, 102.

13. Matriarchs and Kinkeepers

203 "Grandma never threatened. She . . .": Mead, 45–46.

204 She's perceived as highly competent . . . : personal communication, Sandra Halperin, Ph.D., November 13, 1998.

210 . . . the inevitable outcome of being placated all the time . . . : Barker, 67.

211 Of the four types of matriarchs . . . loving mothers they never had: personal communication, Kathleen Moges, Ph.D., psychologist in Beverly Hills, Calif., November 13, 1998.

212 Yet granting absolute power . . . : Baronowski, 577.

214 The typical kinkeeper is a . . . : Carolyn J. Rosenthal, "Kinkeeping in the Familial Division of Labor," *Journal of Marriage and the Family* (November 1985): 969–72.

217 Her most likely replacement is . . . : ibid.,
    970–71.

PART IV: Mother of My Mother
15. Woman to Woman

247 Sixty-one percent of the women . . . :
    Mother of My Mother survey, question
    14.
247 Twenty-five percent were older . . . : ibid.
247 And nearly one-third of them . . . : ibid.,
    question 21.
247 . . . conducted a national survey of 208 . . . :
    Lynne Gershenson Hodgson, "Adult
    Grandchildren and their Grandparents:
    The Enduring Bond," in *The Ties of
    Later Life*, Jon Hendricks, ed. (Amity-
    ville, N.Y.: Baywood Publishing Com-
    pany, 1995), 155–70.
248 . . . so too can the relationship . . . : Barranti,
    99.
249 Physical proximity continues to play . . . :
    Barranti, 90.
250 Adult granddaughters tend to expect . . . to
    act as role models: Joan F. Robertson,
    "Significance of Grandparents: Percep-
    tions of Young Adult Grandchildren,"
    The Gerontologist 16 (1976): 138.
260 A 1976 study of eighty-six . . . : ibid., 139.
260 More recent studies have confirmed . . . :
    Kennedy (1990), 45–46; Nieli Langer,
    "Grandparents and Adult Grand-

children: What Do They Do for One Another?" in Hendricks, 171.

260 Of the thirty percent of women . . . : *Mother of My Mother* survey, cross-reference of questions 15 and 21.

260 More than half of the women . . . : ibid., cross-reference of questions 21 and 29.

264 "Always with the jokes, they can . . .": Joy Horowitz, *Tessie and Pearlie* (New York: Scribner, 1996), 12.

17. One Woman Leads to Another

277 Behavioral geneticists now believe . . . : Malcolm Gladwell, "Do Parents Matter?" *The New Yorker*, August 17, 1998, 56.

279 From these studies, we know that . . . : Jay Belsky, "The Determinants of Parenting: A Process Model," *Child Development* 55 (1984): 85; Michael Rutter, "Intergenerational continuities and discontinuities in serious parenting difficulties," in *Child Maltreatment: Theory and Research on the Causes and Consequences of Child Abuse and Neglect*, Danti Cicchetti and Vicki Carlson, eds. (New York: Cambridge University Press, 1989), 317–48.

279 The death or divorce of one's parents . . . : Margaret H. Ricks, "The Social Transmission of Parental Behavior: Attach-

ment Across Generations," in *Mono-graphs of the Society for Research in Child Development* 50 (1985): 218; also see Belsky, 85.

279 These include the amount of . . . : Bertram J. Cohler and Henry U. Grunebaum, *Mothers, Grandmothers, and Daughters* (New York: John Wiley & Sons, 1981), 43–65; Susanne Frost Olsen, "Inter-generational Transmission, Genera-tional Differences, and Parenting," diss., University of Georgia, 1992; Richard A. Hanson and Ronald Mullis, "Intergen-erational Transfer of Normative Pa-rental Attitudes," *Psychological Reports* 59 (1986): 711.

279 . . . nearly all of these studies indicate . . . : Marinus H. Van Uzendoorn, "Inter-generational Transmission of Parent-ing. A Review of Studies in Nonclinical Populations," *Developmental Review* 12 (1992): 92; Belsky, 85; Ricks, 220–21.

280 As British psychoanalyst Michael Rutter . . . : Rutter, 321.

280 The first is the ability to express . . . : Hicks, 220–24.

282 Psychoanalyst Nancy Chodorow . . . : Nancy Chodorow, *The Reproduction of Mothering* (Berkeley: University of Cali-fornia Press, 1978), 89–90.

283 A poignant example . . . fed that way her-self: G. L. Engel, F. Reichman, V. T.

Harway, and D. W. Hess, "Monica: Infant Feeding Behavior of a Mother Gastric fistula-fed as an Infant: A 30-year Longitudinal Study of Enduring Effects," in *Parental Influences: In Health and Disease*, E. James Anthony and George H. Pollack, eds. (Boston: Little, Brown, 1985), 29–89.

18. Reclaiming a Culture: Helie's Story

292 "I am who I am . . . they so proud people": Helie Lee, *Still Life With Rice* (New York: Scribner, 1996), 12–13.

20. Saying Goodbye

300 "During her dying I felt . . .": Suzannah Lessard, *The Architect of Desire* (New York: The Dial Press, 1996), 312–13.
302 "It feels like the most violent . . .": Cynthia Kaplan, "Better, Safer, Warmer." *The New York Times*, Monday, February 1, 1999, Op.-Ed.
309 She knows the loss is . . . : Therese A. Rando, *Treatment of Complicated Mourning* (Champaign, Ill.: Research Press, 1993), 498.
310 They're the symbolic losses . . . : Therese A. Rando, *How to Go On Living When Someone You Love Dies* (New York: Bantam, 1991), 15–16.

Acknowledgments

To Susan Kamil, my editor, and Elizabeth Kaplan, my agent, my gratitude is endless. Your insights, patience, and confidence in me are the reasons this book exists.

My thanks also go out to Wendy Sheehan and Christina Chang, the research assistants who tirelessly tracked down source material, and to all the family members who shared their memories with me, particularly my sister, Michele. I am especially indebted to my aunts, for giving me access to my grandmother's writings; to the NYU and UCLA library systems for giving me access to their extensive collections; to all the granddaughters who participated in this book for their cooperation and their candor; to my students at the UCLA Writers' Program for their energy and enthusiasm; to Arthur Kornhaber, Vern Bengtson, Sandra Halperin, Evelyn Bassoff, and Naomi Lowinsky for their insights and their time; and to the members of my writing group — Toni Frank, Karen Kasaba, Deborah Lott, Danny Miller, and Spencer Nadler — for their feedback and encouragement at the end, when I needed it most.

My husband, Uzi, is an unwavering source of love, support, and humor. My daughter, Maya, is my greatest joy. To both of them, my devotion has no bounds.

My mother, Marcia, and my grandmother, Faye, are the source of everything to me. I miss them more than I can possibly convey.

Hope Edelman is author of the international bestseller *Motherless Daughters: The Legacy of Loss,* and editor of *Letters from Motherless Daughters: Words of Courage, Grief, and Healing.* Her articles and essays have appeared in *The New York Times, Glamour, Self, New Woman, The Washington Post,* the *Chicago Tribune,* and *The Iowa Review* among other numerous publications. She lives in Los Angeles with her husband and daughter.

The employees of G.K. Hall hope you have enjoyed this Large Print book. All our Large Print titles are designed for easy reading, and all our books are made to last. Other G.K. Hall books are available at your library, through selected bookstores, or directly from us.

For information about titles, please call:

(800) 257-5157

To share your comments, please write:

Publisher
G.K. Hall & Co.
P.O. Box 159
Thorndike, ME 04986